BWB
1.00
③
W9-BZM-943

MY LAST STEP BACKWARD

Tasha Schuh

Inspiring Voices®
A Service of Guideposts

Copyright © 2012 Tasha Schuh

All rights reserved. No part of this book may be used or reproduced by any means, graphic, electronic, or mechanical, including photocopying, recording, taping or by any information storage retrieval system without the written permission of the publisher except in the case of brief quotations embodied in critical articles and reviews.

Inspiring Voices books may be ordered through booksellers or by contacting:

Inspiring Voices
1663 Liberty Drive
Bloomington, IN 47403
www.inspiringvoices.com
1-(866) 697-5313

Because of the dynamic nature of the Internet, any web addresses or links contained in this book may have changed since publication and may no longer be valid. The views expressed in this work are solely those of the author and do not necessarily reflect the views of the publisher, and the publisher hereby disclaims any responsibility for them.

Cover photo: Becky Beissel

ISBN: 978-1-4624-0417-9 (e)
ISBN: 978-1-4624-0418-6 (sc)

Library of Congress Control Number: 2012921860

Printed in the United States of America

Inspiring Voices rev. date: 11/16/2012

DEDICATION:

To Mom, Dad, Angie and Ryan... for your never ending support and sacrifice that has helped me become who I am today.

Acknowledgements:

THERE ARE CERTAIN people that I have to thank for their support throughout this project. Without them, this book would not exist.

To all of my wonderful and amazing friends—you know who you are. I wish I could list you all by name because you all mean so much to me. You have been here for me, whether I met you before or after my accident. You have believed in me, encouraged me, made me laugh, supported me in difficult decisions, and have helped me more than you'll ever know.

Nancy Dumke, who directed me to finally start this project—thank you for your perseverance in knowing that this book needed to get done; the medical staff from Mayo Clinic, who saved my life and helped me believe that I could overcome; Jan Pavloski, who has spent hours upon hours, sacrificing so much in putting this book together. Thank you for using your amazing writing abilities and creativity to guide this to completion. Your patience and your fun-loving attitude made this project so much fun to work on and would've never happened without you; Cassandra Lokker, whose professionalism influenced me from start to finish; my caregivers, whose trust and devotion I will cherish forever; to Doug, who had the courage to jump on board my journey and has made my life so wonderful— I am so excited for our future; my nieces and nephews who remind me every day how much I would have missed had I not lived; you bring so much joy to my life—I hope my success inspires you when you are faced with adversity.

Finally, with heartfelt gratitude, I lift this project up to God who orchestrated this, for without Him and His great faithfulness, I would not be where I am today.

Contents

Prologue

"Well life has a funny way of sneaking up on you
 When you think everything's okay and everything's going right
 And life has a funny way of helping you out when
 You think everything's gone wrong … isn't it ironic."

AS MUCH AS I like Alanis Morissette's classic anthem on irony, I can't help but think that rain on your wedding day is just plain bad luck. The weather is always a fifty-fifty thing, right? A bride half expects a cloudburst.

Or when your bus fare is paid and you immediately find an acquaintance with a car soon departing for your side of the city. Bad timing? Sure. Ironic … not really.

Here's irony: When people meet me for the first time, they immediately focus on what I can't do. At first glance, I am defined by my losses—the loss of my limbs … the loss of athletics … the loss of an acting career … the loss of dreams. What they don't see is that *loss* is the last word I would use to define my life. *Loss* couldn't be further from the truth.

Ironically, my life is defined by what I have gained from becoming quadriplegic. My life is richer because I have endured such drastic change. My life was saved by a disaster. I have learned that a greater power guides my destiny. And I have taken my last step backward.

Introduction:

My Story

"WHAT HAPPENED TO you?"

"I was in an accident. I got hurt."

"What's this for?"

The little girl points to one of my chair's many control buttons. "And what's this?"

I explain another feature of my chair that fascinates her so.

Ha, ha, ha. The adults around me—I'm guessing one is a parent of this girl—laugh at her curious yet bold questions. I admit, she's cute. And it's easier when a child is not afraid of me. So many are.

But I'm here to watch Ryan's game. Ryan, the football coach. Ryan, one of my closest friends from college. I couldn't wait to get situated in the stands, surrounded by people who share one thing—we all love Ryan and want him to have an amazing career as a coach. Football is his passion. Family and friends from all over have come to this game, meeting in one section, in hopes that Ryan's team will prove he's a worthy head coach.

Yet one little girl—I'd guess four or five years old—draws the attention away from Ryan's game and brings it all to me. Frankly, I am ready for this. I have become accustomed to telling my story, or at least part of it, every time I meet new people.

"How did you get hurt," one of the adults asks. I notice sincere and attentive looks from everyone but the little girl who is counting the number of bubble buttons on my chair's control pad.

This is my cue to start sharing my story. I have learned to be grateful for curious children who give me permission to break the ice so we can focus on more than me. So I explain. Just a little bit. Just enough to ease the natural concern that comes from viewing all six-foot-two of me in a chair that weighs as much as a Prius.

"I was in a theater accident."

"A theater accident?!"

"Yes, I know. Crazy, isn't it. A theater accident."

"Oh, my gosh, that's awful. You poor thing. I remember when ..."

Pity ... which I could do without. But the ice has been broken. The sharing begins, because everyone has a story.

Yes, I mean *everyone* has a story. Whenever I tell my story, which I do all the time—visiting a local classroom, dealing with curious customers in restaurants, presenting as a paid professional at a national seminar—people quickly begin to share. Whatever detail I start with—the accident, the long hospital stay, learning to drive my modified van—people can relate. I hear lots of stories.

I could be annoyed by this. I could think, "Come on, *you* didn't survive a sixteen-foot fall to concrete, or endure a coma for eight days with a fever peaking at 108 degrees, or learn to drive to the Mall of America using only the hinge of your right wrist." I could justifiably be irritated each time my story is cut off prematurely. But I'm not. Instead, I am amazed.

I am amazed that so many people can relate to how a split second, a quick movement—in my case, a step backward—could alter the course of a life forever. I am awed and saddened by the endless tales of tragedy I invite by being so open about my own.

Early on I believed that my step backward was unique, one of a kind. I was one of the few with a "story" to tell that might move others to reflect on their own good fortune, their own personal blessings that make their lives seem charmed when compared to my accident. I really thought my story was unrivaled, that talent and youth and optimism like mine had never been struck down so abruptly. But as I am once again interrupted—

this time by a kind elderly couple in the parking lot of Woodbury Lakes Shopping Center—I realize this couldn't be further from the truth.

"Yes, a theater accident," I reply with sincere appreciation that others care. My appearance in a wheelchair, especially when I emerge from my van alone, triggers the most compassionate response in people.

So for all who have stories to share, for all who know what it is like when the life you expect is stopped short, here is my story in full.

Chapter 1

A Step Backward

THE STORY I am about to tell you is the true story of my life—of Natasha Lea Schuh, born on December 19, 1980. Though my story could start on that day, this written record begins with Tuesday, November 11, 1997. On this date, the new Tasha Schuh was born. The Tasha Schuh who will never again *stand* over six feet tall. The Tasha Schuh who panics at the sight of a sore on her leg because she knows it may take weeks, maybe months to heal. The Tasha Schuh who painfully mourned the death of Christopher Reeve because she could relate so well to his struggles. The *new* Tasha Schuh ironically remembers almost every detail of her birth, from the first moment of that day.

The morning of November 11, 1997, brought the first real snowfall of the season. Another Wisconsin winter was here to stay. My fall sports season had just ended. I'd had a wonderful experience playing varsity volleyball, definitely my favorite sport. The *Pierce County Herald* covered our games, and I felt pride in seeing my stats and name mentioned each week. But gears had shifted to our school's fall musical. *The Wizard of Oz* would open that upcoming weekend.

Securing the part of "chorus girl" in *Oz* might have been a let-down. This proverbial step backward, after playing Sandy in *Grease* the previous year, likely caused some talk. "Wow, Tasha couldn't even get the part of a witch this time around. She must be devastated." But I wasn't.

1

Although some saw this as being demoted, I wasn't a bit surprised. Our director, Mr. Dulak, had a fair-minded approach to lead parts. My prayers for the part of Sandy were answered the season prior to *Oz*, so now it was someone else's turn. In fact, I saw this as an opportunity to learn all about theater—to study every aspect of something I fully intended to pursue as a career after high school. I wanted to perform! Everything I experienced in *Grease* convinced me this was now my path. I would squeeze volleyball, basketball, and work hours at my parents' grocery store into my remaining high-school years. But my college plans were rock-solid: I would major in music and theater.

Knowing that I shared my stage performance dream with countless American girls, I was determined to get the edge on others. Even at sixteen, I was willing to admit that the road to professional acting would be bumpy, but not impossible. I needed to learn every aspect of theater in order to have an advantage over other talent.

Like so many high school girls, I spent far too much time making sure people liked me. Events from my childhood—dark secrets that triggered instant shame when my memory drifted back—brought self-doubt about the littlest things. Acting was an escape. I believed I could become someone else. Yet there was pressure to be the best. Because I knew that other students had lost out on the audition for Sandy, I felt compelled to do superior work in the role—to justify a sophomore girl being chosen over older students for the lead in *Grease*. And I had to do this without becoming a diva. I had to maintain friendships, win back girls who perhaps resented me, keep the rehearsals positive. It was exhausting, but I loved every minute of it.

Oz brought a lighter role. I was still onstage quite a bit, but this time I had the leeway to worry less about my character's appeal and more about the skills I needed to enter a college theater program. I wanted full knowledge of how a production materialized from start to finish. What's not to love about this chorus part? I was eager to help others with makeup, lighting, costumes, set design—anything, just so I could learn about the complete show.

I did feel some apprehension on November 11, but it had nothing to do with *Oz* or my own insecurities. I wouldn't see Sarina at school that day, and from the weekend talk, I didn't know if or when I would ever see her again. Sarina Murray, my friend and sports teammate, had survived a very serious car accident that Saturday. Nobody really knew what had happened because she was by herself when she apparently rolled her vehicle within miles of the restaurant where she worked. Wearing no seatbelt, she was ejected from the car and suffered a critical head injury. The extent of her brain damage was not known, although the doctors speculated traumatic brain injury (TBI). I wanted to see her. I needed to see her. Yet I knew I had a frantic full day ahead of me and would not have time to drive to the hospital. School and play practice would consume every moment of November 11. All day long, I struggled with this cloud of fear for Sarina—I worried about her future, and ignored signs that my own fate was about to change.

"Tasha, you have to get going. You don't want to be late for school. Grab your backpack. Do you have money for your break tonight? Just buy supper at the bakery." My mom was so organized. Still is. That morning, she had just returned from a warm Las Vegas vacation with her best friend, bringing back a semblance of routine to our home. My easygoing dad was no longer in charge. I needed a boot out the door that morning, and Mom got my focus back on track. I'm sure she'd bought out a full row at the Sheldon Theater through the advanced ticket sales. Mom would make sure I was prepared and doing my share of the work.

Besides the snow and my concerns for Sarina, and a little bit of resentment over Mom having a fun "girls" weekend without me, the morning of November 11 was the typical start of a busy school day. Mom the manager reminded me of everything I had going on. I listened, was grateful, and prayed for Sarina. While my friend fought for her life, I maintained my own ironic delusion: I still believed I controlled my destiny.

"I see you did a little shopping." Mom noticed my new jeans and sweatshirt as we each headed for our cars in the driveway. Mom was leaving for the grocery store to put in a long workday. She knew that a weekend away meant things were piled up, just waiting for her.

Kathy, the *K* in D&K Family Foods, did a little bit of everything at the store. Duane, my early-bird dad, opened the business. He was long gone by the time I got up for school each day. Mom, on the other hand, stayed home until her three children were off to school. Even though Ryan and Angie were out of the house, living on their own at this point, Mom kept the same hours for me. Her biggest tasks included scheduling, payroll, and the store's accounting. These things were often done after I went to bed. Every member of my family has had the experience of waking up at one or two in the morning to find Mom finishing the bookwork. On November 11, she would stay at the store with Dad until closing time to play catch-up after her Vegas weekend.

We both looked down at my sweatshirt, which boldly stated, "Thank God I'm Female."

"I agree. Thank God," Mom said. "Tasha would be a strange name for a boy."

"Very funny, Mom." I hesitated after I hugged her good-bye. "The guys are going to tease me, aren't they?" Self-doubt made me wonder, *Should I run back to my room and change? I can already hear Stevie saying, "Female? Really? Are you sure? Let me check for you."*

"Aw, you can handle Stevie! Have a good day, and I'll see you at home after rehearsal."

Mom was right. My sweatshirt asked for comment, and I was prepared to give it back. I'd had fun shopping over the weekend for this and my new jeans. I loved shopping! Shopping was a passion of mine—always has been. So the morning of November 11 was even more memorable because I wore new clothes that I chose, with a little help from Dad's wallet.

"So who drove you to the mall?" Mom was fishing for info that morning. Always the careful questioner, she managed to find out that I spent quite a bit of the weekend with friends—including my boyfriend, Travis. The entire weekend brought good times without Mom's usual curfew. Within a month I would turn seventeen, and lately the thought of being eighteen, entering my senior year, and facing true independence was constantly on my mind. I wasn't wishing my life away, but I seriously looked forward to the adult world of college, parties, and independent living—without my parents' supervision. Independence would come, more than I bargained for, but not remotely the way I envisioned it in my head.

Although I tried to keep it light by proudly wearing my new sweatshirt and jeans, Tuesday, November 11 belonged to Sarina. I can still remember the talk between classes. The bell would ring and we would wander from student to student asking, "Have you heard anything? Do you know how she's doing?" In this final decade before cell phones, our word-of-mouth network was not considered gossip since we were asking out of genuine concern for a friend.

The last bell released us with the knowledge that Sarina remained in critical condition. I ran home for a quick break just before loading four cast members into my 1989 New Yorker for our ride to the Sheldon Theater. The chorus needed to start rehearsal by 5:00 p.m. sharp, and the twenty-minute drive from Ellsworth, Wisconsin, to Red Wing, Minnesota, would take longer on snowy roads.

I called the store before leaving home to check in with Mom or Dad. With Sarina's accident fresh in their minds, my parents expressed concern for the threatening weather. "Drive carefully, okay?" Mom begged. "It's so slippery out there. Ellsworth High School doesn't need another student to worry about. All of our prayers need to go to Sarina, right? Promise me you'll be careful?"

"I promise, Mom. We'll take it slow." She was right—Highway 63 was slick. Nonetheless, we arrived safely, ready to rehearse.

Exceptionally cold and dark that day, the Sheldon seemed to have Sarina's cloud of worry hovering just below its ornately painted ceiling. Maybe it was the winter weather. Maybe it was Sarina's cloud. Maybe it was the fact that kids kept referring to the Sheldon as a haunted theater. We had been practicing in this beautiful historic building for a few days now, and some cast members tried to spook others by bringing up this old superstition just as a hidden closet was discovered or a trapdoor had to be opened. There were times we wished our school had its own theater. But we were grateful that our high school director could secure the Sheldon for big productions like *Grease* and *The Wizard of Oz*.

My way to avoid the gloom of this practice: when Mr. Dulak gave us a break, I hustled across the street with a few friends to the local bakery for donuts and hot chocolate. But the comfort food didn't do the trick. I can't tell you how many times Stevie said, "What's up with you? You are not

5

yourself today. Snap out of it, will ya?" I couldn't shake it. I could not let go of this anxious feeling. Plus I knew we still had to tackle a scene-change problem that cropped up the night before. The bakery break provided minimal motivation to get back to practice and attack this problem.

This scene change—this six-minute scene change—needed the magic of *Oz*. Ruby slippers ... a wave of Glenda's wand ... *something* supernatural was needed to transform six minutes into thirty seconds by opening night, a mere seventy-two hours away.

I remember lots of doubts. Few believed this scene change could be done in thirty seconds. Our director brought our attention to a door where he had posted a list of new tasks related to this transition. What? We were wiping out most of what we had rehearsed in those six minutes. We would have to learn a whole new approach to this scene change right now, tonight. With opening night so close, the cast and crew definitely had their doubts about saving five and a half minutes in this part of the show.

"Come on, everybody. A six-minute scene change? Good lord, the audience will up and walk out!" Our director was right. Six minutes was ridiculous for this transition. No one takes that long to change scenes. "You'll get this. Really, just look at the new list."

After some objections, we put our doubts aside and cooperated.

We eyed the posted list of duties: name followed by prop and task. My job was to move a prop that displayed Land of Oz flowers on a painted piece of wood. Various props, including mine, would be loaded on a movable bridge and then wheeled onto the stage. Crew members like me could take our designated items off the bridge and quickly move them to their precise locations.

In this scene, a spinning bridge would create a magical effect for the audience. I was eager to learn new technical aspects of theater, so I was completely onboard with this revised attempt to transform the stage in thirty seconds. However, as I walked away knowing my personal task, one important fact evaded me: the bridge was going to be moved over an open trapdoor. I read the assignment listed next to my name, but I did not grasp the concept of a gaping hole in the floor as the bridge, carried by two others, found its destination.

Some of what I'm about to describe is rather sketchy. Some of this I precisely recall. Other details were told to me later by those who watched but could not stop my fall.

I remember it being so dark that I struggled to follow the progress of the stage crew. The houselights were out since we needed to mimic what would happen on opening night. The cast and crew had to adapt to complete darkness—the blackness of a choreographed scene change.

"Places everyone."

One cast member told me later that someone said to her, "Rachel, be more careful. You almost fell through the trapdoor last night, remember?" Why hadn't I heard that warning? Why did it seem that everyone knew and comprehended this revised scene change but me—as if everyone but Tasha Schuh got the memo?

I stood in the dark, waiting for the bridge that carried the prop assigned to me. The bridge was moving closer when someone said, "Tasha, move out of the way." Quickly I took one step backward, and my body went through … nothing.

One moment I was standing there waiting for the bridge, waiting to grab my prop, and the next moment, the stage was gone. I was falling, flipping. Seconds later, the back of my head crashed onto a concrete floor—a crash like Dorothy's house, with one ruby slipper still on the stage. I had stepped right out of my Reebok athletic slide, which stood neatly in front of the trapdoor while the other shoe remained on my foot after the fall. I slid backward out of my shoe and dropped sixteen feet to the hard cement floor. My head hit first; my body weight came next, falling on top of me. I heard the crunch, and then I just laid there.

Confusion took over. Screams flew through the air above me, bouncing off Sarina's cloud.

"Oh, my God."

"Tasha! Tasha!" I heard my name a hundred times.

More magic. I have no idea how everyone got to the basement of the Sheldon as fast as they did. I found out later that one music teacher, the pit-band director, was down there and saw me hit.

Immediately I was surrounded by friends and teachers. Rachel and Stevie told me later I was lying as if sleeping in the fetal position. Imagine this six-foot baby rolled up on the concrete floor.

This is the freak-out part of the scene change.

"Please don't touch me—don't move me." I'm not sure if these words got out, but I know I was thinking them. I didn't want anyone to lay a hand on me, but at the same time, I was trying to get up. I remember pausing, looking up, staring at the trapdoor from the cold basement floor, wondering how it all happened. My fall took seconds, but I can replay it in slow motion in my mind, like it took days to land in this uncomfortable position. I felt like Land of Oz royalty. *Relax everyone; I've landed. Now, don't touch me!*

Rewind: Fall ... head/neck crunch ... what feels like a broken shoulder ... intense pain ... can't move ... and now, call an ambulance!

Ms. Huber, another music teacher, yelled, "Someone call 911!" She put words to my thoughts. "No one touch her! We're not going to move you, Tasha. Try to stay still, all right?" From the Sheldon's basement phone, a cast member called for an ambulance. Again, no one had a cell phone.

More irony. I was kind of joking at this point, but petrified at the same time. "I'm such a klutz! I can't wait to hear what they say at school tomorrow! Only Tasha Schuh could manage this, right?" Again, words or thoughts, I'm not sure.

What saved me from complete panic was the delusion that I would be okay. I imagined my friends making fun of me the next day at school, and the embarrassment momentarily outweighed the physical pain. I struggled to get up, still believing that I could brush this off and walk away.

Pushing to get up ... excruciating pain ... it'll be fine ... paralyzed ... scary word! But how serious can this be?

I never lost consciousness, which kept my delusion alive.

Okay, relax. I had fallen down the stairs as a child, so I already knew what it was like to not feel my legs. That had been scary too, but it passed. This will pass, right? Fear began to overtake me as the word *paralyzed* silently drifted in and out of the crowd who surrounded me on the basement floor.

This word, *paralyzed,* carried hidden fears ... the demons that creep in during moments of shame ... memories of allowing others to control me. Self-doubt threatened to swallow me up.

Timing is essential in matters of irony. As the paramedics prepared me for the ride to the local hospital, where arrangements for my Rochester airlift were already being made, I fought my greatest fear—a foresight I had revealed to a friend just three days before my accident.

That very weekend, with Mom gone to Vegas, I had viewed part of a televised benefit involving Christopher Reeve. I rarely took time to watch TV in high school, but this caught my attention until my friend picked me up that Friday night.

I don't recall why our conversation turned to this topic, but for some reason my friend asked me, "So what would be the worst thing that could happen to you? What scares you the most, Tasha?"

Without hesitation, I answered, "Being paralyzed. In a wheelchair for the rest of my life—like Christopher Reeve. I could never do that."

As paramedics entered the basement and took every precaution, I recalled all the times accident-prone Tasha Schuh had bounced back from a close call with only short-lived, minor injuries. My delusion was strongest when I needed it most. I would be fine.

Extreme pain started shooting up and down my right arm. I thought I had broken my shoulder and received electric-shock therapy all at the same time. I knew I couldn't move or get up. I believed if I gave my body some time to recover from the fall, my mobility would gradually come back. But doubts crept into my mind with one recurring question: *Am I paralyzed?* I would ask this question so many times within the next few hours. Whether it was a nurse, a doctor, my parents, or my closest friends, they all answered with the one thing I did not want to hear: "I don't know."

My right arm was lying over my body. I thought if I was paralyzed, I shouldn't be able to move it. I took my arm and dragged it across my body. Here was hope! My friend Tiffany, sitting near me, read my mind. "Tasha, you're going to be okay!"

"What do you mean?" I asked, trying to understand how she could say this when I was in so much pain. "How do you know?"

"Your toes are twitching!" Tiffany answered.

Irony again. I was not trying to move my toes; they were twitching involuntarily. Panic engulfed me as the ambulance crew continued their work.

I asked Tiffany to go with me to the hospital. I did not want her to leave me. I grasped onto Tiffany, my oldest friend in the building ... friends since third grade ... my closest *family* until my parents came.

By now, the EMTs had secured my neck in a brace and clamped all of me onto a body board. People were trying to manage my escape from the lower level. With incredibly steep steps plus a sharp turn at the top of the staircase, the normal exit would not work.

Someone came up with the idea to lower the orchestra pit as far as it would go. Kids scurried to clear out all of the instruments. Strapped onto a gurney, I was raised from the orchestra pit onto the stage. Once on the stage, I could be wheeled out of the building via the Sheldon's traditional theater ramp. Everyone called out to me as I was loaded into the ambulance. "Tasha. You'll be okay." My name echoed in the theater over and over as the ambulance door closed.

I was openly upset when they didn't let Tiffany go with me in the ambulance. Thankfully, they agreed that Ms. Huber could follow closely to the hospital, where she would stay with me until my parents arrived. I don't think I ever got the words out, but I wanted Ms. Huber to bring Tiffany, too. I certainly didn't know it at the time, but this was the start of no longer getting my way.

"Okay, I have IV access," one of the EMTs announced. "Let's drive." Although it was only a few blocks to the Red Wing Hospital, the paramedics were in trauma mode. My head was throbbing, and they were rightfully obsessed with the potential for brain hemorrhage. No one cared to shield my feelings. No one spoke in code. I don't recall precise words after the IV went in, but I do recall the feeling that I was now a medical science project. The goal: to save me, and with some luck, stabilize me for an airlift to Rochester Mayo. This was about an hour's drive away, but would take only minutes in a helicopter.

At this point, I just wanted my mom and the comfort that family brings. The doors of the ambulance opened and I read the sign: EMERGENCY. I can't tell you how relieved I was to recognize the mother of one of my friends on duty as the ER nurse. It took only minutes for my parents to arrive to sign papers authorizing the airlift, but in that moment my friend's mom magically erased my panic. Coincidentally, this nurse would be in the audience at one of my speaking engagements many years later to hear me talk of the calm that came over me in her presence.

Cautiously, I was moved to an x-ray table, and then my family appeared, along with my boyfriend and one of my closest friends, Sarah. Mom told me later that, as she came up beside me in the examining room, it broke her heart to see me quietly crying.

"Mom, I can't feel my legs!" I finally said in a panicked whisper.

"It's going to be okay," she whispered back, her face close to mine, her tears flowing also.

A helicopter ride—every kid's dream, right? Be careful what thrill rides you wish for. I was getting an experience I had often begged to have on family vacations. Hawaii, the Rocky Mountains, the German Alps— every time our family encountered a helicopter excursion ad, I begged for a ride. I always imagined that Mom or Dad would ride with me. But there was no room for my family on the airlift to Rochester.

"Please, Mom, don't let me go alone." Once again, I would not get my way. The flight nurse closed the helicopter door, and my parents made the long painful drive to Rochester's Saint Marys Hospital without me.

Almost immediately into the flight, basic physiology stole what remained of my free will. I vomited donuts and hot chocolate while the flight nurse, unable to roll me over, did her best to wipe away the mess. Doctors later deduced that I had aspirated. This would prove life-threatening to lungs destined for a hospital traction bed.

The next few hours are a jumbled memory of pain meds and worried whispers. Inventory of my injuries led to a laundry list of complications. I quit listening.

My world succumbed to dreams. I lived in the past, gaining consciousness long enough to see family and friends rotating to and from my bed—some crying, some cheering me on, all worried beyond my understanding. I drifted away from the pain and dreamed of my life before the trapdoor.

Chapter 2

Before the Trapdoor

THE YEAR BEFORE I was born, Duane and Kathy Schuh purchased a grocery store in Ellsworth, Wisconsin. This small town with a population just under three thousand is located about an hour east of Minneapolis, making Ellsworth a rural farm community, not a suburb. Prior to this career change, my mother had worked at the Creamery, a cheese factory aligned with Ellsworth area dairy farmers, and my father worked in a furniture store.

My parents discovered they were expecting me right about the time they made this leap into small business ownership. I can only imagine the emotional confusion, since doctors had informed my mom five years earlier that she would be unable to have any more children. My sister, Angie, born in 1973, and my brother, Ryan, born three years later, would round out the Schuh family nicely. Yet my parents, making the best of every curveball ever thrown at them, referred to me as their "unexpected miracle." The timing was horrible, but as far as they were concerned, I was a Christmas gift for my brother and sister. I literally came home from the hospital in a holiday stocking on Christmas Eve, with no talk of "stress" or "bad timing" from anyone.

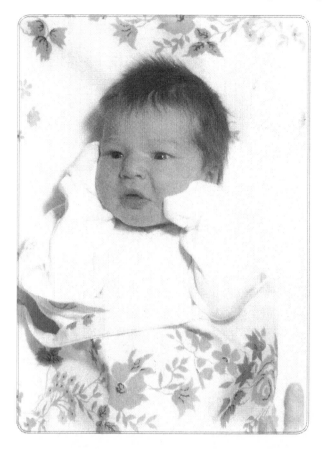

Natasha Lea Schuh, born December 19, 1980.

My parents were determined to raise their children expecting only the best—for and from us. We were required to work hard and earn good grades in school. In return, our parents would provide us with every opportunity to succeed. Essentially, my folks made a pact: growing up would be significantly better for their children than it had been for them.

Although they were brought up in extremely different households, both Mom and Dad experienced gaps and setbacks that they didn't want their own children to experience. My dad was raised in an alcoholic family, and my mom grew up never hearing from her parents the words, "I love you." Mom and Dad's first and foremost daily goal was to show and to tell their children that they were deeply loved. Despite this goal, and as loving as she is, my mother's strict, worried ways kept us from being spoiled children. She set rules and boundaries, which I understand now as the parameters of good parenting. Adults who want to foster self-discipline and respect in their children must set rules. Most days, Mom was the rule-maker as well as the enforcer.

My dad, on the other hand, cultivated my free and creative side. No worries with Dad! He loved to say yes to his children, and so I got away with a lot more when Dad was in charge. Yet I frequently heard the famous words uttered by most moms when their kids need reining in: "Just wait until your dad gets home!" These were the times when I knew Mom and Dad were united as a parenting force. They fully intended to raise respectful and caring children who were mindful of the consequences of their behavior.

Like most kids, my sister, brother, and I had our differences growing up, but we generally got along. Eight years older than me, Angie babysat while our folks ran the store, or when they tried to squeeze social lives into an already full schedule. Ryan, my older brother by five years, adored me when I was a baby. Once I was old enough to play in the yard, I became the annoying little tagalong sister. We fought a lot, but deep down, we loved each other. Clearly, as the youngest, I had the security of siblings who would protect me. This is something I didn't appreciate for many years.

While my parents ran their business in small-town Wisconsin, I attended Hillcrest Elementary. I would be a "townie" kid from kindergarten through graduation, and I loved it. I loved the convenience of having everything close to home. It allowed me to take an active part in all of my school's activities, despite my parents' demanding work schedules.

Learning came easy to me—so much so that I remember feelings of frustration since the lessons were too simple. I would wonder, "What do you mean we're counting to ten? I already know how to count to one hundred!" Thankfully, I was picked for the Omnibus program which provided more intellectual stimulation. I enjoyed this challenge and was grateful that it made school more exciting again.

One obstacle could have really set me back in my education, but Mom and Dad stayed on top of it. I was born with extremely small ear canals. Endless ear infections deteriorated my hammer bone and resulted in significant, permanent hearing loss in my left ear. Surgeries had to be repeated numerous times because of my active nature. I loved the outdoors, especially riding my bike—something I truly miss to this day. Despite my klutzy ways, I learned how to ride a bike when I was four years old. Wipeouts, road rash, and constant scraped knees did not slow me down from loving the freedom of my bike, and more than once my new hammer bone popped out of position.

I started building my reputation as "the klutz" at a very early age. In kindergarten, I broke my arm trying to block a playground ball that a child randomly kicked during recess. Visualize this—I saw the ball coming, and to protect my face, I naturally put my arm up to block it. How can a midsized rubber four-square ball cause a broken bone? Even the teacher wouldn't believe me when I said I should call my mom. This teacher was so used to my playground injuries, she showed me a little comfort but refused to let me call my parents after a recess injury.

"Tasha would have been on the phone every day!" she told my parents years later. We all laughed and agreed. She usually wiped up a little blood, put on a Band-Aid, and I was back in business. But this time, since I complained so much about my throbbing arm, Mom took me to the hospital emergency room for x-rays. Sure enough, my arm was broken.

In first grade, I broke my leg on the parallel bars. Already by age seven I was more legs than my coordination could handle. However, in my mind's eye, I could do anything. As I attempted to spin around one bar, my left leg rotated too fast and hit the other bar. This resulted in a clean break, which was not only painful, but bad timing. I had a dance recital within weeks, and the leg cast was not coming off for a while. Lessons at Helmer Dance Studio, steady since age three, were a big expense in time and money to my parents. My mom would see that the recital was not a complete waste because of my injury. I can only imagine the conversation with my dance instructor.

"Well, yes, she'll be on crutches, but she can still be onstage during the recital."

"Crutches. Hmmm … That's going to be a little tough, Mrs. Schuh. The girls have to leap and make a sweeping run across the stage at this point."

"You know, I can help you re-choreograph this. Really, if you skip this leap, and have only half the girls circle up ..."

My mother's smile radiated throughout the audience as I hobbled onstage for the recital, displaying my showy costume and crutches. This was an early lesson, well before *Oz*, that the show must go on.

Dance recital—the year after my broken leg healed.

Besides these few injuries, the only other trouble I had in school came from my passion for talk. I was social. When I drew attention in school, it was because I couldn't hear just how loud my own voice was. And I certainly didn't want to miss what others were saying. Whispering with my classmates turned into public conversation for me. Teachers always heard my voice over the others, so I was the one to get into trouble. My mom would say, "Tasha, I go to teacher conferences and they say what a great student you are and how carefully you do your homework, but they cannot get you to shut up." It would be years before this talking problem would become my greatest asset—God's gift that essentially secured my recovery from the trapdoor fall.

Dance and my gift for conversation made me a social butterfly at a very young age. I lived for the weekends, even as a grade-schooler. Although I loved my family, I wasn't about to sit home with them when I had free time. My mission was to make things happen. I became a social instigator. I either had a friend over or I was packing a bag to go to someone's house whenever the opportunity presented itself. My parents again sacrificed for their children when they paid to have an inground pool put in the backyard when I was five years old. We would barely have the pool's cover off in April or May, and I would somehow fall in. I didn't care how I entered the pool for the season—I loved swimming! Having the neighborhood pool made me automatically *cool*. Every kid within a mile-long bike ride wanted to come to my house on a hot day.

In addition to dance, I was active in every available sport at a young age. My dad loved this, so he often coached whatever team I happened to be on at the time. I joined youth programs for softball, basketball, and volleyball. However, in the winter, my whole family worked around school, store, and basketball schedules in order to get as much skiing in as possible. We hit the local slopes—Afton or Welch—and visited the Nelsons with their cabin near a Northern Wisconsin ski resort. Skiing brought my family closer together, since it was something we all loved to do.

With such a busy family, about the only other unifying activity for us was church. Every Sunday we would all attend our small country church, where my dad sang in the choir and my mom taught Sunday school. I believed in God and knew that He was real, but I had the idea that He was miles and miles away, and must have other big concerns that trumped mine. I know now that God did not play a significant role in my life at this point. I was going to church frequently; I was making my parents happy. I went along with the idea that my whole family was attending so I should too. But when church was over by mid-Sunday morning, I never really gave God another thought until the next Sunday rolled around.

One Sunday highlight for me was that after church, my parents would take the family to Pizza Hut for lunch if we had all behaved well during the service. I believed that dining out with my family was the bonus for good behavior and church attendance. I had earned a pizza lunch for cooperating with this church commitment that cut into my weekend plans and forced me to get up early on a free day. I had so much to learn about the spiritual growth my parents worked to instill in three self-directed children.

Tasha, Ryan, and Angie—six months before my accident.

In addition to family, faith, and love, my parents taught their children the value of money management. Owning a grocery store did not make us millionaires. We watched my mom's attention to bargains. She cut coupons for our family's personal needs, found deals on food items for the store, and bought clothing only when it was on sale. These things saved money at the time, plus taught us habits of careful spending that everyone should follow as they work hard for their income.

My parents' careful money management through the year helped finance family vacations. Colorado, Hawaii, Disneyland, Tortola, Mexico, and Europe were my most memorable traveling experiences. These vacations created positive family memories and motivated me to dream of trips I wanted to take once I was an adult. My step backward would complicate this dream but not kill it.

As my childhood progressed, I began to feel loss for the first time in my life. My sister, my second mom, graduated from high school and moved out of our house. Although she only went as far as the Twin Cities for college, I felt the loss—a subtle reminder that I didn't control things around me. I wasn't the center of the universe. Someone or something else was allowing things to change. When Angie moved out, I felt lost. I was a child again, with no one to count on or play with.

As Angie left for college, Grandma Barringer became one of my closest friends. Despite her tough exterior, Grandma had an amazing heart. We cooked and baked, made dollhouses, and simply spent great quality time together.

I was really close to Grandpa as well. He was a retired farmer who had a weak heart. For five or six years, doctors claimed that less than 20 percent of his heart was functioning. I was nine years old when I began to help take care of him. As Grandpa got weaker, I learned to pitch in with things like shaving his beard, cutting his hair, and bandaging his wounds, since he'd had fingers and toes removed due to gout. I didn't mind taking care of him. Believe it or not, I thought it was fun. I loved my grandpa.

I found myself spending more and more time with my grandparents. There were so many times that we believed Grandpa was so ill we might lose him, but when the end finally came, it was without warning. The night of his death, Grandma told us later, he woke in the night, called her to his bedside—a hospital bed in the living room. He gave her a hug and a kiss, and then said good-bye. Grandpa passed away in his sleep. It was a week before his birthday. I had been to funerals before, but losing someone so close was a devastating experience.

After the loss of my grandfather, I experienced a different kind of loss—that which comes from acknowledging the world is not always safe and good. If not at Grandma's, I spent most of my free time hanging out with neighbors and friends who lived near me. I have disturbing memories of the neighborhood boys, as well as one older gentleman who lived down the block from me. Young and naive, I was sometimes tricked into following the boys into the woods. "Playing doctor" was something I thought every neighborhood girl did, but the end result was that it hurt my self-esteem. I felt guilt for complying with the boys' demands. Looking back is like reflecting on another person's life. The objectivity which comes with adulthood allows me to confront these memories without shame since the child involved was clearly a victim. What I struggle with is how this girl—this young Tasha Schuh, with loving parents and supportive siblings—lacked the judgment to put a stop to such violation. Why didn't she tattle? Why did she seem to believe that boys had a right to bully, or use and abuse a young girl?

I share this brief disconcerting memory for two reasons: first, my lack of assertiveness haunted me for much of my young life. The loss of self-esteem that accompanies shame and guilt required some serious recovery time and sporadically threatened the confident person that I am today. Secondly, I hope that girls and young women reading this find the inner strength that I lacked to say "no" or "stop"—that they pursue help right away when confronted with sexual situations that are clearly destructive.

The older gentleman from our neighborhood was an entirely separate story—yet linked, since again I lacked the clear judgment to report the man to the adults in my life who would have gladly protected me. While some of the boys were making me grow up before I should, the older neighbor man took advantage of me in a different way. He would invite me over to his home to visit. Either upon arrival, or as I would leave, this man would somehow lose his pants. They literally dropped to his ankles, and he acted as if nothing had happened. I would look the other way, embarrassed for the man, thinking he just didn't know that his pants had fallen down.

Although I was a smart child in school, I was gullible enough to repeatedly accept this neighbor's invitations into his home. He had his own children who were around my age, so it never crossed my mind to tell anyone. I would later find out that this disturbed man continually stalked me without my knowledge. Eventually, an investigation revealed that he was watching me through my window as I dressed. In the years to come, he would harass me over the telephone, which authorities discovered, he had done with other girls as well. My sense of security and trust in others was damaged. My self-confidence was impacted beyond my understanding, and it was difficult to move forward with all of this looming in front of me. Consequently, my attitude changed just as I was heading into my last year of elementary school.

Chapter 3

Eat, Pray, Act

SIXTH GRADE BROUGHT more change and more self-awareness. I started to care about how I looked, how I appeared to others. Suddenly, life was not about playing with just any neighborhood kids. It was about establishing loyal friends and making myself attractive to boys.

I always had friends, and we certainly had our differences, but when conflict hit, I would just go hang out with someone else. However, something changed by sixth grade. I started caring about acceptance, appearance, and popularity.

At this time, there was really only one girl who I considered to be my best friend. We did everything together. Naturally, the two of us positioned ourselves to join a bigger group of girls—a clique we believed was made up of the most popular girls in school. Life was so fun for these girls, or so everyone thought. They would enter the classroom on Monday morning and openly talk about all of the cool things they had experienced together over the weekend.

Somehow it was made clear to my friend and me that the group only had room for one of us. The decision came down, and they picked me. I witnessed my friend's devastation at the rejection she felt. I should have been appalled as the clique shunned this girl. Although I was saddened to lose my closest friend, I started hanging out with the *chosen* girls. I couldn't deny it—it was so much fun. From then on, I became preoccupied with acceptance, acting cool, and maintaining my bond with girls who were considered popular.

The irony of popularity is that most teenagers can't avoid its lure, yet unpopular behavior earns them this status. As I entered junior high, our group of popular girls grew. I would tease those excluded—it made me feel better about myself. The rest of the group did the same. We were very different girls with one thing in common: we artificially boosted our self-esteem by criticizing others. We were mean-spirited, petty girls who deliberately hurt our peers in order to secure our popular status. This need for popularity fed my deepest insecurities.

As my school years went on, and my popularity went up, my self-image spiraled downward to the point that every look in the mirror left me with feelings of self-hatred. For one thing, I already towered over my classmates, quickly on my way to being over six feet tall. I despised what I saw—in particular, I hated my nose. What I targeted as my most unattractive feature preoccupied my inner thoughts. I had a bump on my nose that led one of my uncles to tease me relentlessly. Every holiday, every family event, my uncle never greeted me without a comment. "So, still smilin' with a schnoz like that? Amazing." This man predicted that my nose would become my trademark, the source for tireless teasing by the boys. "Kids must give you the hardest time."

My uncle's warning came true. One boy at school nicknamed me "Ski Slope." This brought me attention while other girls floated through adolescence unnoticed by boys. I should have been flattered by the attention, but my dramatic reaction to the name Ski Slope encouraged the boy, and I feared this label would stick with me forever. I would have to carry out my deepest secret plot to correct my genetic distortion.

I had fantasized my plan for a long time: I would perform my own plastic surgery and remove the bump on my nose with a kitchen knife. With Ski Slope threatening to become my iconic symbol, I left school one day resolute in my bloody design to remove my greatest cosmetic flaw.

Then it came to me—the insight that words could fight words. What made this boy think he was any more physically attractive than me? In fact, his nose was noticeably larger than his face could conceal. So while my mom did book work at the kitchen counter that night, oblivious to her duty as butcher-knife security, I invented my comeback.

The next morning at school, this boy halted in his tracks after his greeting of "Hey, Ski Slope" was met with "Hi, Tweety Bird."

"What? What did you call me?"

"Tweety Bird. Nice beak—something we share, right?"

Within minutes I negotiated a deal never to call him that name, if he would forget Ski Slope forever.

The tables turned again in seventh grade. My popularity did not protect me from a student who rejected the hierarchy of middle school social status. Taunted and verbally degraded, I was repeatedly harassed by this boy. The hostile names I fired back at him fell unnoticed. I suffered as this fiend whispered insults into my ear every chance he could. Even after my teacher moved him across the room, I dreaded going to seventh-period English.

One day, I just couldn't stand it any longer. I refused to be tormented, at least for today. I called my mom at the store and told her I was sick. Typically, Mom would pep-talk me: "Do your best. You can make it! Classes are almost over, then you can come home to rest." But she explained later that she could hear something different in my voice. Something told her this was not Tasha trying to get out of an afternoon class. Once we were home, my mom disappeared into the kitchen. I sprawled out in the living room with a blanket, pretending to be sick. I could hear Mom working. She would run the blender, and I would start crying. She would turn the blender off, and my tears would stop. This continued for three or four cycles until my mom finally heard me and asked what was wrong.

I cried out, "I'm ugly!"

"What?" She laughed a little and then quickly realized I was serious.

"Tasha, you're not ugly!"

"Yes, I am. And I'm so sick of feeling ugly! I look in the mirror and I hate what I see!" I let it out and already felt better for sharing my secret self-loathing.

"But Tasha, you're beautiful! Where would you get such an idea? You are so blessed to be a beautiful girl!"

I continued to cry, but I was listening.

"Okay, it's true; some girls are not blessed with pretty features. But you are! Why would you spend one minute of your day worrying about this?" Mom laughed again, trying to persuade me that she was right and I was wrong, that this was silly.

But I continued to cry. I told her I believed she was saying all of this simply because she was obligated to … because she was my mother. With my defenses down, I told her my biggest hang-ups. "I hate my nose and I hate being tall!" I cried out, relieved that she knew it all.

With her blender on hold, we sat on the living-room floor for almost an hour. At thirteen years old, I never thought my mom could help me through this. Clearly I'd never shared my insecurities with her before that day. I couldn't fathom that she would understand what I was going through—my mom, who was always busy, who was difficult to talk to because I knew she had a million responsibilities weighing her down. As we talked, she even admitted how she had hated her nose too. Wrapped in the security of a blanket, with no one else home, I let Mom convince me of the simple truth that everyone was different and that it was a good thing. In time, she assured me, I would grow to love myself.

From that point on, I went into my seventh-period English class refusing to hear what the harassing boy had to say. His voice faded with my insecurities, but it would be years before I understood that the power of God's gift of beauty was not found in any mirror.

My struggle to grow up, kept alive and well by the narrow-minded nature of the teenage mind, did not end despite some wonderful lessons. I was still guilty of faking a smile, stretching the truth, and perpetuating the gossip if it kept me in the loop with the junior high elite. At times, I myself was the subject of school rumors, but I could hardly feel like a victim since I routinely contributed to this negative climate.

About half of my energy was devoted to maintaining my position within the popular group. The rest went toward securing a boyfriend. At this point, it was monkey-see, monkey-do—conformity at its worst. If some of the girls were starting to have boyfriends, I should, too. Despite my insecurities, I took an interest in a boy named Adam who happened to be two inches shorter than me and a year younger. This was actually a leap of independence for me. Instant feedback from the group let me know who approved and who did not.

Adam wasn't a part of my group, which helped open my eyes to the myth of popularity. A major shift in my friendships resulted, since I gravitated toward people who accepted Adam and didn't judge our relationship. At this point, my best friend was Emmy—a free thinker who made me laugh and forget about others' harsh judgments. Adam and Emmy inadvertently helped me detach from a social circle that thrived on petty elitism. Emmy never looked down on others who struggled to fit in. She seemed to navigate school with a healthy disengagement from the whole mean-girl experience.

Adam was not so self-assured; he often questioned why I even dated him, wondering if he was worthy. Our relationship felt the strain that comes when two self-deprecating people seek the remedy for self-doubt. Although Adam brought some positive changes to my life, he would eventually influence me in a dark way, mostly through the culture of his favorite music.

The decade of the 1990s brought angst, grunge, and Goth into fashion. Even small-town Ellsworth followed trends influenced by heavy metal bands and alternative idols like Marilyn Manson and Kurt Cobain. Moreover, we had a meth crisis right here in our own backyard, as law enforcement declared Pierce County, Wisconsin, one of the hotspots for "cooks" who found easy access to the agricultural chemical anhydrous ammonia—a necessary ingredient for methamphetamine. This decade of prosperity ushered in a new rebel without a cause, as upper-middle-class teenagers sought artificial highs. Our high school experienced a rash of bomb threats and drug-dog-navigated lockdowns. It was a negative time to be a teenager.

Although I managed to fight off the allure of illegal drugs, the darkness found within Adam's favorite heavy metal music consumed me. I never dyed my hair or tattooed my skin with satanic messages as some kids did. But I began to dress almost entirely in black. My pseudo-Goth appearance worried my parents. It was clear that I had sworn off pastel colors forever. Heavy metal music brought dark drama to our lives, since I was not strong enough to simply listen for fun.

This was the period of time when my parents were pursuing legal action against the neighborhood sex offender. By now, he was calling me up to thirty times a day. Other local girls were also victims. The authorities were on to the fact that the laws were rather weak regarding sex offenders who exposed themselves. Those who stalked their victims by watching, following, or phoning, but not touching, rarely were prosecuted. Things escalated, since I was truly afraid of him and what he might do to me. Finally, this man was ordered out of Pierce County. He could have no contact with me or our community, regardless of the fact that his own children resided in Ellsworth. Since I was not the only teenage girl to whom he exposed himself, the multiple complaints helped my family pursue some level of prosecution. The stress of this case, tied with my secret belief that I was somehow to blame, nurtured my negative attitude.

Angst grew between Adam and me—the trouble that festers from a faithless existence. I began to argue with him about subjects I didn't even know concerned me.

Adam didn't believe in God. I found this disconcerting. I wasn't exactly the poster child for religious growth, yet I couldn't tolerate his open declaration of atheism. Evidently, Adam's rejection of God's existence was the first push I needed toward a relationship with God. Although I was in no position to help Adam with his lack of faith, every argument ironically pushed me closer to the spirituality that would save me. Unaware of the importance of this particular conflict between us, I fixated on the fact that Adam and I spent far too much time fighting. It was time to break up with him, yet I lacked the willpower to do so. I didn't call on God to help me. In retrospect, I should have.

My grandma often told me that I shouldn't bother God with my petty problems. He was busy with really serious issues affecting people with real needs. I took this to heart and thought that God truly didn't pay attention to me other than watching my attendance at church every week. Outside of Sunday morning, I would only go to God if I really felt desperate. As soon as things would work in my favor, God was gone from my life until the following Sunday, or the next crisis.

Despite my detachment from real faith, I recall an amazing Sunday school class for teens. It intrigued me, and I felt hopeful that some of my doubts and questions could be answered in this class. Admittedly, I was very irreverent toward God at this point. But I knew God loved me. I just couldn't understand faith beyond this fundamental fact.

One thing I did acknowledge was that God created me with a passion for so many things. Besides sports, I was fascinated by theater, music, and any opportunity to perform. Most of my family participated in the performing arts. Dad sang professionally with the Sheldon Singers and the Country Gentlemen, and he performed solos at local weddings and funerals. My sister played piano beautifully. Like Dad, Ryan was involved in musicals; probably the most memorable for me was his role in Ellsworth High School's *West Side Story*. I loved that production so much that I couldn't wait until I was old enough to take part in these plays.

Feeling the pressure to perform as well as other Schuh family members, self-doubt reared its ugly head again. Despite my fears, I took what I thought was a first step in pursuing the family performance tradition: I auditioned for a singing solo at school. I felt equal parts of fear and excitement at the thought of getting up and singing in front of so many people.

Just before the director announced the winner of the solo spot, I whispered to her, "Just so you know, I can't do a solo."

She responded, "What? I thought you wanted this chance. Are you sure?"

I said, "Yes, thank you, I'm sure," and I took my seat in the choir room.

Later, I learned that the director had in fact selected me for the solo. I was so disappointed that I missed my opportunity. I blamed myself and made a silent promise: next time, I would give my best audition and have the confidence to stick it out.

In the early spring of eighth grade, my friend Jesse Carr called and said, "Tasha, we need you." Here was my chance to stick to my word.

Jesse's church was putting on a musical and had been practicing for a long time. She explained, "The girl who had the lead just quit. If we can't replace her, we're going to have to scratch the whole thing. Do you think you could do it? You'll have to sing some solos."

I said, "Jesse, I don't know if I can even sing in front of people. I've never really sung a whole song by myself before."

Jesse begged me. They really didn't care if I could sing well. I finally agreed, even though I would not be available the whole week before the opening performance since I would be in Europe with my family. These kids had been working on this play for so long, they just wanted a willing participant to learn the lines and take the part.

To this day, I am eternally grateful to the girl who abandoned her part. This role just fell into my lap, and since I felt needed, I was compelled to do my best job without the pressure of too much judgment. The cast was grateful no matter what my level of talent, since the show would be cancelled without a volunteer lead. Performance experience without pressure ... what an opportunity.

I played the part of Nanny Bird. And, yes, I actually had to squawk like a bird. I remember very little about the actual plot, but I vaguely recall spending most of the play dressed as a giant bird, searching for my glasses. I am sure I was a horrible actress, even for the likes of this childish plot, but it was so much fun. The following year, I was singing solos and not backing down from any performance challenge.

At the age of fifteen, I finally attained the same status as every other member of the Schuh family: I was employed, albeit part-time, by my parents at D&K Family Foods. I dreamed of ways to spend all the money I would make, while Mom reminded me of the college savings account I needed to fill. I stocked shelves, cleaned and organized the store, and worked as a cashier. I loved my job since it was compatible with my hectic schedule. In charge of scheduling all the workers, Mom finagled my hours around sports, music, and other school activities. I generally worked two nights a week and on Saturday mornings.

Besides the store and the occasional choir concert, most of my time outside of school was consumed by sports. Through eighth grade, basketball was my favorite game to play. However, this would change my ninth-grade year when a new coach entered the scene. Some coaches emphasize sportsmanship or team-building, but for the first time I was led by a coach who was all about winning. He was dealing with junior high teams, yet his manner was that of a college or professional basketball coach.

As this coach tried to build players who shared his passion for winning, he destroyed my confidence. And I believe he had a similar effect on many of my teammates. From this point on, basketball had to become our top priority "or don't bother to come out for the team." If we had other winter activities, like skiing, "expect to give them up for the next four years. No player will run the risk of injury anywhere but on the basketball court." As freshmen, our first official season under his rule, we listened to his demands as he robbed us of the joy of the game.

Prior to my freshman season and the new coach, I had always received a lot of playing time. My game-time minutes on the court developed confidence in me that contributed to the success of my team. This suddenly changed. Insecurity grew as my playing time diminished. I played about twenty seconds during our first game that season. Silent self-questioning started—why was I contributing all the hours to practice if I couldn't perform on game day? Sitting, waiting, watching while others subbed in and out gave me time to think. Was this decision to bench me the right one? The same self-esteem demons that told me my nose was too big attacked my confidence as I waited to play.

Finally, Coach called me to sub into the game. Here was my chance to prove myself ... but nervousness hijacked my skills. With the eyes of a doubting coach on me and the pressures to play flawless basketball for a few short minutes, I made a fool of myself and was abruptly pulled from the game.

I later sat on the bench so much that I became great friends with another girl on the team. Sarina, a feisty little guard with blonde hair and a sarcastic tongue, made the best of any situation because she loved to laugh. She couldn't get down on herself—it wasn't her nature. If a coach didn't want to play her, it was his loss. On and off the court, if you disagreed with her, she'd be the first to let you know. I knew for a long time that I'd rather be her friend than her enemy. Sarina and I created our own fun as we both sat during games and made the best of our ninth grade season together.

Honestly, I stuck with basketball because my parents persuaded me to see through any activity that I started. I recall having my complaints at home answered by my dad: "Just remember, we are not quitters in this family. No driver's license if you quit before the end of the season." This threat and Sarina's friendship helped me tolerate my ninth-grade winter. Self-proclaimed "bench buddies," Sarina and I formed a bond that remains today.

Just as the basketball season ended, the high school drama department announced the tryout schedule for the fall musical, *Grease*. Wow—my absolute favorite movie would be performed at Ellsworth High School! I had to get a part. I already knew every line of the script by heart. I was obsessed with John Travolta, and I had just seen the Broadway revival of *Grease* in New York that previous summer. My New York trip boosted my confidence that I was meant to be a part of this cast.

Since these were the days when Ellsworth High School housed grades 10-12, and Ellsworth ninth graders still attended the junior high, it was rare for a freshman to earn a part in a high school production. The director simply didn't know the younger kids. Traditionally, upperclassmen got the big roles in our plays. However, Ms. Huber, our junior high choir teacher, consulted with the high school director for auditions. I figured I had a small chance of getting a chorus part. With *Grease* on the line, I didn't care what role I secured—I just had to be a part of this play.

Tryouts held in the high school choir room ran like any theater audition. I was warned by others to simply walk in, give my name, sing, recite my lines, and then wait to be told, "That's enough ... thank you." Don't expect the slightest hint from the staff that you will be cast as a lead—or picked to sweep the stage floor.

We were told to prepare one of the songs from the play. I was so nervous! One girl trying out, a senior who looked exactly like Sandy from the movie, rehearsed confidently in the hallway as we waited to be called. I was certain she would get the lead part.

Timidly, I went in, sat down, and waited my turn. I heard my name, stood up, and when given the cue, started singing my song—the slow version of "Look at Me, I'm Sandra Dee." The director's jaw dropped. When my audition song ended, the room was silent. I didn't know what the silence meant. I wasn't sure if I had impressed everyone or if I had just embarrassed myself. As I sat back down, people began praising me. Once all the Sandy candidates were finished, the director of the play approached me with positive comments about my performance. I didn't sleep very well that night. I wondered if my very first high school role could possibly be a lead part.

The next day in choir class, my teacher read off a list of names—callbacks for the high school musical. I was included. Nervous, I reported back to the high school as directed. By then, it was clear who was going to be Danny. The director asked three of us to act out a scene alongside him for the other leading role. I knew I had a chance at Sandy, since one girl lacked a strong stage voice. But the Olivia Newton-John lookalike was also there. Since I didn't look like Sandy, I felt my chances for the part were slim.

As Dad can tell you, with callbacks completed, I jumped into our van and, with hands folded, declared, "God, please give me this role. I will do anything! I promise! I will become a nun. If you give me this role, I will serve you and do anything you want me to. If I get this part, I will be so happy! This will be the only thing I will ever want, and I promise to be happy for the rest of my life."

The next morning, the high school band director came over to the junior high to personally deliver the casting results. She made it clear that she wanted me to come up and see the results first. I walked up to her, and she removed her hand from the list. Written next to the name *Sandy* was my name, *Tasha Schuh!* Everyone in the choir room started clapping.

Adam was not happy that I had tried out for the play. He knew that if I got the role of Sandy, I would have to kiss another boy. I looked over at him as he pouted in jealousy, another clue that we were not meant for each other. Everyone else cheered for me while I freaked out with excitement. As I left the classroom to call my parents and share that I had gotten the part, thoughts of breaking up with Adam hovered in the back of my mind.

Up until that point, I had often wondered about my purpose in life. I had such a shaky sense of self-worth, but securing this role gave me hope that life could be wonderful, even beyond this high school play.

Scripts were distributed at our first cast meeting, where we were instructed to learn our parts by the start of the new school year. I took voice lessons that summer and practiced my songs for hours. Before these lessons, one of the few times I sang in front of people was in Jesse's church, playing Nanny the Bird—the lone part on my musical theater resume! The voice lessons boosted my confidence so much that I agreed to sing for my sister's wedding. Summer also meant I had time to think about the Sandy look-alike who had lost out on the lead role her senior year. I fought my self-esteem demons, but this time with a grateful attitude that I owed everyone my best performance in *Grease*.

The summer ended, and so did my relationship with Adam. Life would be freed up to focus on school, sports, and most importantly, my new obsession. There would be a different kind of drama in my life now—Ellsworth High School musical drama.

Chapter 4

Time, Place, and Motion

LIKE A CLICHÉ high school movie, Adam's prediction that I would be attracted to the lead of the play came true. During my sophomore year, I spent extra hours practicing the kissing scenes with Jake, my surrogate Danny Zuko. However, Jake challenged my myth of popularity by refusing to officially "date" me. Burned by his previous girlfriend, he swore off commitment until graduating years later from the air force academy.

"We're not dating. Just remember that."

"So you can spend time alone with me after play practice, almost every weekend, and *not* call me your girlfriend?"

"You got it. We're not that couple. If you're okay with that, I'll see you tomorrow night."

We spent the vast majority of our time alone having this very conversation, which clearly conflicted with every established notion I had of dating. I fought it, but Jake was so fun! I had never been treated this way by any of my boyfriends or by boys who chased me. I tolerated Jake's unwritten rules, perhaps because Jake was a senior, more likely because Jake was a wonderful guy. He was fun, secure with himself, and ironically offered less drama than I expected in a relationship that publicly did not exist.

Because of the demands of *Grease*, I spent more time with not-my-boyfriend Jake than most official couples spent together. This was the inaugural year of a class called Musical Theater, a ninety-minute course

33

under a new block scheduling system that granted every cast member an elective credit. We met in the choir room second period every day for *Grease*, in addition to the lengthy rehearsals that were added in the evenings as opening night approached. I loved the schedule, since it freed up two hours after school for volleyball. I didn't have to abandon sports for the demands of the play.

With opening just weeks away, the class-time practices gave our directors the luxury of time that should have guaranteed a superior performance. Yet one factor threatened a quality show despite a talented cast and crew: our ridiculously small stage.

EHS did not have a theater. In previous years, we sold tickets for folding chairs in our old junior high gym, where a small stage stood behind the basketball court. With an enormous cast and complicated set, Mr. Dulak sought and secured the Sheldon Theater in Red Wing, Minnesota, for our weekend run of *Grease*. Once we moved everything to the theater, we had five days to pull it together. We practiced from five to eleven-thirty p.m. those final nights in the Sheldon, where my parents purchased ninety-four tickets for family and friends, guaranteeing that I had loyal fans applauding me at each performance.

I was so nervous. Gossip that I was too young to handle this big role drifted throughout our town. I was sure that when the curtain opened, I would vomit all over the stage.

But the thrill of performance propelled me. I recall shocked looks from people in the first few rows as I started to sing. It felt so good to feel unique—to have people staring at me and getting lost in the performance. All my friends were petite and cute, but I was this towering mast who transformed into something special when given the freedom to sing.

Grease was an amazing experience! My insecurities were at least weakened by well-earned confidence. After our final show, others moved on, while I focused on the change *Grease* seemed to bring to my life. The show convinced people I had a voice—"like your dad and Ryan." I received compliments that indicated I was another talented Schuh who should pursue more musical opportunities. Thus, *Grease* remained a part of me, became a piece of my identity. It built confidence that spilled into other aspects of my life, like dumping Jake and his rules. *I deserve better,* I thought. *People know me—they are paying attention to me. How would it look if everyone realized I was sneaking around with a senior boy who doesn't acknowledge me as someone special in his life?* Obviously, I was still too concerned with public opinion, but in this case, it was positive motivation to move on from Jake.

Performing as Sandy in Grease, November 1996.

The play closed, and I prepared for basketball tryouts. Promised more playing time, I was duped into joining the Ellsworth Panthers for yet another disappointing season. Sarina and I deepened our bench-buddies friendship while secretly swearing we would not repeat this decision again. If I could have valued the team experience for what it was—a chance to be with friends, a healthy activity, an opportunity to unselfishly support others' success—I might reflect on basketball as positively as my time in theater. But no one mentored me through this sport in that way. It was all about playing time and catering to favorites, and it fed my own need for the limelight. Embarrassment from being overlooked at game time trumped the benefits of the team experience.

In the final game of the JV season, I subbed in for my token few minutes of play. I couldn't hold back my tears. With my parents in the stands and the Ellsworth bench wondering what was wrong with me, I cried up and down the court.

One of my teammates, Missy Halverson, told me later that Coach was rather confused. "What's up with Tasha? Is she hurt? Should I pull her?"

"No, she's all right. Leave her in till the end. This is her last game," Missy tried to explain.

"What do you mean her last game? She's only a sophomore."

"She's done. She's made up her mind. She won't come out next year."

Later that night, Coach tried to leverage to keep me playing. I suppose he figured he was doing the right thing—that promising me varsity playing time in the upcoming regional would convince his tallest player to keep trying to improve in a game that seemed designed for her. But I refused the offer. I cried through the last minutes of this game and walked away from it forever.

I knew I was not crying because I would no longer play for the EHS Panthers. Quite honestly, this decision brought me nothing but relief. I cried because this was the last time I would play basketball. I would never play another organized game of a sport I truly loved. I don't know why I knew this—that I would never again run up and down the court with nine other players. A lot of students played college intramurals or adult league ball. But I knew. Intuition, premonition, or God's message to feel every last moment on that court—I knew this was something I would never experience again.

High school life moves fast, and *Grease* soon became nothing but a yearbook snapshot to most of the kids in my school. The honor of portraying Sandy faded along with the charm of playing by Jake's rules. My friend Sarah convinced me to take a call from a boy named Travis—someone who would apparently pick up where Jake refused to commit. One night, I informed my dad that I was expecting a very important call that would interrupt our "wedding singers" rehearsal (we were booked as a duet that weekend).

The phone rang, and my dad answered. I ran to our second phone in another room for privacy.

"I've got it, Dad. You can hang up now."

"*If ever I would leave you ...*" Dad's version of his favorite song from *Camelot* echoed through the phone.

"Dad, hang up. Please. Dad ..."

"We have some practicing to do. *It wouldn't be in summer ...*"

After apologizing to Travis and making a date for Friday night, I ran to the living room to scold my dad.

"Really, did you have to sing the whole song? A few bars would have done as much damage."

Dad laughed and reminded me, "Let him know right away what he's dealing with."

Friday night came. As covertly as a small town would allow, I went to the movie *Jerry Maguire* with Travis, not Jake. He opened doors for me, paid for my ticket, bought me a late supper—shocking in an era of gender equality. But more than that, Travis was sensitive and generous, and more attentive to me than any other boy had been. I let Jake know that I was no longer in the game, and Travis and I became official.

I was back to my comfort zone of steady couple-hood. Travis and I were inseparable. Throughout the second half of my sophomore year, Travis and I fit "together like ramma lamma lamma ka dinga da dinga dong." That is, if *ramma lamma lamma* is alcohol.

I occasionally joined in at drinking parties as early as age fourteen, but with Travis as my collaborator, we made this the center of our weekend social lives. We used the typical small-town complaint, "There's nothing else to do in Ellsworth." So every weekend we instigated plans to hang out in a cornfield and drink beer. The established popular group welcomed me to their weekend retreat, where Travis was already accepted. These were fun, social people, some of whom proved to be incredibly loyal friends after my accident; others cared only superficially for their drinking buddies. All of us were taking risks that strong character—the character that comes with faith and Christian values—would have helped us avert.

By day, many of us were the achievers—the top athletes in our coaches' eyes, the conscientious students worried about ACT scores and college applications, the musical-theater talent who entertained our community. It is hard to measure the damage done from hiding illegal behavior that comes with teen alcohol use. For starters, most of us lied to our parents. "I'm at Trisha's house watching movies." Or "We're bowling in Red Wing—going for pizza after that."

"Sorry I'm late and didn't call—Samantha had a flat tire, so we were all out in Trisha's driveway helping. Time just got away from us."

Of course, some kids had folks who condoned their drinking. "Could be worse, you know. At least they're not doing drugs. In a few years, they'll be legal. Gotta learn how to handle their beer sometime. We have rules—no driving. I take the keys from the kids and make them sleep at our house when the bonfire's done."

Hangovers, pure poison the next day, reminded me of the lies to my parents. They weren't the "cool" types who winked and approved of my nightlife. I fell into the category of those who chose to keep our drinking a secret out of some warped respect for the adults who held us in high esteem. We justified our behavior with the same corrupt reasoning. "Could be worse—could be drugs; could be smoking pot and trying ecstasy, or doing meth."

We actually said these things out loud: "What's the big deal—all of our parents did it. Heck, the drinking age was eighteen when they were kids. You can fight for your country in a foreign war, but you can't drink a beer until you're twenty-one? That's just wrong."

We had thought of everything—every defense that seemed to justify our lies, our promiscuity, our pseudo adult behavior. But we never talked about the lousy feelings that accompanied the lies. We analyzed lots of topics at our parties, but the awful guilt from sneaking around never was confronted.

Despite our weekend pattern, Travis was far more than my partner at parties. I totally fell in love with him. I was sure that Travis was the one I would marry someday. We made plans to move in together after high school and talked about our futures often. We both had career goals, although very different ones. Travis would join in his family's business, and I would go to college to earn my bachelor's in performing arts. We fully intended to support each other's plans and maintain a relationship along the way. Meanwhile, I cheered Travis on at his wrestling matches, and he joined the guys in the bleachers at my games. Then the spring of my sophomore year brought an unexpected opportunity to perform again.

Ellsworth High School only pursued "the musical" every other year, partly because of production costs and partly because of the demands placed on the student cast and crew of a relatively small school. EHS had one of those rare traditions where over a hundred students contribute in some way to the chosen play. Actors, musicians, stage managers, set builders, a publicity team, a lighting and tech crew all bring large numbers of students to the experience. Since *Grease* pulled in so much revenue, talk of another big production led to plans for *The Wizard of Oz*. The success of offering the musical as an accredited class confirmed that back-to-back shows could be the start of a new school tradition. So the Sheldon Theater was once again procured for the elaborate spectacle that would prove to be the very last Ellsworth High School production in that venue.

Chapter 5

The Wizards of Rochester

"CAN YOU FEEL this?"

"Can you feel this?"

"Can you feel this?"

X-ray beckoned and put an end to the repetitive quiz for which I hated the answer. *No, I can't feel whatever it is you are doing to me, but your question stabs my soul more painfully than that prodding tool.* Heavy medication numbed my consciousness while doctors demanded that I stay awake. It was eleven p.m.—four and one-half hours after the fall. I had been at Saint Marys Hospital, part of Mayo, for most of this time without any family contact. While I endured careful inspection, my parents faced the overwhelming news that I would never walk again.

In the final hour of November 11, one doctor entered a private lounge where close family and friends gathered to support my mom and dad. With a businesslike tone, this doctor stated what the initial screening clearly showed:

- "She's broken her neck at the C5 level. She has a fractured skull. That bony bump on the back of her head apparently hit the concrete first, thus making this a sixteen-foot fall—ten feet from stage to basement, but remember her head already stood six feet above the stage. This makes it sixteen feet of force when she falls from standing position to headfirst contact on the basement floor."

- "She has C5 vertebrae broken off, forming a perfect arrowhead that's pierced her spinal cord—a triangular sharp point. Surgery will address this."
- "She has a crushed spinal cord—not 'severed.' Same outcome: paralysis."
- "She's suffered a cerebral hemorrhage—bleeding that threatens brain damage. Every precaution is being taken to minimize the bleed."
- "Bottom line: she's a C5 quadriplegic. She'll never walk again. She'll have limited use of her arms, but she's going to be in a wheelchair for the rest of her life."

No one said a word. Did they wonder if the doctor would follow with some kind of consolation like, "Well, if she works hard and stays focused, physical therapy might …" *Tasha's that girl! If there's a glimmer of optimism, Tasha's your candidate.* But the doctor followed up with nothing.

Finally, my mom broke the silence. "And who is going to tell her this?"

The doctor replied, "She already knows."

Hmmm … she already knows. She already knows. Even if I recalled being told such harsh news, which I don't, do you think that for one moment I accepted it? Who would buy this grim prospect only hours after a fall that did not even knock me unconscious? Who would comprehend the finality of this doctor's announcement without doubts and denial?

This much I recall from the last hour of November 11: that I couldn't move, that my body wasn't responding the way I commanded it to. I fought the heavy sleep that comes with IV painkillers and believed I simply needed time. I needed time to heal, the antidote for stubborn nerves knocked senseless by an extreme fall.

My mom called Angie in Sioux Falls, South Dakota, where she and her husband, Scott, lived. "Don't drive tonight. This is too far on bad winter roads in the middle of the night. Come tomorrow morning."

My sister didn't listen. She filled a laundry basket with clothes—no time to dig out the suitcase. While she hurled random items into the bin,

Scott tried to translate the few details that Angie acquired during her frantic phone call from Mom. He then tossed his own change of clothes into the basket and jumped in the car with Angie for their five-hour trip to Rochester.

My brother also received a phone call from Mom just before midnight. Ryan, a junior at UW-Stout in Menomonie, Wisconsin, took Mom's advice and chose to wait until morning to see me. I can now only imagine the level of despair my family felt from the grim facts conveyed by the businesslike doctor. Yet I will tell you that everyone showed strength in my presence, while I demonstrated utter cluelessness.

"Thank you so much for coming. You didn't have to drive all this way. I'm doing okay. I just need to heal. It's definitely going to take time. You guys are awesome. How's Sarina?" To this day, my family says that I asked far more about Sarina's status than my own.

"It's just going to take some time" was my mantra for the next few days as I comforted friends, grandparents, aunts, uncles, and some relatives I didn't even recognize. My revolving ICU door withstood constant use as the staff tried to monitor my small-town celebrity status.

My parents and I were in awe of the love and support that came to the neurological intensive-care unit, eighth floor of the Mary Brigh Building. Visits were challenging with my haloed head and constricted body in a seasick rotation from the traction bed. Yet we turned away no one. People's concerns were an inspiring gift that motivated us to stay strong and hopeful.

For three days, I slowly swung from my left side, then to my right side. Don't misunderstand—this was not a leisure hammock design. The bed was hard, and in my med-induced drowsiness, I imagined I was lying on the surface of my school's Formica lunch table—hard, thick, and unforgiving to my masked pain. The temporary halo, hooked to a hundred-pound weight hanging behind me, elongated my vertebrae. The hope was that my shattered neck bones would settle into place like jigsaw-puzzle pieces seeking a comfortable new arrangement. My vertebrae were in my spinal cord, surgery pending.

Despite emotional outbursts from many of my visitors, I still did not grasp the magnitude of my injuries. I told friends that I couldn't wait until the weekend "so I can get out of this place and party with you."

Travis sadly whispered, "You know, you're going to be here, in the hospital, for quite a while. We're talkin' a few months." Travis was one visitor who struggled to show optimism. He cried, looked worried, and couldn't cover his true feelings. In retrospect, I believe he had one of the most realistic understandings of my grave outlook.

I, on the other hand, thrived on cluelessness. When my bed rotated toward the direction of my girlfriends who were visiting, I asked if they would "make sure all my teachers know that I won't be in school for a while." I worried about my art class—a clay pot was my culminating masterpiece for the semester.

"Sarah and Brooke, you have to talk to Mr. Ruppe. Make sure he keeps my clay covered so I can finish molding. It has to stay wet or it's ruined. Hey, are you even listening to me?"

Afraid to disagree, my friends were silenced by my absolute disconnect from the gravity of my predicament. One of the girls later confessed that when my bed rotated away, tears would roll down her face; when my bed rotated around again, she pulled herself together and promised me anything I wanted.

"Sorry, Tasha. Sure, I'll talk to Mr. Ruppe right away, in the morning."

"Good. I don't think he'll take late points off my grade, right? That would stink. I worked so hard on that piece. I've remolded it so many times. I know exactly how I want to paint it," I said while my friends apparently stifled their cries behind me. Back at the Sheldon, *Oz* was being performed each night, yet right here in my hospital room was some of the best acting Ellsworth students had ever achieved.

My boyfriend, on the other hand, had never taken an acting class in his life, and it showed. One of the first nights when we were alone in my ICU room, he completely lost it. "I can't believe this has happened to you. It's so unfair."

Call it inner strength, God's support, or maybe just a naive state of denial, but I often comforted others who came to my bedside to comfort me. And here I was doing it with Travis.

"I think we need to break up." I gave him some tough love.

"What?"

"I know you. This isn't going to work. This is your senior year, Travis—the year you've waited for. I don't want to hold you back. You have so many friends. You should be spending time having fun. This is not what you signed up for."

Here's where he got strong. "No—no way. I don't care—that's not important to me. It's going to work." Travis convinced me that no matter what the outcome, he was going to stay with me. Knowing his lifestyle and the things Travis hoped to do, I knew I would not be in the picture for very long. It was not a criticism of Travis. It didn't mean I no longer loved him, or that I didn't feel loved by him. We were simply not going to survive the change that comes with such profound adversity. At this point, however, I trusted in what Travis wanted. I backed off the topic for the time being. I wanted my boyfriend by my hospital bedside.

The final day in my traction bed, talk of surgery filtered in and out of the room. I remember one doctor coming to check my vitals, studying some notes but not sharing much.

"So, this surgery's a step in the right direction, right?" I asked.

"Yep."

"When will I be able to get up and work on walking?" I was polite, but persistent.

No response—just that "Are you kidding me?" look that comes when someone is trying to deduce whether you're being sincere or a smart aleck. I'm sure he thought I had a warped sense of humor. These couldn't be genuine questions.

"Any talk of release?"

"You're paralyzed," he shot back at me. "You're going to be paralyzed for the rest of your life. You broke your neck." His abrupt comeback robbed me of my next breath.

I found out later that my parents had made one clear request. This news should *not* be delivered without my family in the room. "I don't care if you think Tasha's already been told her diagnosis. Have you listened to her? Have you been in her room? She either doesn't remember this newsflash or she's blocked it out completely. Do not tell her she is *paralyzed* when she is alone."

My primary doctor agreed with Mom during that conversation. Yet within hours a different doctor, unaware of this agreement, left me strapped in rotating motion after delivering my heaviest fear.

As I sobbed uncontrollably, one question overwhelmed me—why hadn't I died? My biggest nightmare, life in a wheelchair, had come true. For the first time, I truly wanted to die. As the dread of truth surrounded me, Angie returned to my room, panic on her face.

"What's wrong, Tasha? What happened? I just left for a minute. I thought there was a doctor with you? Why did he leave if you needed something?"

This was one of the few times I cried so hard, I couldn't talk. I was absolutely devastated by information that had been stated so matter-of-factly that most people would have thought the man was reading the weather report. Somehow I sputtered out the truth to Angie.

She was livid. A doctor had gone against my parents' request. Somehow, I told her to stay with me … let him go … "Don't leave; I'm so afraid. He was just telling me what you already know anyway."

Angie's anger melted as she began to focus on the fact that I was now acknowledging the harsh truth: regardless of the surgery's outcome, I was not expected to ever walk again. I sobbed because of this cold reality. I cried even more because I knew that family and friends had already accepted this prognosis.

Slowly, Angie helped me piece everything together. *This is it. This is my diagnosis. This is why everyone keeps telling me that I will be in the hospital for so long. This is why my pain seems endless and heavy doses of medication drip steadily through my IV. This is why my halo digs into my head, and my feeding tube weaves through my nose and down into my stomach. This is the reality for a quadriplegic patient waiting to have a neck-saving procedure. This is the start of a long healing process that cannot be rushed.*

If this frank doctor's proclamation did not give me a reality check, the fact that my accident made Minnesota and Wisconsin state news confirmed it. Both Sarina and I were covered by more than one local news channel, as well as a slew of newspapers with far-reaching circulation.

On November 14, three days after falling *sixteen* feet, the new Tasha Schuh, age *sixteen,* endured a *sixteen*-hour surgery. The surgical team's objective was to fuse my C4 through C6 vertebrae in order to stabilize my shattered C5. Bone taken from both of my hips was fused to my neck, and metal fittings finished out the required hardware. A neck collar would replace the halo.

That morning, I entertained a new delusion as people encouraged me to defy the odds.

"You're going to prove those doctors wrong ..."

"They don't know how strong a person you are ..."

"I know someone who broke his neck and he's walking ..."

These were common words of encouragement from family, friends, even staff that fed my fantasy that this procedure would fix everything. I would come out of the surgery, work in rehab with physical therapists, and soon prove that all of my movement had returned. I would eventually be walking again! Despite the sobbing episode with Angie only hours earlier, I was back to my fantasy—that I would be the old Tasha in no time at all. I would defy the doctors' predictions. One of the most respected neurosurgery departments in the world would be proven wrong.

I awoke from my surgery just as the breathing tube was pulled out. I had been intubated all sixteen hours of the procedure. My team of doctors feared that my lungs would become highly dependent on the vent. They watched for minor difficulty in breathing when I initially came to. With some oxygen for support, I should gradually breathe on my own.

But without warning, pneumonia crept in. Low oxygen levels required a series of bronchoscopies that should have revealed precisely why my lungs were not functioning. "Ready to re-intubate." This order upset my family, as they were allowed to observe and stay in the room for support.

Each bronchoscopy brought more confusion, as everyone watched and waited to see what the next move would be. Alarm in the staff's demeanor told my family that doctors were baffled and not in control of the situation.

The next bronchoscopy request came with a need to "clear the room." Panic attacked my family as they were ushered to a waiting area this time. Resentment fueled their anxiety as they waited for some change in my status. Why had an hour gone by with no explanation? As my parents stood helpless in a nearby room, the sounds of an alarm and the words "code blue" echoed throughout the eighth floor. Medical personnel of every rank stampeded down the hallways and burst into the ICU as the Schuh family stood and watched, frozen in fear that the worst had already happened.

In my room, doctors frantically worked on a flatlined patient whose blood pressure registered zero. Someone on staff speculated, "Pneumonia," while another injected heavy amounts of saline into my veins with hopes of raising my blood pressure.

As time dragged on, one doctor made his way to the waiting room to inform my family that the specialists were unsure about this sudden turn for the worse. "You need to come back to Tasha's room and say your good-byes," he told them.

In disbelief, Mom, Dad, Angie, Ryan, and Scott entered my room, where I was fighting for my life. Doctors and nurses scrambled to do what they could to keep me alive. At the center of the chaos, I laid motionless, tubes doing most of my living for me. A constant push of saline kept my blood pressure from crashing.

I was told later by staff who witnessed my family's faith and encouragement that no one in the room was ready to say good-bye. Despite the directive that led them to my bedside, not one Schuh cried tears of farewell. The staff was awed by my family's spontaneous plan to cheer me on.

"Hang on, Tasha!" Angie started the pep rally by getting right in my face as she found me within the maze of tubes. "Don't you dare go on us!"

After a few moments of momentum from everyone, staff decided to continue on their quest to keep me alive—this time without the Schuhs in the room. Reluctantly, my family made their way back to the waiting room with the announcement of a new game plan. With frantic urgency, the hospital pay phones dialed every number known to my family, this time with one request—pray for Tasha! Within minutes, prayer chains were activated and family, friends, neighbors, and even strangers prayed for my recovery from this sudden brush with death.

Throughout the night, every test and procedure known to modern medicine was ordered in hopes that a remedy would rear its welcome head. Equipment rolled in and out—every mobile instrument owned by the Mayo Clinic made its way to Tasha Schuh's bedside.

By morning, with my blood pressure up to a functional level, a new phenomenon attacked my body. Low blood pressure escalated my heart rate. I was immediately induced into a coma.

Through a process of elimination, doctors investigated two theories: either a stomach blockage or a blood clot was the culprit. A CT scan was ordered to pinpoint the problem that delayed my postsurgical recovery and threatened my life. For the second time, my family was advised to say their good-byes. This scan could not be completed in my room, and doctors were uncertain of my ability to survive the trip to another floor for the procedure. Yet this high-risk exam might solve a mystery that, without treatment, meant imminent death.

The slightest movement of my body threatened my life. I cannot imagine the fear my medical team felt as they carefully prepared me for transport. We would all read later in my records that doctors conveyed, "Natasha is *very sick* ... family knows gravity of situation ... family understands the severity of situation and wants to proceed."

As I was wheeled to another floor for the CT scan, my family marched to the hospital chapel. Prayers for a miracle felt more empowering to them than any medical procedure. Prayers for my survival ... prayers for understanding why God's plan seemed so harsh ... prayers for acceptance if the field trip to CT proved fatal. My family and our prayer chain persevered at the darkest time.

When I had been safely wheeled back into my eighth-floor ICU room, doctors once again marveled at the resilience of one whose vitals showed no hope for survival.

The risky CT scan only deepened the mystery. The procedure revealed there was no blockage, no blood clot. Out of possibilities, the team lacked logical reasoning for my current medical state. Though they recorded "septic shock" in my chart, there was no medical explanation for my body's extreme condition.

For eight days I tolerated a roller coaster ride that required round-the-clock medical staff devoting ICU shifts to my care only. We had always heard about the world-renowned Mayo Clinic and how lucky we were to live so close to this level of care if we should ever need the very best. Well, I needed the very best. Had I not gone there, I believe my outcome would be much different.

Chapter 6

The New Meaning of Thanksgiving

MY DREAM SUDDENLY changed. *I am trapped—I can't move my body. I can't talk. In fact, my mouth feels imprisoned by a garden hose shoved down my throat.* "Pull it out—someone, please, pull it out so I can talk." But in my dream, I had no free will. This part had not changed from my nightmare with Sarina. The strongest sensation I had came from ice-cold rocks that surrounded my neck and shoulders. My eyes felt heavy. I knew they were fluttering, trying to open, which they finally did.

I saw shadows at first, silhouettes of people. I recognized one now. It was Travis—he was talking to me, getting the attention of others in the room and then coming back to my face, shouting, "She's definitely awake this time. Hey, Tasha. I love you! Can you hear me?"

I heard my name a hundred times. I felt confused by the smiling, cheering faces that also shed tears as they bounced in front of me and said they loved me. But where was Sarina? She was no longer in my dream. I was worried about her—did I escape from the old hag and leave Sarina behind? Tears rolled down my face too.

"Don't cry, Tasha! You're going to be fine. Everything's going to work out." I heard my mom's voice. "You didn't come this far for nothing. Be happy! All our prayers are being answered!"

Prayers—did I pray during my other dream? I should have. Even Grandma Barringer would have approved. Trapped in that house, unable to reach Sarina—if that wasn't a time for God's help, nothing was. I had never felt so lost and frustrated in my life.

The longer I listened to my family, the more real this dream became. I was back, awake after surgery. This was real—the accident, the hard hospital bed, the ICU staff, my family surrounding me.

Every vivid nightmare must end, as mine did just one day before Thanksgiving. Eight days had passed without my participation, without my existence. I could not fathom this, so I shook off the desire to know everything and focused on immediate needs. I had to get this hose out of my mouth. But I couldn't lift my arms to even pull on it. A perceptive nurse grabbed a small board and began training my family—language lessons for a ventilator victim.

"She's going to have a million questions. This alphabet board will help, but it's tedious. Ask her to spell out words by blinking." Then to me, in my ice-packed bed, fever still hovering at 103 degrees, she said, "Tasha, can you hear me?"

My eyes widened, and they took this as a yes.

The nurse turned back to my parents and Angie. "She may have suffered brain damage—you've been told this by the doctors, right?" Everyone nodded; serious expressions overtook their faces. The entitlement of having my feelings considered before harsh words were spoken was lost during my coma. "Be patient. Don't panic if she doesn't respond right away. But let's teach her. Eventually, she'll find the energy to respond, so you have to keep at it."

I was exhausted. I couldn't fire off the hundreds of questions that overwhelmed me. But the alphabet board promised escape from silence. I listened closely to the nurse's instructions.

Less than two weeks in the hospital, with fifty pounds of weight melted away, I had strength only to blink. One of my family members would point to letters and I would wink my right eye to indicate a yes. I winked my left eye if the letter they pointed to was incorrect. Laborious compared to my iPad today, I could at least form questions about the last eight days. This arduous task tried everyone's patience, but for the time being, this was one way—the *only* way—I could communicate with others.

Thanksgiving arrived. Stuffing and gravy would not fit through my feeding tube, yet a catered Thanksgiving dinner came to the eighth floor. Those who had prayed so long and hard for me knew that a celebratory meal was exactly what my family deserved, although I remember feeling resentful that I could smell but not taste any part of the feast. I settled for my purple liquid nutrition, shot through my feeding tube, destined to be my dietary source for as long as the ventilator controlled my lungs.

I had so many questions. *Why is everyone so shocked to see me awake? Why do people cry tears of joy as they enter the ICU?* Angie showed me a calendar, and I stared in disbelief at dates that did not line up with my concept of time. It still felt like a dream—not quite as frightening as the one with Sarina, but a science-fiction story where time travel erased eight days of my life.

Despite Thanksgiving cravings, I knew illness still owned me. Revolving nurses appeared like angels, squirting syringe-fed fever meds through my NG tube. These nurses comforted me when I complained of nausea. They coaxed me back to reality when my hallucinations seemed too strong.

My family took turns at my bedside, bearing the constant requests to explain how a broken neck could rob me of my ability to breathe. As with my repeated question the night of my accident—"Am I paralyzed?"—no one had answers. Yet everyone patiently allowed me to ask, with the primitive aid of the alphabet board. "Why so sick? Why tube?" It was like an early form of texting where only essential words were asked because of the painstaking process of spelling even simple phrases.

Many tried to redirect my worries by repeating an insight they all seemed to share: it was a miracle that I was alive. At first, I thought these comments referred back to my fall on November 11. I found no solace in revisiting the accident, since this was old news to me. Yes, I was grateful I did not smash my face into the cement; yes, I could have died instantly on the Sheldon's basement floor. I had acknowledged this gratitude. Did I need to show admiration every day for an accident that salvaged just enough of me to be trapped by life-support now? It took Angie to enlighten me that, for unknown reasons, my life nearly ended in post-op.

Angie grabbed the alphabet board. She swept her right index finger over the letters, hesitating long enough to watch for my reaction. When my right eye blinked at S, she stopped, then started the entire process all over again. My right-eye blinks controlled her finger until four letters spelled out "Sick". She immediately began crying.

"You don't know that you almost died? You don't remember?"

My eyes said, "No."

Angie sobbed uncontrollably, taking breaths to find words that could convey what it felt like to be told, multiple times, "Start planning your sister's funeral."

I cried too, finally recognizing all that I had been through—all that my family had suffered while waiting for the worst of the sepsis to end. I remembered thoughts of wanting to die … wishing I had biffed it on the basement floor so hard that I never woke up. Now that I had faced the closeness of death, I realized more than ever that I wanted to live. The fear of death would become my new obsession.

I looked at my sister through different eyes, with the realization that she completely and unconditionally loved me. If there is ever profound goodness to be discovered from utter disaster, it is the revelation that love is the greatest gift in life. My sister, my parents, my brother and others shared the deep despair they felt while facing my possible death. I'm not sure why it takes a tragedy of this proportion for people to believe, "I love you so much, I do not want to live without you." But here I was, acknowledging this immense love for, and from, my sister.

Before this, Angie and I were not all that close. From this point on, all I had to do was look at her and she knew precisely what I was thinking and what I needed. My accident completely changed our relationship, and I would make a far greater effort now to share my love and gratitude in return. This trait found in the new Tasha Schuh was worth holding on to.

As cluelessness faded, a new emotion filled its void. Fear invaded my ICU room for the next two weeks. I had escaped death, but the ventilator served as a steady reminder that I was dependent upon a machine to breathe.

The fear intensified in the dark of night. With bloodshot eyes, I became a nocturnal creature who preyed on the company of any human who would give me a moment's attention. My insomnia subsided as I watched every tick of the clock approach six a.m. The bewitching hours were over as lights were flipped on and a new shift of workers scurried around the ICU.

By midmorning, doctors, nurses, and sometimes medical students joined my family for daily "rounds." My nurse would often apologize for the heavy traffic in my room. If she only knew this was my favorite time of the day—when a medical field trip came to me. There is power in numbers, the power that multiple lab coats carry when infiltrating the ICU, armed with knowledge that could save me from crashing O_2 sats.

My family tried their best to stay awake with me during the night, calming my fears by taking turns in the chair next to my bed. But jobs and health were threatened by my frenzied need for constant companionship. Since no one knew how long this demanding care would go on, family friends began to take shifts so Mom, Dad, Angie, and Ryan could tend to some of their own needs. Many volunteers sacrificed entire nights of sleep to ensure my comfort. Yet my night fears worsened, especially if Angie disappeared from my sight for very long.

Angie was my most vocal advocate through this stage of my recovery. She had a unique way of showing complete sensitivity to all my fears while calming me at the same time. My sister possessed the gift of logic. If a fear was legitimate, she attacked it and eliminated it. If a fear was illogical, she dispelled it like a lawyer, exposing it for what it was—an unfounded fantasy that could not harm me.

Many doctors and nurses later admitted that they would break into a nervous sweat when my sister approached them. Angie questioned everything. It wasn't that she didn't trust the staff—she just knew that I would ask for an explanation later with the alphabet board. She was an efficiency expert, with Tasha's emotional well-being on the top of her concern chart.

Like a clairvoyant, Angie read my eyes as soon as staff walked near my bed. She jumped up and assertively asked for details. She knew she could skip the alphabet board later if she could prompt a doctor into sharing an open explanation, whether about adjusting the ventilator or drawing blood.

"Drawing blood again? That's the fourth time today. Why is this so frequent?"

The lab tech sent to do the deed looked confused. "Well, I'm doing as I was asked. If a doctor writes an order, Lab has to respond."

"Who is the doctor writing this order? I'd like to speak with him or her before you poke Tasha again." Angie was firm enough that the attending nurse stepped in.

"Angie, you know the blood reveals so much. Everyone wants to see how Tasha is progressing. This is pretty common procedure … frequent blood draws in ICU."

"I get that. But to the point where she needs a transfusion? She's had one already—I don't understand why blood can't be drawn just twice a day. You have plenty of other instruments that can measure her distress or progress in a given day."

Within moments, the lab technician returned to my room with the physician who had written the blood-draw order. Angie voiced the same concerns directly to him, and *voilà*, a new order was written. Blood draws were cut in half.

Angie read my smiling eyes. As the staff walked out, she gave my right shoulder a victorious squeeze. In all my years of sports, I never felt the loyalty of a teammate quite like I felt at that moment with Angie.

Even with Angie's militant defense, I grew frustrated by ICU's inability to communicate with me. In care conferences held in another room, staff told my family play-by-play details of procedures and protocol. But without warning, I was often approached with another invasion of privacy. Privacy—a luxury reserved for nondisabled, healthy people—could not be honored in situations like mine. Yet I wanted to mentally prepare for each procedure. Just once, I wanted to yank my respirator tube out long enough to say, "Hey, what are you doing? What are you checking now? Any changes? Any steps backward?" With every invasive approach to my bed, anger joined fear in my defense against the medical force that battled to save me.

Before the next care conference, I managed to spell out to Angie, alphabet-board style, that I wanted to be involved.

"Really? You want to hear everything the doctors say? You may not like what you hear. You know they have to tell you the bad stuff just in case something goes wrong. You want to hear all that?"

She spelled out *yes* on the alphabet board as fast as she'd ever done, then looked at me in time to see my eager eyes. I was going to get my way for the first time in weeks.

Angie worked her magic, and the following day I participated in my first care conference, right in my room. With family and staff surrounding me, what started as my proudest moment in the hospital became my first encounter with clinical claustrophobia. I had difficulty breathing, even with the ventilator's support, but I stayed strong because I wanted to hear what was said.

The rehab doctor, Dr. Christopherson, reminded everyone that I would be in a wheelchair for the rest of my life. "Tasha, you will need assistance with transfer in and out of your wheelchair, and you'll require assistance getting dressed." Gradually, the claustrophobia consumed me. Angie was right—these were dreadful things to hear, which may have translated better through Mom and Dad.

"Because your paralysis includes your stomach muscles, your voice will be weak. Don't expect to sing from a stage again. Also, we're not sure how a prolonged respirator will impact your voice at this point."

Then the most surprising words came out of his mouth. "With all this said, you *will* be able to drive." How a person unable to fasten the buttons on her shirt could steer a vehicle down the highway was beyond belief. Yet I had attained my driver's license six months prior to my accident. To be able to keep it—earn it back, I should say—was an unexpected gift amid the depressing news. The entire room read the joy in my eyes this time.

Chapter 7

Gifts of Heart and Courage

THE ICU APPEALS to two types of nurses: those with the courage to confront suffering patients and those with the heart to minimize their misery. My favorite ICU nurses had the capacity to do both.

This hospital was loaded with heart and courage. Who wouldn't love a one-to-one patient-to-nurse ratio when faced with the fears that come with critical care? Ginny, the nurse on duty when I crashed, knew the power of angels. She dangled one from my IV pole—a little winged cherub that lifted every visitor's spirits, if only for a moment, during my darkest days. Martha, my favorite night nurse, didn't scold me to "shut your eyes and go to sleep," something I heard from some of the other night nurses. Instead, she pulled up a chair to tell me stories. "You aren't going to sleep anyway, are you? Well, let's pass some time together."

Enter Nurse Marni. She would get credit for my very first hint of hope after my accident. Despite my limited speech, Marni listened and understood one of my biggest fears. I found the courage to ask, "Will I ever be able to get married and have children?" She told me I would, and shared enough success stories that I felt a lift I hadn't felt, and so early in my recovery. Years later, Marni shared a story that told me I had helped her that day as much as she had helped me.

"Tasha, I was driving to work that morning, the day you asked me questions about life after your recovery. I really thought I was burned out on nursing. I asked God, 'Show me sign … give me something that says, yes, stay in this profession—or no, find a new challenge.' Then *you* happened that day. You asked questions that made me feel so useful, such a relief to you. I could feel your worry lift. And I knew I was making a difference. I mattered. Tasha, you helped me as much as I helped you, maybe more. That was the sign, and that's why I still do this job." Our private conversation was a hope-builder for me and a game-changer for Marni.

Despite care and attention from nurses like Marni, hallucinations like my frightening nightmare with Sarina controlled my world of recovery. Triggered by medication and sleep deprivation, hallucinations magnified my fears and phobias.

I made daily appeals on the alphabet board to Angie, Mom, or Dad, "Can't breathe. Pull tube," in hopes that I could shed the ventilator. But staff and family knew I could not breathe on my own. In fact, there was now care-conference talk of a tracheotomy. Visions of another invasive procedure, one that would require an incision through my neck, threatened the vocal cords I begged to use. This only heightened my fears. With moods ranging from lethargy to manic anxiety, I often lost touch with reality.

During this stretch, I believed I was waking up in a different room every morning. If I gave in to sleep in the dark of night, someone on staff would move me—or so I thought. To this day, I vividly recall one ICU room with wood-paneled walls; then, after a midnight gurney ride, I awoke to freshly painted walls. What disturbed me most was when I ended up on a different floor than the nurses' station.

I spelled out to my mom, "Stop moving rooms!"

"Sorry, Tasha, I think I goofed on the alphabet board. You want to stay in the same room?" I wanted to yell, "Yes! That's it!" But I could tell she believed she was lost in translation.

Mom followed the letters again.

"Tasha, there is no way you are in a different room. See—here's the ventilator; here's the white board where your shift nurse writes her name; here's your window in the same spot as yesterday." I could hear my mom's frustration.

59

Yet somehow she understood my biggest fear—that I lacked the strength to press my call button in the night. No one would hear me if my breathing machine suddenly quit. I ruminated over the thought of a power outage. If I closed my eyes, the power might go off and I would be left to suffocate in the dark. Every alarm, every hospital noise, affected my nerves and tensed my body, leaving golf-ball-sized knots in my shoulders.

Comfort came on the nights when I imagined a fireplace in my hospital room. This fireplace appeared more than once, usually when I had an overprotective nurse assigned to me. Some nights, its warmth would wane, and I feared the fire had gone out along with the ventilator. Yet most often, if it appeared, the fire gave me sanctuary enough to sleep for a few hours.

At their worst, my hallucinations grew into the most far-fetched fantasies. The nurses were against me. They mocked and mistreated me behind my family's back. Once I was placed on a metal cart instead of a bed—a cruel joke to see if I could feel the difference. I awoke one morning with a body-sized blood-pressure cuff squeezing my frail torso, calculating and then releasing, squeezing again and then releasing.

After two weeks of vent air, panic attacks were common, as the oxygen never seemed enough. This constant need for more air drove me to steady complaints through the alphabet board. I pestered my busy nurses, "Can't breathe. Can't breathe." Some would appease me by tinkering with the machine—that is, until I discovered it was already set on its highest level.

The ventilator led to anxiety ... which triggered claustrophobia ... which caused sleep deprivation ... which brought an order for heavy meds. I had the perfect formula for paranoia. Every topic of conversation led to obsessive mistrust, producing even more worry. Gifts from concerned friends suddenly became objects that might rob me of lung-saving oxygen. "You know, balloons take up oxygen. Maybe that's why you're having difficulty with your breathing," one nurse said nonchalantly after carrying in another bouquet of cheerful balloons. O_2-sucking, egg-shaped monsters stole the very air I craved! Poor Dad—he was my company that afternoon. I spelled out on the board, "Deflate the balloons."

"What? Let the air out? But they just came! What do you want me to do? Spell it again." He was sure he had misread my winking eyes.

"Deflate the ba—!"

"Really? But they're so colorful."

My eyes indicated, "If I have to spell out 'deflate' one more time …!"

"Okay, okay, I hear you! But how about if I just take them out of the room. Maybe down the hall to the waiting room. They might cheer someone else today."

I reluctantly agreed, although my mind still fixated on the notion that oxygen was being stripped from Mary Brigh's eighth floor. If a panic attack ensued, I was sure to spell out, "Pop the darn things before I suffocate to death!"

One of the oddest hallucinations came one night when I thought the TV was talking to me. Cher Horowitz, played by Rachel Blanchard in the television series *Clueless*, was trying to tell me something. She spoke directly to Tasha Schuh. (No, I am not making this up—Cher from *Clueless*. Apropos, I know.) Although I cannot recall her message precisely, she definitely conveyed that I would not survive. This should have amused, not terrified me. Cher's character wasn't capable of anything as threatening as a death wish. I should have said to myself, *I'm delusional again!* But in true *Clueless* fashion, I believed the hallucination. I cannot tell you how disturbing, how powerful this vision was. The main character from a bubblegum sit-com that ran for three short television seasons wished me dead! After this I vowed, no more TV.

Actually, one show I could watch without fear of interactive characters was *The Flintstones*. I longed for a *Flintstones* cartoon marathon. I relaxed and often slept as Fred and Barney's antics played across the box mounted on my ICU wall. If I woke up in the middle of an episode, no problem. I had memorized every rerun and could jump right in to narrate if necessary. Oddly, this active student, with little time for TV prior to the accident, soon became a *Flintstone* cartoon junkie.

One day pixelated into another, with little change in my status. My family labored to break up the mix of monotony and fear, although my brother's visits became less frequent. Ryan supported me, not always at my bedside, but by covering Mom and Dad at the store. Attending college less than an hour's drive from Ellsworth, Ryan returned home on weekends, helping at the store, earning cash for school expenses, and visiting his girlfriend, Nikki. Now he would work additional evening hours so Mom and Dad could be bedside with me.

My life changed Ryan's. He sacrificed the typical college experience so he could free up time for our family's business. Mom and Dad could devote so many hours to Rochester because they could count on Ryan to cover things at home.

I don't quite know how, but Ryan managed to squeeze many visits in. A bit intimidated by my fragile condition, he shrank from cares that most of the family did as regularly as the staff. For instance, I begged for water, even though the vent prevented me from drinking. My family members had permission to squirt water into my mouth with a syringe, as long as they agreed to siphon the water back out quickly with a suction tube. Relief for my dry lips and tongue! My mom trained Ryan and then left the room to make some phone calls.

I gave Ryan a clear look of, "I'm ready for a shot. Hit me."

"So you want some water ... now?"

I blinked, "Yes."

He fumbled with the syringe while I waited. Looking like a guy who was appointed to defuse an enemy bomb, Ryan slowly sucked up some water while my parched mouth begged for relief. *Mom or Angie would have shot and extracted three rounds by now,* was my thought. Sometimes it was a good thing that I could not speak my thoughts.

Slowly he put the syringe up to my mouth, dropped one bead of water, pulled the syringe away, and suctioned instantly. The vacuum stuck to my tongue.

What, do you think I'll drown from one molecule of water?! I thought. I actually laughed. I think for the first time since my accident, giggles escaped me. This is not an easy task with ventilator hardware plugging your mouth. Ryan, ready to press the nurse's light or yell down the hall for Mom, instantly relaxed. He began to laugh with me, and then he tried it again.

Time cruised by on the days when friends came to visit. I could only listen, but the drama back at school seemed fascinating to me. Stevie, Sarah, Jesse, and my boyfriend, Travis, were the most frequent visitors to my parents' new living room—the ICU waiting area. My family welcomed everyone and would usher the kids in to see me as soon as they arrived. Any request to visit met a resounding, "Yes. Please come." Even my doctors observed how my family understood the innate healing power sparked by new and different people. Although I could not form words, visitors seemed to feel my appreciation. Miles and time sacrificed during the long, ventilator-plagued days made such a difference.

One visitor, Darcy Pohland from WCCO-TV in Minneapolis, came a little too early. Still in my coma, I couldn't even blink in reply to her questions. Yet my parents welcomed her with open answers. Later they wondered … were they more impressed by Darcy's genuine confidence that I would be fine or by her self-assured rolling entrance and exit in a wheelchair similar to one I would use? My parents approved of any TV coverage that might bring the power of prayer from viewers. But they were especially taken with Darcy Pohland, who had survived a diving accident more than twenty years before. This optimistic reporter brought hope for my future because she was quadriplegic too.

With enough information to air an initial report, Darcy wheeled out of the ICU to share my story on the news that week. My folks agreed to further coverage once I regained consciousness. My entire family felt a surge of confidence from Darcy's visit—a feeling I discovered later as Darcy and I became friends.

Despite frequent visitors and the positive distraction they produced, I continued to drop into the depths of depression once my room cleared out. More than anyone, Angie felt my wrath. Honestly, I showed anger every time she made a move toward any concern for herself. If she needed to go eat, I complained. If she wanted to shower, I whined. Even when she stood from her chair to go to the bathroom, I squawked—silent protest in the form of ugly facial expressions. Others were hurt as I displayed this possessive need only for Angie. But I didn't care. I was not shy about hurting others' feelings. This was survival mode, and my most selfish traits were temporarily blown out of proportion.

Travis dealt with my obsession for Angie's attention, but his patience wore thin. I loved that he was there, but I made it clear we couldn't be in the room alone. If I crashed, he wouldn't know what to do. My sister, mom, or dad always had to be with me.

Angie, still my most trusted ally, saw that Travis deserved time alone with me.

"You'll be fine, Tasha. Travis can call for help just as fast as any one of us if something happens."

Despite Angie's testimonials to Travis's competence, I somehow got my way. Travis would continue to hold my hand with a constant chaperone in the room.

The time had come for a tracheotomy. I neared the maximum number of days a ventilator could be in place. The good news: the vent tube would no longer be lodged in my mouth. The bad news: a long incision would be made a few inches below my Adam's apple. Placed through the opening, a tube would meander its way toward my lungs. Artificial oxygen would continue to circulate throughout my body, but in a less restrictive way.

The trache would hold my vocal cords hostage indefinitely. No sound could be emitted while I healed. I could mouth words after the surgery— once I felt strong enough, that is. This language system would be a vast improvement over the alphabet board.

My chart read, "Surgery successful." *By whose measure?* I wondered. Large pockets of fluid remained in my lungs, suctioned by a long, invasive tube every half-hour. I cannot exaggerate the relief I felt whenever those fluids were suctioned. Effortless breathing kicked in; free-flowing movement filled my lungs. But half-hour intervals became an eternity as I craved the clear air that followed each procedure. As I anticipated the chronic secretions, I'd start my vigilant watch of the clock again.

Angie began planning for the day she would leave the hospital and return to her husband and job. We cried whenever the subject came up, and Angie would literally climb into bed with me. "You will be fine," she'd assure me. "You are so strong. You have proven this all along. You have Mom here every day ... Dad and Ryan when they can get away from the store ... Travis and so many friends. I will come on the weekends."

Angie's best defense was not working. But there was comfort for the moment; cuddled together, we both fell asleep.

Eventually, it happened. My nurses took over as surrogate Angies. Trust builds over time, and since time was abundantly available to me in Rochester, some gifted nurses soon won me over. During my long days without Angie's constant companionship, I began to notice the personal concern my team had for me all along. Of course, the Angie replacements had directives—doctors' orders—to challenge me with new tasks. It was time to mimic some of life's "normal" situations, and lying in bed 24-7 was not one of them.

The physical therapy department implemented its own strategic plan, with one nurse in particular becoming obsessed with sitting me up in a chair. "You'll love the view, Tasha." She wrapped my legs in Ace bandages, tightened my stomach with an abdominal binder, and then solicited help to transfer me from a prostrate to an upright position.

"Your blood pressure is still really low."

I gave her my best, "I know. I'm not ready for this!" eye contact, which was ignored.

"This binder will help keep the oxygen circulating. You'll like the change, really. Must be so boring to lie in bed all day."

"Boring and *safe*." But she couldn't read my eyes like Angie did and missed my point completely.

"Here we go! Just try it for a few minutes. If you are showing any signs of distress, we'll move you back immediately."

Okay. That's long enough, I thought within seconds of being placed, unattended, in the hospital recliner. *I'm good. Really, this was interesting, but I'm done!* Still, no one read my eyes, so I tried to mouth my anxiety—let them know I'd had enough. Light-headedness, a symptom of low blood pressure, zapped my strength. I had no energy to even mouth the word, "Enough!" My eyelids began to drop.

"Hmmm, that's a pretty faint pulse. I think that's enough for now," my nurse said to her accomplice. "Sorry, Tasha. Field trip's over. Back to bed for now. We'll try it again later."

No! Please, don't trouble yourselves. Hardly worth all the effort to move me. Let's wait until I'm much better—maybe next week. No one heard me, and I had to endure another chair-propping episode a few hours later. The staff was right, of course, and each recliner adventure got longer as I gained strength.

Another team of staff frequented my ICU room in hopes of busting me out of there. Occupational therapist Barb softened my knots, while physical therapist Neil stretched my limbs. To withstand long hours in a wheelchair, I had to show stamina beyond mere moments propped up in a chair. Perhaps I was ready for the big move a few floors down to Saint Marys rehabilitation unit.

Rehab ... this required a hard sell from Barb and Neil. Barb, about thirty, single, and fashion-savvy, could cheerlead me into the most challenging tasks. Neil, although closer to my dad's age, was fit and buff from his own work-out regiment which made him seem youthful yet wise. Saint Mary's couldn't have put two more credible people on this mission to enlist me in rehab duty.

I started somewhere in the area of total resistance, but they soon coached me to the point of pure excitement. The athlete in me woke up as I imagined myself physically working out in a facility that, in my mind's eye, rivaled our national Olympic training grounds. Trache in place, little to no feeling in my body, fifty pounds underweight, I readied myself each morning for the rehab move. Clueless again? Perhaps, but I envisioned myself going to this gym and surprising everyone with physical prowess that no quadriplegic had ever achieved. I would defy my diagnosis. I would go back to school one ripped and fit girl.

My final days of ICU were spent daydreaming of rehab "boot camp," where I planned to astound my coaches, both PT and OT staff. Every time Neil said, "Let's get you ready for the gym," I pictured basketball and volleyball courts, a state-of-the-art weight room, and every kind of cardio-building machine. Barb and Neil said over and over, "Tasha, you'll be moving in no time." However, their definition of moving—navigating life in a wheelchair—greatly differed from my powerful vision that had me walking, perhaps even running and jumping again.

Sleepless nights without Angie helped neutralize my fantasies, however. Doubts, fears, and ventilator noise brought back the reality of paralysis, yet incited me to overcome my fate. I'd never personally known anyone with a spinal-cord injury, but I could not recall seeing one happy person in a wheelchair. Indifferent faces of people who coped, who tolerated their circumstances, came to mind. I was too animated for this role. My stereotype of a wheelchair-bound patient both appalled and inspired me to defy the odds. *I did it once—right? I survived the coma stage of septic shock!* I told myself. *Wheel me into rehab tomorrow. I want to break the odds again.*

I shared this request somehow with Neil the next morning.

"The only thing that's keeping you from rehab, Tasha, is your dependence on the vent. Let's get the respiratory team in here." After some consultation—nothing's ever changed without a group approach—respiratory therapists began aggressive efforts to wean me off the breathing machine.

Mike, a respiratory therapist who always seemed eager to get rid of the very equipment that gave him job security, came in one day while Ryan visited. Mike loved to tease me about my reputation for incessant talking. He reminded Ryan that my family was getting "a long-needed rest from having to listen to Tasha all the time." He joked, "She'll get her revenge, you know. That vent tube will be out of the way soon, and you won't be able to shut this girl up." Ryan's courtesy laugh told me he was slightly suspicious of Mike's visit.

Mike approached my bed with a devious smile, like a teenager about to break the house rules. "I bet you'd love to talk with your brother. How about trying it without the ventilator. Get some noise through that motor-mouth again."

I'm not sure whose eyes looked more questioningly at Mike—those of the fearful patient or her cautious brother.

Both afraid but ready to take a risk, Ryan and I consented by not responding. Mike plugged the hole in my trache, unhooked me from the vent, and told me, "Try it. Say something."

I went to mouth the word "what," wondering if Mike had completely lost it ... and then it happened. A sound whispered out of my mouth.

"What?"

"Hey! See? I told you that motor-mouth still worked. Try it again!" Mike egged me on. I could feel my heart race with the excitement of getting my voice back.

It only lasted about a minute until Mike took out the cork and put me back on the ventilator. But a brief moment of talking with my brother gave me a jolt of energy to start living again by leaving critical care behind. The three of us shared the most amazing breakthrough feeling. Sixty seconds of inspiration. I wanted more than ever to get to rehab!

The very next day, I was unhooked from the ventilator and put on a portable unit. This would help me make a smooth transition toward breathing on my own. It went well for about the first twenty minutes, and then Mike said, "Okay, Tasha, we're going to unhook you from this machine."

No, I'm too scared! I thought. I gave him my best "no way" look.

Smiling, he replied with a smug tone, "Um, Tasha, you have been breathing on your own for the last ten minutes now."

Joy, relief, pure love for life! I was elated for the first time in months and wanted nothing but to show gratitude for everyone who helped get me to this point! "You saved my life. I love you. Do you know what heroes you are?" I said to every person in the room.

Mike was right. They couldn't shut me up! But I was stuck on one topic—thanking every single member of my medical team.

I paged everyone. One by one, staff members either called or popped into my room. "Tasha, what's wrong? Do you need me?"

"Yes! Hey, I'm talking—I'm breathing on my own! Thank you, thank you, so much! I love you! I can't believe it—you saved my life!"

Mom told me later that she saw a big, burly teddy bear of a man at the end of the hall crying. It was one of my nurses. He couldn't believe I called him—included him in the celebration. "I can't believe how far she's come." Mom did her best to let this man and everyone know how blessed we were to have their care and support.

I vowed that since I hadn't been able to speak for over three weeks, everyone would hear everything that I was feeling. I called the school and paged Travis from the wrestling practice room. "Travis, do you know who this is?"

"No …" I could hear the confusion in his voice. No one interrupts wrestling practice unless it is an emergency.

My voice still raspy and hoarse from the trache tube, I said, "It's me—it's Tasha! I love you!"

Like a malfunctioning robot, I spent the next few hours in constant talk, listening to no one, monopolizing every conversation. However, I had created a new problem for myself. I was overexerting my vocal chords. I was given a new order: if I didn't give my chattering a rest, I would be hooked up to the vent indefinitely. Mute again, I had hopeful daydreams of talking soon.

My dad entered my room that evening, thrilled by the news of all that had happened. When others left for the night, I cheated a few whispers to Dad.

"Amazing! I'm so proud of you! Our little secret," he winked. Quiet talk in the dark—my gift to Dad, sure, but proof to myself that today was not a dream.

Chapter 8

Chair Wars and Other Rehab Battles

ON DECEMBER 5, 1997, less than a month after my date of birth into the world of quadriplegia, my things were packed and moved to a double-occupancy room in Saint Marys Hospital's rehabilitation unit. I would live alone. My possessions—the books, videos, angel figurines, plants, posters, and stuffed animals that made up the menagerie of gifts bestowed upon me by so many concerned people—collectively became my roommates.

My hospital room at Saint Marys.   *Missy and Rachel visit.*

Ventilator-free and strategically placed near the nurses' station, I found some relief in knowing I could verbally call out for help. Some of the nurses looked familiar, which was another comfort. The intensive-care unit encouraged the rehab nurses to swing into the ICU to meet patients who were destined for their locale. Wise technique—it made me feel welcomed immediately.

Despite all the planning and precautions, transitioning from ICU to rehab was dreadful, even though it was only five floors away. My first objection: moving forward without my sister's fastidious watch. Although Angie promised that she would visit every weekend, I refused to hide my anxiety over facing rehab without her support. I reluctantly accepted her plan as "Well, if that's the best you can do ..." although I recall thanking Angie over and over again for the sacrifice of each ten-hour round trip to help me.

Everyone else began to transition back to their normal lives too, as my dad and brother took care of an expanding grocery business, already committed to a brand-new building. Mom secured a spot in the overcrowded Ronald McDonald House just blocks away from me. I squealed with approval when I heard that she leveraged for a room—always the shrewd business dealer. She wouldn't sleep there for weeks, still staying on a cot in my room. But she had a home base in Rochester until I was discharged to Ellsworth.

Although I was off the traditional ventilator, the problems with my lungs would continue.

"Pockets of fluid are still present, Tasha. These fluids need to be loosened up and suctioned out through your trache tube," explained one of the respiratory therapists.

In a constant effort to keep my lungs clear, nurses were ordered to roll me onto my side, place a massager on my back, and loosen up the secretions in my lungs. The massager often failed, so I was vigorously patted by hand. I became a bongo drum to each nurse who pounded me like a cystic fibrosis patient. Nebulizer treatments every two hours interrupted my sleep, zapped my energy, and interfered with my rehab agenda. Yet rehab staff persevered. Sleep-deprived and exhausted from coughing, I was wheeled into the gym every day for my "workout."

"Sorry, Neil. I don't think I can do this," I argued to postpone my very first day in the gym. "The lights flipped on at two a.m., at four a.m., at six a.m. If it wasn't a neb treatment, it was the nurse pounding on me and ordering me to cough."

"Good! Sounds like this team is really going at it. Get those secretions down and you won't believe the energy you'll get back. Okay, let's get you in this chair." Neil ignored my request to pass on physical therapy.

"So I don't have a choice?" I asked. By now I was transferred into my wheelchair and moving down the hallway. Clearly, Neil's selective hearing allowed him to ignore my plea to skip Day 1 of rehab. I looked at Barb for rescue, but her eyes were on the gym doors as well. *Okay*, I thought, *I finally get to see this amazing gym that Neil and Barb have been boasting about.* As we made our way down the corridor, I felt a burst of anticipation for the facility.

I'm sure my face told all. Disappointment jolted me back to reality. I was not here to get buff! The "gym," a twenty-by-thirty-foot space, housed mats like Travis's wrestling room back home. I saw a fake car for the driving simulation and parallel bars for those with the goal to walk again (not on Tasha Schuh's rehab agenda). Rubber balls, like the one that broke my arm back in elementary school, reminded me that, in here, the biggest sports challenge most patients achieved was playing catch.

The sudden realization that I had arrived only to learn how to live in a wheelchair unnerved me. My enthusiasm for the long-awaited rehab stage of recovery vanished in one split-second glance at the gym.

I have no idea how Neil or Barb got anything productive out of me. Devastation stole my memory on that first day of therapy. But Neil worked his magic. He made me laugh, he praised my bad attitude with just the right timing, and he gradually sold me on everything I had to do to get out of Rochester.

I spent a few weeks getting used to the schedule. Wheeled from my room into the gym, I was stretched, pounded, rolled over, and massaged whether I liked it or not. The rigor of therapy didn't slow down despite plans to celebrate my seventeenth birthday. The old Tasha's birthday, December 19, was quickly approaching. Stevie and others from the musical-theater class had dropped enough hints that I would be surprised by a big group of students that day. (Teenagers don't do well with surprise parties.) Although I was excited for new visitors, I panicked at the thought of everyone seeing my ugly feeding tube spilling out of my nose.

"I don't know if it pays for a bunch of people to come here." I tried to discourage their plans. "You know how long my rehab sessions are. People will just end up sitting in my room waiting for me."

"We thought of that," Stevie said. "Even Neil agreed—he'll call it early on your birthday. Big day! Number seventeen! You don't do that more than once. Save room for birthday cake!"

Birthday cake? I could only eat soups, ice cream, popsicles—things that would not stick to the tube as I tried to swallow. I hadn't eaten bread since the last time it became lodged in my throat. The satisfaction of solid foods just wasn't worth the choking. To add insult to injury, I couldn't taste anything. This sense was temporarily knocked out of commission by the head-injury part of my fall.

Nutrition was my new catch-22. If I ate bigger calorie items, I choked and actually consumed less because of the stress of it all. If I stuck with clear liquids, my caloric intake was so low that supplements had to be given through the NG tube. My strength, essential to my rehab success, was completely dependent upon the fuel I fed my body. Falling far short of the desired 1,500 calories per day, I was losing the nutrition battle.

Of course, the longer the feeding tube passed down my throat, the more it hurt. I swore I had a perpetual case of strep throat. Despite a negative strep test, I knew that the feeding tube was the culprit, so I began a campaign to get the doctors to pull it out.

"Tasha, I understand your frustration," one doctor explained. "But we need a show of faith here. You either increase your high-nutrition calories, or we keep the tube in place. You shouldn't be the patient who needs lifelong tube-feeding. You have less paralysis than those patients. Yet you aren't progressing. You're simply a bad eater."

I promised, I begged, and I finally persuaded my doctor to pull the feeding tube. I would eat once the menace was out of my way. So on the day before my party, as an early birthday gift, the orange NG tube was pulled from my stomach, through my throat, and out of my nose forever.

"Count to twelve, Tasha, while I pull." I listened to my doctor as the tube, along with a whole mess of stomach acid, came up and out within seconds. Pain, gagging, and then instant relief.

"Get me a cheeseburger." My first food request without the tube

73

made everyone laugh. However, I started my full diet with something less questionable. The cheeseburger would have to wait while I stretched my stomach with smaller, more frequent meals.

The tube was out. I had my gift even before my seventeenth birthday party started. A modified rehab schedule would give me more time with friends, and sure enough, about forty of them arrived the next day bearing gifts and balloons. Students and teachers snapped their cameras. It was easy to smile, knowing the feeding tube was out of the picture. What a memorable day!

We ate supper together, and although my taste buds were still not working, I held up my end of the bargain by consuming plenty of calories. The choir students sang "Happy Birthday," while I opened gifts. My favorite surprise that evening came in video format.

My classmates captured video birthday wishes from all over the school. Someone sang a "Happy Birthday" solo, and hundreds of kids and staff expressed how much they missed me. I was moved that my closest friends would take the time to do this, and that so many people took part in it. By this point, we had received countless cards, letters, and packages from schools, churches, and people who had been praying for me—some of whom I didn't even know. Spending my birthday in the hospital was not what I wanted, yet the support made me feel blessed beyond belief.

That night, as *The Flintstones* droned in the background, I reran the day in my mind. I wondered how many able-bodied kids spent a birthday without acknowledgement. How often does a shy child go through the entire school day without anyone even knowing it was her birthday?

My seventeenth birthday was a revelation to me; tragedy brings blessings beyond imagination. Sure, the old Tasha would have hung out with friends and enjoyed an excuse to party. But something told me this was better. To see so many classmates genuinely celebrating with nothing more elaborate than birthday cake and a place to gather—there was something almost miraculous about this. I don't know if I told God I was grateful that night, but I believe I was moving closer to the place where I could forgive Him and move on. My seventeenth birthday was a start.

Shortly after my birthday party, Neil showed up for a session with a new chair. Up to this point, my comfortable red *manual* chair meant I had to be wheeled everywhere by staff or family. I liked being pushed into therapy and transferred right back into bed when I was done. I could get used to a constant companion pushing me everywhere. Neil obviously sensed this. Enter a motorized wheelchair.

"Hi, Neil." I smiled, and then paused as I realized the change. "That's not my chair. Where's my red chair?" I asked. Before I knew what was going on, Neil had me transferred into a black, motorized, self-navigating wheelchair.

"Here ya go! Looking good! Drive it around. Let's see how you do." Neil acted like a dad buying a new sports car for his daughter. And I reacted like a spoiled teenager who wanted the red car, not the black one. I broke down in tears.

"Hey, what's wrong? You'll love this chair! *You* will be the driver. Just like when you get into the van. You're the boss. Give it a try."

The chair was jerky. My weak arms gave me no control. I ran into the wall. I banged the first corner. The controls seemed backward. This felt like the first time I tried to parallel park on a busy street.

"I can't do this. I want my red chair back." I was so uncomfortable. The hard headrest was different, and my weak, bony arms teetered on the skinny black armrests. All my progress in therapy over the past two weeks felt erased.

Then the truth hit me. My complaining came down to one thing: the motorized chair was my final transition. Once I mastered its navigation, this was my view of the waking world for the rest of my life. Outside of learning to drive a van, this was the most upright I would ever spend my days from now until I was old and frail like Grandma Barringer.

"Typical female driver," Neil tried to joke. "Running into everything, making us guys have to watch out for you." I was not in the mood for his humor. Sadness faded as a defiant child planned her resistance.

Neil instructed me to use the black wheelchair as often as I wanted over the weekend.

"I'll come back on Monday, and you'll have mastered this thing. Just let the staff know when you want some practice. Have fun with it. You'll be ready for the NASCAR track in no time."

I watched as Neil put my red wheelchair in the storage closet and left until Monday.

The next day, the weekend therapist reported to my room with the black chair.

"Good morning, Tasha. Let's get you in the new chair. I hear you're quite the speedster down the halls."

Not so fast, I thought. *You can't flatter me into changing chairs if I don't want to.*

"You brought the wrong chair. That's not mine. My red chair is in the storage closet," I said calmly, pointing at the closet door.

"Hmmm ... I don't think so. Neil's note said you used this motorized chair yesterday, and to try it as often as you like all weekend."

"Sorry, but that's the wrong chair. I'm using the red chair to go to therapy. The red chair's the one I always use."

The therapist looked confused. His long pause told me I had this.

"But Neil ..." he tried.

"You must have misunderstood him. That's really the wrong chair. Why would Neil store the red chair in my closet if he didn't intend for me to use it?" I felt like Angie, taking on the staff with the argumentation skills of a seasoned lawyer. My words were back, and I was fluently, persuasively getting my way. I had a genuine smile of satisfaction on my face as the therapist pushed me down the hall in my red chair. All weekend, I gloated in victory. Chair Wars: Round 1 goes to Tasha Schuh!

However, when Neil returned the following Monday, he did not find my red-chair victory very amusing. Immediately, against my will, I was back in the motorized wheelchair. The red chair, wheeled away by someone from housekeeping, left my sight forever as Neil reprimanded me for twisting the truth with the weekend therapist.

"So this is the way it's gonna be, eh?"

I didn't say a word, as I could see that Round 2 of the Chair Wars was going to Neil.

"The black chair is it—your ticket to mobility. You know it's time."

I knew when Neil meant business. I stared straight ahead, ignoring contact with Neil as my nurses transferred me from the bed. "Let's get a driving lesson in, so you can stop fighting this change, all right?"

I finally acknowledged his presence. "Okay. But I'm gonna suck at this."

I had to admit, the comfort level of the chair improved once I got used to the operating the controls. However, it was like learning to drive all over again. And let's face it, I wasn't a great driver back in the New Yorker, trying to dodge speeding tickets. I always hauled a boatload of kids, but I managed to throw a bit of fear into each of them as my lead foot passed a police car headed in the other direction.

"Tasha, you are so lucky!" This was a common cry from friends, especially those who had already paid a ticket plus an insurance hike.

Now I was in a much stranger vehicle, trying to manipulate a joystick that made this rear-wheel-drive chair feel like a go-kart on ice. The controller had to be pushed in the opposite direction, like turning a car's steering wheel in order to back up a boat trailer. I just couldn't wrap my mind around it. The collisions continued.

"Whoa, careful. Maybe slow down a bit." Familiar words from the rehab staff. The unit doorways were huge, yet I managed to rip off padded trim and put nicks into every corner edge.

In my defense, this chair was not exactly custom-made. My tall, thin body looked lost in its cushion. To this day, my ten fingers have absolutely no movement, and in the early stage of rehab, my fine-motor skills were essentially nonexistent. Without a grip, it was my arm—my bicep muscle to be precise—that provided the leverage to push the chair's joystick. Still underweight, I lacked the strength to move the stick, so an extension was added to the regular armrest of the wheelchair. Pure physics allowed me to muster enough pressure to push the joystick and jerk my way down the hallway. I feared I would cause new damage to my neck from the whiplash that came every few feet.

Surrendering to Neil's wishes, I persevered. What was my alternative? Of course, I communicated quite clearly to Neil that, like the princess and the pea, I felt every imperfection of this substandard chair.

"It's just so awkward, Neil."

"What do you mean? You're doing great! You haven't run over anyone's toes for two days! I'd call that progress." He knew exactly how to pump up my confidence.

And so, my rehab phase began to take shape. Barb and Neil had their work cut out for them. They aimed to maximize my list of non-paralyzed body parts. This included my biceps, my deltoids, my shoulders, and my right wrist. Although I knew that my *left* wrist had potential, clinical evidence would not back me up.

"See, watch," I'd say to my nurses, my parents, anyone who would take a moment to look. I was like a kid with a magician's set of lame tricks. *Watch and you will see the coin disappear!* In this case, "Stare long enough and you will observe as my left wrist moves oh, so slightly." I needed a witness to prove that I wasn't crazy. Was I seeing things, or more accurately, feeling a phantom movement?

Despite a variety of onlookers, my left wrist, hand, and fingers remained motionless before their eyes.

"See! Did you see that? I felt it. A little move. Did you see it?"

"Nah, not really." No one wanted to squelch my enthusiasm, but most felt I should focus on the strength I could indeed get back. It would be six months before I would prove my theory and show off the start of a little hinge control that remains in my left wrist today. As far as rehab was concerned, we had a final inventory of body parts that worked. The left wrist and hand were not on the list.

"We should strengthen the things that can rescue your independence, Tasha," Neil reminded me. At this point, all of the tasks that Neil knew I could eventually do for myself were being done by others *for* me.

Sympathetic to a teenager's need to sleep in, Barb, my primary occupational therapist, scheduled OT as late as possible—eight a.m.

"This is the best I can do, Tasha," Barb explained. "You have to finish your OT work before you enter the gym for PT. I know it's early, but OT is just the start of your day." So true—I was scheduled for OT and PT twice a day, recreational therapy, counseling sessions with the psychologist, while still fighting to keep my lungs clear. There was also talk of tutoring sessions to tackle some schoolwork. These were very full days.

Barb saw the dismay on my face and knew my aversion to mornings was legit. I still couldn't sleep at night, even though the days of Demerol for pain were long gone. In rehab, I took nightly Benadryl to make me drowsy. This and a *Flintstones* rerun relaxed me but rarely put me to sleep. It seemed as if the moment I dozed off, someone would enter with a nebulizer or suctioning tube, and before I knew it, a nurse would be at my bedside, ready to change my clothes for the next day.

My silence made Barb try one more angle. "You'll have your evenings free for your friends. If they drive all this way, you want to be available to visit, right?"

Barb who probably had a million friends herself, knew just how to motivate me. She was right—I was so lucky to have people still driving to Rochester to see me. I didn't want them sitting in a lounge, waiting for me to come out of the gym. I stopped my whining and accepted the eight o'clock start time.

Although I have never been a fan of early morning starts, it is funny how my complaints seem petty now. The before-school routine for old Tasha was completed in record time: turn off the alarm, eat a quick breakfast, hop in the shower, grab comfortable clothes, put my hair up in a ponytail, apply a little makeup, grab my backpack of books and workout clothes, snag a Mello Yellow from the fridge, jump in my car, and pick up Sarah Sans on my drive to school. Total prep time: less than thirty minutes.

For *new* Tasha, a rehab-day routine started with the insertion of the first of four catheters. The "cath team" began rounds at five a.m., and although I lacked the normal bladder urgency most people feel after a full night's sleep, something told me that the cath nurse had impeccable timing. Most members of the cath team had stealth technique. These nurses quietly completed their task without disturbing me. I might hear a whisper of a voice, "Tasha, it's Becky. I'm here from the cath team. You just stay sleeping, okay?"

One or two of them, however, felt compelled to wake me up for the day. "Rise and shine, Tasha," one cath nurse shouted as she flipped on the florescent light above my bed. "Cath time. Let's get this day started!"

If I could get back to sleep after this friendly but abrupt start, I would.

The next item on my agenda: early-morning coughing, promptly at seven. My lungs remained full of dangerous secretions. Lying inert throughout the night, my body was due for a thorough coughing session. With paralyzed stomach muscles, I lacked the capacity to cough on my own. Nurses took turns performing a modified version of the Heimlich maneuver, thrusting the secretions out of my body, clearing my airway for the challenging day ahead of me. On a good coughing day, my nurse would stop the Heimlich and begin changing my clothes within an hour. On a bad coughing day, Barb would have to skip most of her OT agenda to help cough me.

Next, nurses wrapped my legs in Ace bandages and placed a belly binder around my torso, all to increase circulation and minimize my light-headedness. These were also the days of my TLSO brace—thoracic lumbar sacral orthotic—or my "turtle shell," as most of us called it. This customized hard-bodied chest brace brought security to me for three months straight. Initially, the TLSO was as uncomfortable as it sounds, mostly because it pressed up against my neck collar. It resembled a bad *Xena: Warrior Princess* costume, made for a full-figured woman, not a thin teenage girl.

Over the years, other C5 patients would ask me, "Why didn't you have a halo after surgery?" Funny how I had the foresight to know that despite all the trauma of my accident, I did not want a halo if I could avoid it. I had seen one classmate in a halo after her accident—drilled bolts in her head, all hardware, and no range of motion with her neck. When the ER staff asked whether I wanted a halo or a collar, I remember saying, "Cut me up all you want (to get that neck collar in place), but don't put a halo on me!"

I have met many C5s who indicate they had no choice in the matter, perhaps because their lives were more at risk when the decision was made. Others have wondered why I opted for a neck collar that left me with multiple scars from incisions made all around my neck. All I can say is I have never regretted that split-second decision, which required both neck collar and TLSO. I still view these as the lesser of many necessary evils when trying to save a severely crushed spinal cord. Even after three months of both collar and TSLO, I truly did not mind when later I temporarily needed my Xena costume back.

Finally dressed, bound, and bandaged, I could be transferred to my chair for morning occupational and physical therapies. Although I was thin, my height made things awkward, so chair transfer required two nurses, either using a sliding board or a two-person transfer procedure. There was no such thing as a "lift"—no mechanical transfer, common in hospitals and rehab centers today. Not long after my rehab time in Rochester, Mayo's concern for patient *and* nurse safety led to new equipment in the realm of patient transport.

Since I was still underweight, lifting me without a sliding board should have been quick and easy. But my frequent blackouts during transfer interfered. Two very careful nurses lifted and moved me at just the right angle while Mom nervously watched and learned. She knew that eventually she would be in charge of all she observed.

Breakfast became part of my OT workout. With Barb's coaching, I had been drinking Carnation Instant Breakfast, since it oozed smoothly past my NG tube. Now, even without the tube, I needed to get a lot of calories quickly, so this drink continued as my morning staple. I sometimes ate part of a banana, which took another ten minutes.

Ironic how one of the things I miss most in life is getting myself ready for the day—more than riding a bike, more than serving a volleyball, even more than dancing onstage. Hopping out of bed, scurrying to the bathroom, adjusting the shower to just the right temperature, pulling my clothes from the closet, pouring cereal and milk into a bowl ... these are the things I miss most.

The new Tasha's prep time, from cath team to the end of breakfast? About three hours.

It wasn't long before I realized that the key to some degree of independence was my upper-body strength. My arms, sprouting from my torso and neck braces, possessed muscles so atrophied from lack of use that they may as well have been paralyzed too. I couldn't even scratch my own nose, which became my new obsession. If this sounds petty, just take a day and tally the number of times you scratch your nose or pull a tickling strand of hair away from your face. My itchy nose served as a perpetual reminder that I was dependent upon others. Nothing could be more annoying, especially to the people around me, than the constant request to scratch my nose.

"Say, do you mind … yeah, no … over a bit … a little to the right, yes, there! Ahh, thank you."

Barb was my salvation. With my fine-motor skills at the top of her list, she sought ways for me to not only feed myself but also do my own makeup, pick up my sunglasses, push numbers on a phone, paint and draw, and, of course, scratch my nose.

Neil joked about that last goal. "What's the big deal about scratching your nose? You'll just start back with that nasty nose-picking habit again." Yet he knew that success with Barb carried over into PT sessions with him.

Still, a healthy rivalry ensued. While Barb ran OT in my rehab room, Neil worked me in the gym. He straightened and strengthened my arms, taught me to navigate my chair, and inspired me toward our ultimate goal—driving a van down Highway 52.

"I heard you won a Dairy Queen treat in a card game against Barb yesterday," Neil stated one morning as I entered the gym. "You're gonna have to do more than beat me in Crazy Eights if you think I'm springing for treats. You ready for a real challenge today?"

Neil's charm woke the competitor in me.

"Bring it. I'm dying for another Blizzard." He was my coach, and he talked to me like I was his star athlete. With twenty-seven years of experience, his record of success with spinal-cord injuries spoke for itself. He knew exactly how to read a patient and was uniquely suited to work with sports-minded teenagers. In addition to creating game-like rehab sessions, he could answer virtually any question. Neil the counselor, honest and frank about my future mobility, never shot down a dream—even one as far-fetched as, "One day I will surprise everyone and walk again." He placed faith in medical science and its ability to advance my situation, yet reminded me of limitations if I didn't progress from my *current* potential. This meant I had to build muscle tone within every bit of tissue I still controlled.

"Hold up your end of the bargain, Tasha, and who knows … Twenty-seven years ago, did any of us imagine a quadriplegic driving sixty-five miles an hour down an interstate highway?" Neil reminded me of the balance I needed between reality and hope. "Look how far technology has advanced mobility just in my career. But … if you're not in prime form, look at the risk you put yourself and others in." As he held one of the few healthy joints I still controlled—my right wrist—he reminded me that my hands would manage the wheel of a vehicle in a very different way. "I want this wrist to have the reaction time of a race-car driver."

Neil also acknowledged that his most successful clients were those who believed they could accomplish anything if they set their minds to it. "I'll never say you won't walk. But don't sit in a bed waiting for the next discovery to be made. Live while the search is on, and be physically ready if and when the opportunity for more mobility comes along. You know what that means, Tasha? That means … let's do ten more stretches."

Despite my coughing jags, my therapists worked me like a healthy transitioning patient whose days in rehab were numbered. It was a race to get me ready for discharge. Whether this would take weeks or months, the rigor of the day was the same. Strengthening my neck while I still wore the neck collar was one of many frustrations. Watching my arms refuse to stretch or straighten crushed my confidence on a daily basis.

Damage had occurred during my eight-day coma when my arms were left bent in the same position the entire time. My left arm in particular did not want to cooperate when Neil or Barb tried every trick to elongate the muscles. My legs got a workout too, stretched and exercised in order to help minimize muscle spasms. All of this led to grueling days where I teetered on fragile health that could bounce me back to ICU at any moment.

Therapy all morning … back in bed to be cathed again at eleven a.m. … repeated Heimlich maneuvers … self-inflicted coughing jags … lunch promptly at noon … catnap until two p.m., or at least an attempt to sleep.

"Get some rest, Tasha," Mom would remind me. "You know your afternoon rehab is just as hard as the morning." The afternoon brought a repeat of Barb's OT and Neil's PT along with an additional session from recreational therapist John.

By this time of day, I'd wheel back to my room to find visitors waiting with Mom. It was great to see family. But the teenager in me really lit up when my friends from high school came. I know that they weren't always there together, but it felt as if Sarah, Jesse, Travis, or Stevie were there every other day. Stevie, a year or two younger than most of us, managed to hitch a ride with someone every time a car was headed in my direction. Stevie even risked his life by riding with Grandma Thalacker, my dad's mom, hands down the worst driver in Pierce County.

"I don't want to go home with her," Stevie whispered in my ear as he bent down to give me a hug.

"My dad's coming. I'm sure you can hitch a ride back with him," I whispered back.

Stevie's fear of crashing was justified. Grandma simply expected others to have defensive driving skills. "They can just go around me, if they don't like my driving."

Most of my regular visitors kept me informed on Sarina's status. These students knew the gravity of my diagnosis and understood that Sarina was fighting a very different but critical battle as well. Sometime in the winter, she would be transferred out of Regions Hospital to a rehab facility—Red Wing Health Center. Just when I thought we were in very similar facilities, someone clarified for me that Sarina's stay was more like a nursing home for teens. "Her eyes are closed," one of my friends explained. "But when you ask her a question, sometimes she'll give a thumbs up! That's something, right?" The class of '99 had more than homework to think about if they chose to keep up with our medical progress.

One of my closest friends, Emmy, had such a hard time dealing with all the sadness. She only came to see me twice—once when I was in intensive care and then on my seventeenth birthday. Eventually, I would reflect on how hard it was back home, where two close classmates were perpetually absent from their junior year. For now, I continued to worry about Sarina, and envied my friends like Emmy who simply went to school every day.

Chapter 9

Stuffing It

TIME WAS HARD to track in rehab, although only a few weeks had lapsed. Days couldn't be counted down like at school, where students tolerated Monday, worked steadily through midweek, and greeted Friday like a pre-holiday break. Weekends meant free time, when most kids worked odd jobs for gas and fun money, and chased other interests besides school. This pattern just didn't exist for me any longer.

In Rochester, days and nights blurred together as my busy therapy schedule gobbled up the calendar like a hungry rodent. I had not left my rehab wing since moving in weeks ago. As hard as Travis and my friends tried to help me experience my own weekend break, I could never truly escape the daily responsibilities attached to the life of a quadriplegic.

New Year's Eve 1998 was quickly approaching, and January 1 represented more than a full calendar round as the new Tasha Schuh. This holiday marked the day my mother would move out of my rehab room. She would abandon the cot she slept on and claim the Ronald McDonald House bed she had reserved weeks ago. Angie, too, was banned from the cot during her weekend visits. Dad, Ryan … not one family member could sleep in my room ever again. This terrified me.

Rehab had always praised my family support but now feared that too much closeness was counterproductive to my independence. I got that—I understood that it was easy for Mom to reach over and feed me when weakness sabotaged my fine-motor skills. "You'll need your strength later for PT; let me do that." Mom meant well, and at times her instincts salvaged afternoon sessions that would have been wasted had I struggled with lunch. Yet I knew there were things I could be doing for myself, and I would do them if the eager help of a loved one hadn't been so convenient.

Still, I dreaded the day that Mom would leave my room. I hated the thought for so many reasons, and I fully expected the darkness of night to swallow me up forever. At times, I rehearsed, as if preparing for another high school play. I imagined the moment I would have to call out for a nurse in the night when Mom no longer guarded my bed like a hospital SWAT-team member. Other times, I looked forward to the experience of feeling utterly alone—alone to cry, to dream, to rest from the role of "survivor" … the inspirational little patient who was "making the best of things."

"Stuffing it," I think Neil had called it. I was guilty of stuffing it so deeply, so far down that most people thought I was accepting my plight in the most graceful way. And quite frankly, some of my "act" was not an act. I felt genuine gratitude most of the time when I expressed it. Yet looking back, I agree with Neil … that anyone faced with the change that comes from navigating the world via wheelchair will find stuffing it much easier than confronting it.

December brought so much change, I hardly acknowledged stuffing anything. My birthday celebration along with a family Christmas right within my Rochester rehab room should have been turning points in my health and well-being. Christmas blessed me with visitors and gifts beyond imagination. Everyone put me first! I knew amazing sacrifices were being made to guarantee I felt love and concern from so many people. At times, I fought a meltdown of utter despair that I not only had to spend my favorite holiday in this place but forced my family to do it with me. Other times, I felt blessed that so many people sacrificed their holiday to come visit me. Feeling their gratitude that I was alive brought incredible comfort. Aunts, uncles, cousins, and friends made Christmas 1997 a total celebration for my family.

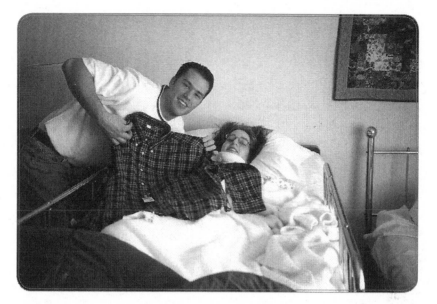

My brother, Ryan, opening his Christmas gift from me, December 25, 1997.

Despite all the support, shortly after the holidays, depression consumed me and made an already-challenging recovery even harder. I was stuffing it, down, down, and for the first time, my dark hole was becoming increasingly obvious to those around me. I quit objecting as my nurses pushed to have my mom move out. I caved, and fell deeper into the abyss that comes with indifference.

Although Barb and Neil took notice, they let the crash occur. Likely they knew that a dark stage was unavoidable. They persevered with therapy while my motivation faded.

"Here's your hairbrush, Tasha." Barb reached out with my modified brush. She had added an extension that wrapped around my hand for stability. This customized hairbrush, like my toothbrush, allowed me to use personal-care tools on my own. Yet if it were up to me, I wouldn't have wasted the energy to brush my teeth or mess with my hair at this stage of rehab. *What's the point?* I thought. *Who cares what I look like?*

In fact, for some time now, I had been opting out of personal cares in exchange for more sleep. Once the cath-team nurse left each morning, I dozed off and only woke because it was time for a bed bath. Thankfully, every-other-day showers occurred at night. I hated showers but found more tolerance for them at the end of my day. Lying down on a special gurney made of some type of netting, I was wheeled into a big shower stall. While the water drenched me, it drained through the plastic mesh gurney.

Did I mention I hated showers? In addition to an attack on my modesty, showers made me dizzy. The whole thing was so uncomfortable. Soon the mesh gurney was abandoned, and I began using a shower chair—likely because this resembled what I would do at home. I fought fainting spells in the shower chair; I just couldn't breathe at the angle this chair tilted me. Yet this every-other-day process, which included my bowel-care program, has become routine in my life.

Bowel care—what can I say? Normal human functioning, right? The biggest false assumption: "bowel care" means wearing diapers. This is not true. My body is on a schedule, but I do need assistance. Those of you who have a spinal cord injury know the challenges of bowel care, but I'll spare all of you the details. When I share my story, especially at schools, the outspoken children will ask about this. Others are shy, like one employee of mine. After about two years of caregiver support from her—everything *but* showers and bowel care—she found the courage to ask, "Tasha ... do you poop?" Inside, I laughed so hard at her. *How could I devour the food you make for me*, I thought, *if I don't get rid of the waste somehow?* But I patiently explained the process, and why only my employees with shower cares know the program.

"Tasha, are you with me?" Barb brought me back from my thoughts of declining personal hygiene. I watched while she secured my grip on the hairbrush.

Along with morning OT, I still endured suctioning through my trache. To keep the NG tube at bay, I held up my end of the birthday bargain. I increased my caloric intake, gained a little weight, and worked hard in rehab to boost muscle mass. Although I struggled to eat everything expected of me, I smothered my food in salt to generate some flavor.

Of course, it helped that, beyond a bit of breakfast or snack food, I never once ate hospital fare. For lunch, I couldn't tolerate anything mushy, so Mom made my favorite version of Kraft Macaroni & Cheese, noodles barely cooked. We could have renamed it Kraft Crunchy Mac & Cheese. The spiral noodles worked best for this brittle pasta effect. For supper, many family cooks—along with Mary and Gary Allyn, catering friends of my parents—whipped up my odd requests. Every evening, I could count on an Ellsworth delivery of the most mouthwatering home-cooked food. These wonderful people accommodated my strange cravings.

When people asked, "How can we help? Let us cook for Tasha," Mom tactfully trained them to create the foods I liked. The Allyns' fattening cheesy soup, sodium-enriched, topped my request list every week. My great-aunt modified her chow-mein casserole with extra-crunchy oriental vegetables—something I could have eaten every day. Minimally cooked to a precise consistency, these dishes kept my food aversions from taking over.

Despite all the cautious cooking, unexpected attacks of nausea set in, and sometime that winter I found myself vomiting most of my meals into a hospital barf tray. Some doctors speculated that my physical illness was actually symptomatic of clinical depression. I admitted to having sad moments throughout each day, but I knew deep down something else was wrong with me. After several tests came back negative, I began to wonder if my illness was in fact in my head. Someone planted the idea, and like a true hypochondriac, I began to believe it. Before increasing my antidepressant, however, one doctor ordered a final blood test. Recalling a patient with similar symptoms, he checked my calcium levels. Sure enough, these levels came back extremely high. Nausea and vomiting are in fact the most common symptoms of this condition, called hypercalcemia. The best treatment: IV fluids.

Prior to my accident, I had been incredibly mobile. Over time, as I went from overactive teenager to sedentary quad patient, my minimal movement practically guaranteed a toxic buildup of calcium. My body simply did not know what to do with it. The IV flush made me feel worse before a sudden turnaround. After a weekend of forced hydration, the nausea thankfully disappeared, my appetite picked up again, and I was reminded to drink my prescribed ten glasses of water between six a.m. and six p.m. every day.

Rehab always pushed the fluids, and I had been dodging them. Now, with concern for a relapse of hypercalcemia, my nurses stalked me with water refills every moment they could.

"Can't it be soda?" I asked my nurse, hoping I could go back to my pre-accident Mello Yello habit. Thankfully, soda counted ... as did popsicles, soup broth, and every cc of liquid I could con my nurses into counting. But water was the easiest to quantify, and I truly hated it! Nurses lectured and scolded me for not drinking enough.

Ironically, after liquids were banned for the night at six p.m., I felt intense thirst. As I begged for an evening drink, the same nurses who pushed liquids in the late afternoon reminded me of the long wait before the morning cath nurse's arrival.

All day long, I ducked the water nurses and then complained to Barb. "I couldn't possibly become dehydrated. I'm waterlogged! I'm drowning from all this liquid!" By night, I endured parched-mouth syndrome. I hated the two extremes.

One bonus from all of this was that I improved my power-chair driving skills. I zoomed out of my room just as a nurse refilled my water bottle. She would literally chase me down the hall, water in hand, as I sped toward the gym for therapy.

"Wait, Tasha, I just refilled your bottle. Here's your water. Tasha?!"

I smiled as I glided around a corner, pretending my chair's motor was too loud for me to hear the nurse trailing behind. Focused ahead, speeding down the hall, I escaped a few ounces of water, at least for the moment.

My water wars became extreme on the weekends. I begged my nurses to let me sleep in on Saturdays and Sundays, and some gave in. Others insisted that I maintain my weekday ritual of early "rise and shine." These were the nurses who never let me sleep past eight. My favorites gave in to my pleas and sometimes let me sleep straight through till noon. The downside to this: I was now four hours behind on H_2O intake.

One Saturday, as I choked down the ounces needed to play catch-up, I asked my nurse if I would have to adhere to this schedule for the rest of my life.

"Once you leave the hospital, you and your family can decide if you will continue the water schedule or not. The thing is, you'll have to find a healthy level of fluid intake to match your level of activity." This was all

I needed to hear. I saw myself swearing off the water bottle for pop and lemonade. I'd have to work on Mom and Angie and their by-the-book rules, but Dad and Ryan would come to my corner for sure. Oddly enough, the water wars became motivation to work harder toward discharge.

Ultimately, the New Year's holiday was only slightly tarnished by the empty-cot rule. Family was banned, but the care team still allowed friends for sleepovers. Jesse Carr was one of my favorite visitors that winter, since I could truly be myself in her presence. She watched as I counseled company who broke down in tears, devastated by my condition. I knew I would upset people if I cried, so I faked my way through and comforted those so saddened by my situation. Jesse, who came often, let me do the crying if I wanted to, although I was generally happy when she visited because we talked about other things.

Jesse and me, hanging out at school.

On the days when my tears flowed alone, I would pull the covers up over my head and beg God to wake me from this nightmare. Even though I held on to hope that I would walk again, I wasn't seeing any sign of progress. I needed a sign. My fragile faith waned to its lowest point as I realized my condition was permanent.

As I wallowed in self-pity, two nurses, Gayle and Val, surprised me.

Determined to flip my attitude upside down, they would bring a party with them during their shifts. No words of wisdom, no pseudo talk therapy like I endured every day from the psych department—just simple, old-fashioned fun. Gayle switched on my CD player, and with her dancing partner, Val, they sang and danced to, of all things, the Carpenters. They knew every word to every song! I don't think that I ever listened to the Carpenters before or since. But as Gayle and Val grabbed a toothbrush or comb as microphone substitutes, I rolled my eyes. My negative attitude fought them until, in a matter of minutes, I was singing along. Soon, with the biggest smile on my face, I was swaying and bobbing my head and feeling a whole lot better.

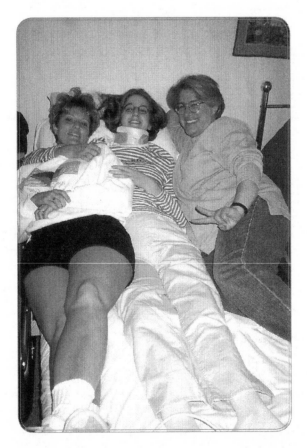

Val and Gail get me laughing by jumping into bed with me.

By the weekend, when Travis and others came to visit, we all agreed I needed a change of scenery. January was a horrible month for anyone with a serious illness. Patients couldn't go outside for fresh air. The sun seemed nonexistent that winter, so even sitting by a window seemed futile.

"Why don't you try the meditation room?" one nurse suggested. A Middle Eastern country that provided free Mayo healthcare for its people had donated this space to promote Eastern peace and tranquility. A trickling fountain, soft New Age music, and unique artwork made this an inviting room for quiet thoughts and prayers. Not exactly a party room. But my friends sensed I needed to break some rules in order to shake up the rehab routine.

So with directions that led us down long hallways, Travis, Stevie, Jesse, and I set out on my first excursion away from rehab.

"Tasha, wait—give me a ride," Stevie said as he grabbed a doctor's wheeled stool from under a small desk in my room.

"You're gonna get me in so much trouble," I said, but I conceded as my power chair—with Stevie swinging behind—zoomed down the corridors in the direction of the meditation room.

"See any Scrubs?" Stevie asked. No staff was spotted, so Stevie squealed all the way to the next corner turn like a kid on the Tilt-A-Whirl at the Pierce County Fair. The meditation room became one of my favorite field trips that winter.

Mom was pleased that I had found a change of scenery in the meditation room, but she knew instinctively that there was not a whole lot of praying going on there. She voiced her ongoing concern. "Tasha, you haven't been to church in a long time."

My family went to the hospital chapel frequently. The church service on Sunday mornings was at ten a.m. and proved very convenient to Mom, Dad, Angie, and any other family or friends who happened to be visiting at that time. I started to argue the point that the Saint Mary's Sunday service just wasn't convenient to me, since Sunday was one of two mornings each week that I was ever able to sleep in. Mom, however, felt that so many of our prayers had been answered. "You need to give back, Tasha."

It was an arduous trip for a quadriplegic patient to navigate through an enormous hospital campus. All down the long elevator ride to Saint

Marys Chapel, I argued that the effort would steal whatever strength I had left. "Isn't this supposed to be a day of rest? Come on, Mom. I can watch the same service on the TV in my room." The truth was, I didn't want to give God any of my time since He had stolen so much from me. But Mom won, and the following Sunday I was prepped for the long indoor commute to the chapel.

Although I had been stuffing it most of that winter, my devious side emerged just as I confronted something I did not want to do. In this case, I would make Mom regret my chapel visit. If I got my way, no one would ever try this again.

My light-headedness still controlled me, so as always to combat the feeling, I reclined my chair as far as I could. Consequently, fatigue drained my arm muscles almost immediately as I operated my joystick from this awkward angle.

The chapel, on the opposite side of the hospital and down a number of floors from rehab, couldn't be any more inconveniently located. As hoped, I ran out of gas early on during the trek.

"Mom, can you push my power stick? I'm so afraid I'm going to pass out if I sit upright. My arm is shot already." Mom was more than willing to help get me to church.

"Oops, watch it. Careful, there's a corner coming up." Mom could drive for me, but I never said it was easy. She crashed into walls, ran over her own feet, and spun around in the middle of the hallway even on a clear straightaway. By the time we arrived at Saint Marys Chapel, Mom was so beaten up and bruised that she wondered if she needed the emergency room for herself.

To me, the chapel service was boring and uninspiring at a time when I truly needed to find my faith again. Battered and exhausted, Mom agreed that until I had enough strength to navigate myself to the chapel, I should stay back in my room and watch the service. Silent victory for the teenager! In my triumph, I disregarded the fact that I actually wanted God's help. I was stuffing it again, but this time I was ignoring the truth—that I was starved for faith.

Two Christian family friends from Ellsworth visited and prayed for me often during my coma days. As my health improved, they came to visit again. They talked of Jesus and his suffering and showed me books that discussed God's love. I honestly couldn't understand this, since God was the only one I could blame for my accident. Even if He did love me, He chose not to deliver me from what I was going through. Why did they think I would be anything but angry with God?

The last thing these women would do before leaving was pray for my healing—pray for a miracle. I wanted a miracle and believed in it so strongly. I heard of so many people who were walking after breaking their necks, so I did have hope. Once these women left after each visit, I sunk lower and lower, feeling that all their unanswered prayers were proof that God had left me. This was *not* helping my faith—or so I thought at the time.

While I struggled to find any connection with God, I truly connected with Kate, the hospital chaplain. She was a single woman with two therapy dogs, Grace and Alleluia. She was the kindest and most gentle person, and I indeed saw God in her. So content and sincere, she encouraged me by simply listening as I voiced my frustrations. I felt so much peace when I was with her. She helped to alleviate some of my worries, and she never seemed stumped or offended by my questions about God.

Frustrations were piling up for my parents as well. With the constant decision-making about my future, one of the hardest things they faced was that our home could not be modified to accommodate my needs. The house that I grew up in was over a hundred years old, with steps everywhere. Mom soon made the decision that we needed to build a new house that was accessible for me. As if we weren't facing enough change, now our home was being stripped from our lives. I took it out on Mom, knowing that my dad didn't like the news either.

"No one wants to move, Tasha," Mom tried to explain. "Our home is our place of comfort. Don't you think I miss it too, all these weeks in Rochester? That's been my home for twenty-six years—seventeen of those years with you. I feel terrible that you have to face one more change. But what is the alternative? There just isn't a choice to make here. The fact that the house is such an old design makes the choice for us. We have to live where you can get around."

Things got pretty quiet. I couldn't argue. Mom was disrupting her life

95

one more time for my sake. Calmly, she added, "Our home is wherever we are—our home will be where we finally settle together again. Just wait and see. You'll love having everything new … just the way you want it. Start thinking of design ideas—you can pick any colors you want for your room."

Once again, I was acknowledging the sad impact my accident had on my entire family. After life-altering damage like this, it's not only the injured who must confront the fallout. As I listened to my mom's defense of a new home and watched my other family quietly comply, I thought of the hundreds of visitors who pitied me as the "victim." I flashed back to the repeated comments—"Oh, poor Tasha. It's a miracle that Tasha has endured so much. Tasha's life has changed forever. Poor Tasha—what a survivor."

In that moment, as Mom finalized her testimony for our new home, I felt profound sadness for every member of my family. No one could rescue them; no one could turn back the clock. Not one of them had the kind of character to run away and leave me to fend for myself. Mom, Dad, Angie, and Ryan were ready to give up their lives for me. And eventually they would lose more than their homes to see me through this. Some would lose jobs—some, each other. And what weighed heavy on me was the fact that nothing could stop this from happening. Because of the wonderful people they are, no one could unburden them from this journey they were so willing to share with me. Just as I could not be saved from my transformation into a life without limbs, they could not be saved from the turn their lives would take because Tasha was now paralyzed.

"They're fighting again," I heard Angie say more than once. Bills piled up. Insurance notices indicated high deductibles or, worse yet, items deemed "not covered." The financial stress snowballed. My parents had to manage the grocery-store expansion … plus the sale of our home … plus the new wheelchair-accessible house construction.

Mom and Dad knew I felt responsible, but both kept saying, "This is not your fault! This is not your concern. Stay focused on getting better—that's all that matters. The other things will work out if you just try doing your best in rehab." However, perception is a powerful thing. I blamed myself, I worried about everyone, and I felt responsible for all the chaos *I believed* I had caused.

It was one thing to feel I had created trouble for my parents. It was quite another to endure the loss I was sure I had caused my brother. Ryan, the most quietly impacted by my accident, was definitely the last to voice it. Before my fall, he was big into family time. Rare for a college student, Ryan came home every other Friday to plan some time together. We had to play cards, or pull out a board game, or watch a movie. When he was home, one evening out of the weekend had to be spent together—Ryan insisted. Literally, one day Ryan had a family, and the next, they were gone. He never complained, but by January, one look at him and the loss was obvious. Ryan compensated by working even more, and by visiting family in Rochester where he knew he would find us together on the weekends.

Somehow he managed to keep his grades up. Besides Ryan, other store employees proved to be amazing support, with so many going above and beyond the normal call of duty. Jamie, one worker who literally knew how to do everything within the grocery-store business, helped my family so much. He was like my second brother. He and Ryan shouldered the burden of absentee owners who needed to be by their daughter's side.

Meeting Nikki (who knew she would become my sister-in-law?) proved to be a blessing to Ryan and our family. Without Jamie's and Nikki's support, I don't know how my brother would have dealt with so much change. When Ryan visited, I could see the pain in his eyes, a longing to fix what he couldn't control. But Ryan quietly managed what he could—his studies and the store—and, without complaint, paid a visit to my room whenever possible.

The longer I stayed in rehab, the clearer I saw the burden to my loved ones. They gradually lost their poker faces in a marathon round of five-card draw. As pressures increased, stuffing it would inevitably lead to some sort of emotional meltdown. Yet the thing that triggered my first public outburst was as unpredictable as my fall back in November.

On my way to physical therapy one day, I saw a woman in a wheelchair playing the piano in one of the rec rooms. She wasn't particularly gifted, but she had such dexterity in her hands. I stopped and watched in amazement, wondering if my fingers had moved that effortlessly across the keys.

I paused long enough for the revelation to take hold. I looked down at my hands. Eight years of piano lessons, suddenly a waste of time—a cruel joke. I would never play again. Why had it taken me so long to acknowledge? I had left another piece of old Tasha in that basement of the Sheldon Theater.

Zooming down the hallway, I entered PT in tears. Without speaking, Neil hugged me. With no clue what had triggered this outburst, he comforted me, no questions asked. I raised my face from his soaked shirt enough to see others in the gym. As soon as I realized that people could see me crying, I dried up, stifled my sobbing, and let Neil wipe my face. I wanted to go back to stuffing it. With his best Frasier Crane look of "I'm listening," Neil never insisted that I explain myself.

"What are we doing today?" I asked suddenly, wanting to shift gears.

"Are you ready to work?"

Neil waited. I nodded.

"Okay. Let's get to the mat. Interrupt if there's something on your mind. But we've got plenty to do." I loved that Neil didn't push me for explanation, and I truly felt some relief from letting my emotions loose, even for a few minutes. With time I would learn to grieve each and every loss that accompanied my paralyzed body. For now, I saw this incident as a regrettable show of emotion. I would park a memory of it in the deep recesses of my mind and strive not to let it happen again.

Chapter 10

Turn and Face the Change

WELCOMED OR NOT, change comes with time. "Stuffing it" couldn't stop or even slow the inevitable progress that comes from quality care and the power of healing. In the dead of winter, word came through a care conference that my trache would be removed. Almost as fast as it was taken out, the tube that had seemed pointless for some time now screamed to be replaced. Immediate complications nearly rolled me back into intensive care. Within moments, I was bear-hugged by a nurse who performed the Heimlich maneuver for over an hour.

A new suction order came down. The incision in my throat, now tubeless, was still wide open, unhealed, so vacuuming occurred through the gaping hole. When the painful procedure was done, I thanked God, despite my anger. Within a few hours, however, the fluids built up again. By now, the hole was completely closed. Suctioning through the trache hole was not an option anymore.

At this point, my doctors performed the most painful procedure I endured in all my weeks at Rochester. A tube was shoved up my nose and then down the back of my throat, with hopes that a direct line to my lungs would clear them. This painfully invasive procedure worked, but the following day the doctors ordered another bronchoscopy procedure. They chose not to put me under sedation, for fear that I would crash again. Fully aware of all that was happening, I endured the pain of a tube being shoved down my throat one last time. This would be the grand finale for my lungs, and I can say that since this traumatic episode, my lungs have not required scopes or direct suction. Had another scope been ordered, I would have demanded anesthesia. No one should have to experience what I did, in wide-awake torture.

Paralyzed stomach muscles guarantee that a weak cough plagues me whenever I fall sick or suffer from seasonal allergies. Even after the trache was removed, the Heimlich maneuver remained on my nurse's list of required daily cares. Once I was discharged, I learned every trick possible to prevent cough-related illness. I miss the ability to let out a good, strong cough about as much as I missed my reach for a tickly nose. Although I recouped my scratching ability, using knuckles rather than fingertips, I will never replace the stomach muscles needed to belt out a strong, throat-clearing cough. For someone whose career relies on the strength of her voice, despite my record of good health, concern for my throat will always be in the back of my mind.

With the trache behind me, physical progress seemed to come more quickly. As fragile as my arms appeared, I began to experience the benefits of daily PT and OT muscle-building drills. In addition, after three months of feeling like a sick pet with a cone collar, I finally received the okay to shed the armored neck collar. Doctors read my MRI and declared this brace "safe to remove." I should have been thrilled. Real progress could be measured by the number of invasive contraptions I shed in such a short time. Yet as much as I couldn't wait to get the neckpiece off, I spent the next two days fearing a collarless life. I was convinced that I would re-break my neck if I tested my range of motion. I turned ever so carefully in my chair, shifting only my eyes.

"Tasha, you'll be fine. Relax. You look so stiff! Look around. No more tunnel vision! You don't know what you've been missing. Loosen up and turn your head from side to side." I heard this from everyone—professional staff, my parents, Travis, Angie. But I didn't buy it when they said, "Seriously, Tasha, you can move your neck. You can nod. You can turn to look at something—your neck will not re-break." It took a few days, and the phantom neck collar faded. More and more regular movement was restored, at least for my upper body.

In my defense, unless you've experienced a broken neck, you cannot fathom the warmth and security a neck collar provides. For some time, I would ask for my collar, especially when extremely cold or tired. The warmth radiated by the collar far surpassed that of a scarf or shawl.

With every change, Barb adjusted my OT agenda to complement my medical progress. She challenged me with more difficult fine-motor skills knowing that my biceps, deltoids, shoulder and forearm muscles needed constant attention. And since I would never move my fingers, the upward motion of my right wrist was key to so many personal tasks.

I will be forever indebted to Barb for bringing fine-motor skills back to a seemingly useless pair of hands. While my fingers remained frozen, ineffectual, Barb patiently taught me new ways to comb my hair, brush my teeth, and feed myself—probably the most pride-protecting duty of them all. Other cares can be completed behind closed doors, but eating—being fed—is very public, regardless of the setting. School, a restaurant, the family dinner table ... the total dependence I felt when being fed like a toddler had to end. Barb's positive persistence toward my independent eating skills proved to be her greatest gift to me.

My friends would have fed me forever. I have no doubt they felt this was one way they could help me. Stevie, Jesse, and Travis rarely visited without making a pit stop at McDonald's to buy me salty French fries. One by one, I would beg, "More salt!" I wanted to taste something— anything! My taste buds remained in hiding for months after the head trauma of my accident. I must have looked like Nanny Bird's baby chick, gaping mouth open, long fries being dropped in, one bite at a time. Although I preferred to have Mom or Angie feed me, Travis reminded me often, "It's no big deal," especially if it meant I could come home soon. But Barb knew I had the capacity to learn this task, and I wasn't leaving rehab until I mastered it.

Of course, from my chest down, I was completely paralyzed and had no feeling if touched, hot or cold. So Barb maximized my available muscles using a deltoid machine. This apparatus guided my arms and enabled me to start feeding myself. Essentially, this machine souped up my strength so I could finally scratch my nose! Since I only had the endurance to touch my nose once or twice a day, I usually saved that skillful feat for evening visitors. Months later, after tackling the more complex motor skills needed for driving, we would laugh at the enthusiastic applause I received for my nose trick. However, while I was weaning off the deltoid therapy (since it was not a machine I could use at home), even the tiniest accomplishments were celebrated by staff and loved ones. My confidence gradually grew with each new achievement, but clearly, I was still stuffing it. The deep fear of leaving the security of Rochester hid and festered like a dormant disease.

At night I wore splints on both of my hands in order to shape them into positions that fostered more independence. According to the doctors, the nighttime splints coaxed my hands into closed positions, almost as if I were making fists. During the day, my hands featured a more functional splint design, facilitating my fine-motor tasks. The bottom line was that I had some sort of splints on 24-7 … and I hated them.

Typically, straight fingers can be freely bent, like mini-hinges at each knuckle. What did Walt Whitman say? "And the narrowest hinge in my hand puts to scorn all machinery." How true, the miracle of working fingers! My injury stole my hinge command. I needed to camouflage ten long, flailing phalanges that did nothing but get in the way and impede my grip. The splints would bend my fingers forever inward, toward my palms. My hands would learn a new way to grip a fork or cup, type on a keyboard, apply makeup, and eventually operate multiple touch screens with the technology explosion of recent years.

My family thought the doctors were crazy for wanting my fingers to look curved and atrophied. The splints, along with nighttime arm weights, made sleeping uncomfortable. *So what's new*, I thought.

I haven't said much about my rec therapy time, although John Verbout, my recreational therapist, undoubtedly impacted my rehab progress. To be honest, I initially feared John and the time I was on his watch.

"Barb, he's not a nurse. What if I die when I'm down there? John can't cough me. I'm just too scared to go there. Come with me, Barb." I begged not to have to see John alone.

"Tasha, don't be ridiculous," Barb said, trying to dispel my fears. "John's not new to rehab. He knows what he's doing. He's not going to let anything bad happen to you."

"Can't you come with me?" I begged.

"You'll be fine. I have other patients, you know. While you're with John, I'm not exactly taking a coffee break."

So my hours in RT, recreational therapy, began, and I actually grew to love that part of my day. At times I felt I was back in Mr. Ruppe's high school art class, since I could draw and paint—two of my favorite things. For these weak arms to perform any type of personal expression was quite a feat, although I took more pride in the process than the final product. This was in fact different from my experience in high school art. My family wondered if I would burn out on the idea because of my limited, fingerless grip. But expression is expression. And that brought satisfaction. The fulfillment found in the process of communicating an idea onto paper, canvas, pottery, whatever—that feeling transcended any reluctance that came from the mournful passing of my former artistic ways.

Travis's trips to see me, complicated by a wrestling injury, were less frequent than ever. I will never forget how heartbroken he sounded on the phone the night he broke his ankle to end his advance to the state wrestling tournament. Just one more thing gone wrong in what appeared to be a cursed senior year. I can empathize now and feel sadness for this great guy who'd had everything in his back pocket a few short months ago—a girlfriend who loved him, a potential state wrestling title, and a position in the family business waiting for him upon graduation.

After ten days of healing, Travis promised he would catch a ride with my brother to Rochester. Although I feared a breakup, I stuffed it. I clung to the loyalty I knew Travis felt for me. But loyalty and love are two completely different things.

I guess I have Lisa Beck to thank for speeding up the inevitable. Lisa, the head spinal-cord-injury nurse, visited one day with *the manual*. This handbook explored everything from cath cares to relationships to sex and marriage for the spinal-cord-injury victim. No one had been quite so frank with me before.

Shortly after I'd read *the manual*, Lisa visited again.

"So, this Travis is a good guy I hear. You think he's the one?"

"Oh, yeah. I'm so lucky. We are going to make it. I know you and others don't think we can, but we are different. We are going to get married and be together forever."

"But what if Travis doesn't stay in the picture? Can you imagine your life without him?"

I kept arguing—what was the point of the "what if"? Why bother thinking about my life without Travis? "He's still with me. That proves he's committed."

Lisa pushed the what-ifs a little longer and then left for the day. As soon as she walked out the door, it was as if a shade had been lifted. I realized that others saw this as a failed relationship. I confronted the issue that I could not pretend about any longer. I knew as soon as she walked out the door that Travis and I were over.

Even before his injury, Travis would share things on the phone that seemed like deliberate attempts to start a fight.

"So, you guys went out drinking last night? Was it a big group? Sounds like everyone was partying … So, who drove?" Although we weren't angels, Travis and I had a pact—we made a promise never to drink and drive. Apparently, all this had changed. And the fact that he freely 'fessed up to his risky behavior made me believe he was deliberately pushing my buttons.

"You promised, Travis. You said you'd never drive like that. What is going on? I thought we had a deal?"

This was the source of many phone arguments. Finally, the no-show weekend brought it all to an end—a very overdue conclusion. It was Valentine's Day weekend, and my brother walked into my room … without Travis.

"Where's Travis?" I asked. But the tears started even before Ryan had a chance to defend the guy. The ankle … a lot of pain … can't drive … a visit just wasn't working out … Travis was full of excuses. Looking back, I realize that all his excuses were legit. Life was very hard for Travis, too. But the seventeen-year-old quadriplegic felt no empathy for her boyfriend that night. After ten straight days without a visit—his longest-ever stretch of absence—I faced my fears. Travis might be the only man who would ever love me. He might have been my only hope for marriage. This breakup would likely be the start of a solitary life for which all in rehab wanted me to prepare.

Ryan appeared as devastated as I was. "Don't cry, Tasha. Please. It'll be all right." I could tell Ryan wanted to cry right along with me. I stuffed it for his sake. I stopped almost as fast as I had started because I couldn't bear to see my brother hurt once again because of me. The pending breakup, the official end to Tasha and Travis, would come as soon as I found the courage to deliver the news.

Early February also brought the attention of the *St. Paul Pioneer Press* to my rehab room. They ran a story on my accident, including my near-death experience, plus the recent improvements made in therapy. The journalist assigned to me asked if my e-mail address could be included at the end of the story. "People will want to contact you. They'll want to wish you well. No point in having all of these notes come to me. Can we direct them to you through e-mail?"

Excuse me? What? E-mail? Remember, this was 1997, and I was a rural Wisconsin girl whose family just recently removed the last dial phone from our home. Mom did all of her accounting work for the store by hand, and we finger-punched every price into our cash registers. No scanning wands where we lived. A personal computer with access to the World Wide Web? *Talk to my nurse*, I essentially said to this reporter who looked concerned that his e-mail would soon be flooded with valentine messages for Tasha Schuh.

"She can use my e-mail." Michael Wheeler, OTA—Occupational Therapy Assistant and Barb's sometime sidekick—spoke up just as I was pushing for old-fashioned snail mail.

"Really?" I asked. "That would be so cool!"

"Sure. Sounds like OT to me. I'll teach you how to access e-mail. You can use one of the pointer tools, open each message, and read every word sent to you. It'll give us something to do for a few days."

A few days? More like weeks! We couldn't keep up, especially since we only had a short window of time each day between therapy sessions to access the Internet. The response was overwhelming. Reactions to my story came from all over the country, from as far away as Oregon. I never dreamed I'd have so many e-mails in my lifetime, let alone from doing one interview with a Twin Cities reporter.

"I don't think this is what you had in mind," I said after opening Michael's e-mail to find another huge list of Tasha Schuh messages. "This is way beyond your job description."

"I know, but isn't it great? Did you ever think you'd have this many people rooting for you?" I just smiled and continued opening and reading each message. People cared. I couldn't precisely measure it, but there was unique healing power in knowing I existed in the hearts and minds of others.

Suddenly, comfort and concern transformed into much more. Here was a letter that brought an epiphany: my life mattered. I could help others not only by soliciting care from them but by directly personifying the courage it takes to live against all odds.

> *I was going to kill myself today. I planned it all—I don't know why I bothered to read the paper. But there was your story. I am alive right now because of you ... because you have the courage to face all that your accident has changed in your life. I thank you for saving my life.*

For the first time in months, I knew that my life mattered. All of this had some purpose, but I would have to help myself first. I had so much to learn! I was inspired to say, "If I can do this, you can do whatever it is that makes your life a struggle. And in that struggle lies immense reward for enduring it all."

Not since my family moved me from ICU to rehab had I taken inventory of the heartfelt notes from so many people. Back in December, I watched as Ryan, Travis, and Dad moved five garbage bags full of cards to my new room. Five thirty-gallon garbage bags! When I was too weak or too depressed to do much of anything, Mom would often read from those five bags to help me pass the time. Now, sitting in my chair, tucked up to a computer, with a little guidance from Michael, I read electronic mail on my own. This was one of my most exhausting experiences in rehab, but it was pure therapeutic gold.

Despite my demanding e-mail load, rehab pushed for a new rec-therapy challenge in mid-February—a field trip away from the hospital. My homework was to plan and experience a day trip. I had to choose my location, pick an activity, and delegate a helpful crew to accomplish it all.

Plans were approved for an excursion to nearby Galleria Mall in Rochester. This would require me to enter and exit a vehicle via wheelchair. I had to invite people who would attend to my cares as well as help me enjoy the social time away from the hospital. Of course, I also needed to make a purchase. It was shopping, for goodness sake! I had to spend money. Whether on goods, services, or just good ol' fattening mall food, an exchange of cash for goods had to be made.

The first moments in the vehicle triggered an unexpected déjà vu. I was unprepared for the trip back in time to my last ride outside of a hospital wheelchair. It was the helicopter—my airlift to Saint Marys Hospital. My carsick nausea subsided as I confronted the memory and moved on to the reason for this current van ride. This time, I didn't vomit all the way to my destination. This time, I did not aspirate, but the memory was strong. I stuffed my queasy emotions to the best of my ability and accompanied my entourage into the Galleria Mall.

I felt like a celebrity traveling with my "people": Barb, Neil, John, my nurse, Mom, Dad, Angie, Sarah, and even Travis. I have no idea what Rochester shoppers thought of me—and for a while, I didn't care.

At first, I felt the rush of a pure social excursion. However, just hitting the "open" pad near the parking lot door took huge physical effort. I would soon find out how physically demanding a day at the mall could be. The "professionals"—the rehab staff—had grander goals in mind.

"Okay, Tasha, you are in charge. We're here just to observe. Act like a shopper." Neil was quick to remind me that I had a mission to accomplish.

"I really came just for shoes," I replied.

"You want to try on shoes?" Neil said. "Better find a salesclerk to help you. Sorry … Mom is not tracking down help for you."

Shoes seemed to be the most logical items for purchase at this point. I hated the ugly white high-tops the nurses put on my feet every day. I found lace-ups that were white with blue and green plaid—cute with jeans, and finally some color! Then a pair of Skechers boots caught my eye. Both of these fit and remained in my closet until a few years ago. That's one minor advantage to wheelchair travel—minimal wear and tear on the shoe collection.

This was fun. Mom would have said yes to anything on this shopping venture. I milked it ... Mom pulled out cash at two different stores. I was so excited!

Not long after I finalized my sales, Neil spoke up again. "Come on, Tasha, get us out of here."

"Push the automatic door pad, Tasha." Everyone reminded me I was still on assignment.

"Where's the elevator, Tasha?"

"You need to hit *up* and *down* on your own, Tasha."

"Someday you'll be doing this without help," Barb reminded me.

Right, I thought. *Like I'm ever going shopping without friends or family.* But Barb had a point. The goal was independence.

As abruptly as the shopping high came on, I crashed from exhaustion. The overstimulation was about to win.

Fatigue hit me like a bad sedative. My shopping climax vanished as quickly as it had started. Suddenly I realized that I had been quite secluded within the walls of the Mayo campus, where I was surrounded by nurses and doctors. I was not prepared for the public reaction to this quadriplegic freely exploring the Galleria Mall. As we left that day, my perception, skewed by exhaustion, led me to think that every shopper questioned my right to be out and about in the mall. I felt like a convict with a two-hour pass.

By this point, I couldn't find my way to the van fast enough. I wanted back in the hospital, where people smiled, greeted me, and praised me for every move I made. After a short ride, I reentered my comfort zone: Saint Marys rehabilitation center, where I was safe and accepted.

Chapter 11

Field-Trip Frenzy

My recreational therapist, John Verbout, had prescribed my previous out-of-hospital experience. But Angie and I plotted the next adventure. All of Ellsworth High School was raving about *Titanic*—and we certainly know how that turned out for Leo and Kate. The following weekend, I asked Angie to put her assertive charm back into action, and before long, we had a day pass to the Galleria Mall Theater.

This was big. As we exited the hospital that Saturday night, Angie and I both felt the weight of my first field trip without a professional entourage. Our eyes locked. I read her face. We were both petrified but clearly afraid to voice it. The fear of not going—of chickening out—outweighed our anxiety. What would my life be like if I stayed within the confines of a hospital room or my bedroom at home? Risk prevailed over fear, and we found ourselves loading the van before either of us could object.

Smooth sailing so far—my thoughts went unstated. I was afraid that if I bragged about how easy Angie made this, I would jinx any future field trips.

Positioned in the back row of the movie theater, my coughing attack started almost simultaneously with Jack Dawson's entrance. Angie gave me the Heimlich maneuver throughout most of the movie. How could the audience enjoy this film with someone performing life-support calisthenics nearby? Yet I had no intention of leaving. I selfishly allowed Angie to miss most of the movie while I coughed and remained glued to every visually amazing moment of *The Titanic.*

"I'm so sorry." If Angie said this once, she said it a hundred times that night. "No, really, she'll be fine. Sounds worse than it is." No one could focus on the film out of fear that Angie would cry out for 9-1-1 help at any moment.

But I didn't care. I was oblivious to anyone else's viewing experience. For me, the night was amazing! Not only had I gained the right to my enthusiastic thumbs-up for *Titanic,* I had accomplished a social goal that fed my field-trip frenzy. Although we were both relieved to get back to the hospital, we still felt a boost of confidence from all we had accomplished.

Our next outing took us back to the mall—time for prom-dress shopping. Attending prom in Ellsworth, Wisconsin, became my biggest rec-therapy goal thus far. I was excited on so many levels. Although I had attended Travis's prom as an underclassman, this was *my* junior prom. I felt the pressure—or was it opportunity?—to be an Ellsworth student again after all these months away. Of course, my storybook view of Prom Night seemed tainted by my wheelchair, since entering the Grand March sitting down was never part of my plan. But I felt driven to do this; no one really had to talk me into it. Finding a dress became my new mission in life. I knew that whatever I purchased had to work as a sit-down gown. Plus, it had to be stunning enough so people saw past my chair to focus on me.

Angie and I navigated the mall once again to find a beautiful royal blue dress of charmeuse satin. This bold blue was the color of the year. (Sarina, also healthy enough to attend prom, wore a different gown in precisely the same brilliant blue.) Expensive? Yes, but worth every penny if it boosted my confidence for this important transition back into high school life.

In spite of our frequent arguments, Travis and I still planned to attend prom together. I concealed my conviction that if he broke up with me, nobody would ever date me again. However, I began telling people at rehab that I was going to talk to him—that *I* was going to end it. The next day, Travis would visit, and I'd chicken out. The security of a boyfriend sustained me. As awkward and unattractive as I felt, my courage to break it off disappeared as soon as Travis stepped into my room.

While my relationship with Travis topped my list of worries, I was clearly stuffing so much more. My fears of seeing classmates again ... of returning home unable to walk ... of hiding my struggles with basic things like eating and going to the bathroom. I hid so many anxieties behind my smile, while pretending that I could handle anything.

One day, while Barb worked me through her OT agenda, we chatted about my weekend. I decided to share with her that I would soon break it off with Travis. I just didn't know when, where, or how. I played it as if this matter didn't bother me—just a minor nuisance that needed closure.

Barb saw right through me and asked me outright, "Tasha, are you sure you're okay with this? It's all right to admit this will be hard for you."

I snapped right back, "Oh, yeah, I'm fine, Barb. This is long overdue."

Barb was good. She didn't buy my bravado. I had buried more than the fear of life without a boyfriend. "Now, Tasha, how are you *really* doing? Tell me the truth."

My fake smile quickly faded as I realized Barb saw through my pretense. She tore down my front, although I admit, it was pretty weak at this point. I felt defenseless, while Barb seemed ready for my collapse. No more stuffing it. My resistance was gone.

Tears welled up in my eyes, and the flood of defeat broke loose. I was falling, but not sixteen feet to the Sheldon Theater floor. This time I was falling apart with no strength left to fight. The emotion I had stuffed for so long would not stop gushing forth for hours.

With blurred vision from tears that flowed freely down my face, I motored back to my room where Mom was waiting.

"Tasha! What's wrong? What happened?" She looked to Barb for explanation, doubting my ability to speak through heavy sobs. Barb never had a chance to reply.

"My life sucks! This is so unfair!" I am certain this was the most volume out of my mouth since my last *Wizard of Oz* rehearsal.

"I'm never going to be able to do anything that I want to do! My life is over! I can't believe this is me! Travis and I are going to break up! You guys had to spend all of your life savings on a new house! I'm going to live with you for the rest of my life! I can't believe what has happened to us!"

This was Mom's cue to start crying. She had been holding it in too—for who stuffs pain better than a mother who would give anything to spare her child from all this disappointment. As much as I love my mom and empathize with her now, at the time I was inconsolable. I continued to cry for almost fifteen hours straight.

Throughout the night and into the next morning, I cried even as I dozed, although I don't think I really slept. Ironically, when I finally stopped, I felt incredible relief. I had been carrying this grief within me, and when I cried it all out, I felt release from a burden that I cannot quite explain. My situation had not changed overnight. I was exhausted from not sleeping, but suddenly, I felt some peace. Yes, my life sucked, to put it as bluntly as any teenager would. But what had changed overnight, through the endless tears, was the way I dealt with it: I had decided that I would no longer stuff it. It was my life, after all, and I felt an odd desire to face it—to complain about it, to cry about it, to mourn the loss of old Tasha.

Oddly, it felt as if old Tasha had melted away with my tears. Not like the Wicked Witch of the West, who melted from a bucket of water; old Tasha wasn't completely gone. But she had stepped aside for new Tasha to wheel into the spotlight. Her brave performance was over. It was time to take a bow and become the new Tasha—not an actress but a human being, with fears and hopes for the future.

With puffy eyes, I thanked Mom and Barb for putting up with me and announced that I wanted to plan my next field trip. It was mid-February, and Sarah Sans was a contestant in the Miss Ellsworth pageant. The crowning took place during the Winter Snow Fest, an Ellsworth tradition. After my accident, every time Sarah visited, she reminded me, "I'm entering the Miss Ellsworth pageant, and you are going to be there in the audience. Promise me? You have to work hard so you can come to support me."

"I promise." It was my standard answer, but I had no idea how I would get there. And now that the Winter Snow Fest was quickly approaching, I asked Mom if we could pull this off.

My mom lined up a wheelchair-accessible vehicle—not an easy task. This was another sacrifice, another huge expense at a time when my parents were financially stressed beyond belief. But Mom worked a deal. (One of her many gifts is that my mother can haggle anyone down to her bottom line.) I could take the round trip with Mom to Ellsworth once we received clearance from my doctors. Travis surprised me with a new outfit to wear. (See why it was hard to dislike this guy?) Though I wouldn't look quite as elegant as Sarah and the Miss Ellsworth contestants in their formal evening gowns, I would be more dressed up than I had been in months. With a little makeup and my hair done, I looked like the old Tasha, yet with a new confidence. When Travis saw me, his jaw dropped. I thought, *Hmmm, maybe I can still charm the boys after all.*

Halfway through the evening, the emcees made an announcement that I was in the audience. Immediate applause led to a standing ovation. I was overwhelmed by the warmth of this response. Were people proud of me? Did they think I had done something heroic? If they saw me on a day when I struggled, would they still clap? I was only doing what anyone would do, right? Taking it one day at a time? That night, my hometown support shot a force of optimism through me that had lasting power.

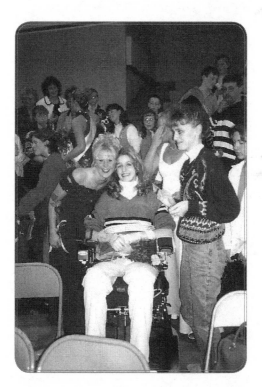

With Hayley, Sarah, and Angie at the Miss Ellsworth pageant.

Sarah Sans was not crowned Miss Ellsworth, but I believe she felt satisfaction in accomplishing one goal—coaxing me home, if only for a few hours. I was more determined than ever to earn my discharge and come home permanently. My last three weeks of rehabilitation became a crash course of all I had to learn to make my release from the hospital a reality.

My most challenging new task: learning to orchestrate a team of caregivers. In other words, several new nurses came onboard whose sole assignment was to listen to my instructions as they conducted my personal cares. I hated this. My regular nurses knew the routine. They just came and did what needed to be done. Now I had to be completely aware of every detail regarding my own needs and train each nurse in meeting those needs.

My mom and Angie would lead my cares, but I would handle the support staff that replaced my family when they were pulled in other directions. My mom's face was full of anxiety with each new duty placed in her hands. She could do anything they asked of her, yet the responsibility must have weighed heavy. Try as she did to hide any worries, she wore her fears openly.

Rochester Social Services worked with Pierce County Medical Assistance to line up caregivers, medical supplies, and other equipment in order to pave my path home. Although we did not have a discharge date, everyone knew the end of rehab was near.

My new wheelchair arrived—another sign that the countdown was on. Manufactured in Sweden and customized to fit my body, this chair was tailored for my back as well as the length of my legs.

"This is what a custom-made chair feels like!" I exclaimed.

"Yes! Worth the wait." I don't know who replied, since I became lost in the comfortable fit. I could finally lose the loaner chair and navigate with ease, just days before I moved on to the next stage: transition time in the Ronald McDonald House.

The new Schuh home in Ellsworth was far from completion. Although we broke ground on February 5, the house was not prepared for my move, and neither was I. Mom and I would share her spot at the Ronald McDonald House, and I would make a daily commute to the hospital for therapy. This proved to be an effective plan. I could bring every new problem met in my nonhospital setting to therapy the next day and troubleshoot immediate solutions with Barb, Neil, or John. When my day of therapy ended, I focused on schoolwork with my tutor, an important part of my academic transition.

I looked at my mom upon hearing we were to be Ronald McDonald House roommates. From here out, Mom would be my primary caregiver, and employees from a local agency would assist her. "Hospital discharge" on my chart meant serious work for her.

"Well, this is it, Tasha." She smiled and sounded excited for me. But I knew that tone. It camouflaged the worry. "You're on your way home! Angie and I have our work cut out for us. Let's get the nurse in here. We need to resolve this cath schedule."

The dreaded cath schedule. The most difficult part about leaving Rochester and the biggest challenge to my caregivers once I left the security of this medical environment was my bladder. A leg bag, fairly standard for patients like me, would grant me independence from bladder worries throughout the day. Unfortunately, I was prone to bladder infections. Kidney scans indicated that I must take this problem seriously. In every written document related to my discharge, doctors declared, "Leg bag ... NOT an option ... cath every 6 hours." Every six hours—this meant getting out of my wheelchair, getting undressed from the waist down, getting the cath in place, getting dressed again, and then being transferred back into my chair. This is not what I wanted!

In my final days as a hospital patient, Mom listened and took direction from the cath nurses. Angie, her weekend backup, learned too. We had recently discovered that once back in Ellsworth, the Pierce County caregivers would *not* cath a patient. Medical assistance was limited to the qualifications available in our area. People have asked me why we didn't fight this. Perhaps we didn't complain for fear it would set back my discharge date. Perhaps we were so overwhelmed by all the discharge responsibilities that we didn't think to question it. We were grateful for all the support we were receiving, so who were we to challenge the system when it had limits?

"I want that surgery," I told Barb and Neil one day in rehab.

A Mitrofanoff, or cathing stoma surgical procedure, would change my

115

internal plumbing so that my bladder could be emptied—by a caregiver, or ultimately by me, all on my own—through a catheter placed in my belly button.

"Ew, through your belly button?" I recall Angie reacting when I first brought it up. "That means a permanent hole? Right? Isn't that what a stoma is? Sounds dangerous."

"I agree." My mom jumped right in. "Sounds like an infection waiting to happen."

"It's the most independent way to handle my cares." *What's more dangerous—that, or an exploding bladder from waiting for one of you to come cath me?* This thought I kept to myself. I wouldn't exactly be handcuffed to Mom or Angie every hour of the day. But the fear of needing one of them as a primary cath technician, precisely every six hours, unnerved me. This was too much togetherness.

"Isn't independence what we're shootin' for? Isn't that the point of rehab? It just becomes a part of my body," I continued to argue.

"I agree with Tasha," Neil explained. Then, turning to me, he said, "But you aren't a candidate until your one-year anniversary."

I did not understand why I had to wait so long after my accident to have this procedure, but clearly my family was relieved.

"Tasha, it's so risky! After all you've been through, why would you want to be put under, take the chance of another coma, with no guarantee that it would work anyway?"

My mom and Angie repeated this same concern so many times. For now, they would get their way, satisfied that my being cathed every six hours was "not a big deal." But I saw the implications. Out with my friends, watching the clock. Like Cinderella, I would self-destruct promptly at midnight, unless my final cath of the day was placed precisely before the ominous hour. And believe me, I heard every horror story.

"Autonomic dysreflexia could result from a neglected bladder," one pamphlet read. Autonomic dysreflexia: the ultimate radar system that quadriplegics rely upon. Since messages no longer carry from the nerve endings throughout the body to the brain, another sense takes over. So if any part of my body—including my bladder—senses trauma, something overt will happen. This unusual happening, different in every patient, is something I should very much fear because it could result in stroke or death. I should proactively strive to prevent it. I promised everyone I would watch for and report physical signs, no matter how minor, in hopes of averting another hospital stay because of autonomic dysreflexia. However, in time, I would come to realize this feared phenomenon would become my best friend—my internal warning system. Paralysis prevents me from feeling danger like a full bladder or a tight shoe. Heat, for instance, is an enemy of arms and legs that have no feeling. Once, my caregiver tried to blow-dry some glue used to repair my chair. "Ooo ... I have the chills!" Immediately, my autonomic dysreflexia kicked in with the goose bumps to warn me that another few seconds of heat and my leg would have suffered a severe burn.

To ease Mom's fears of a cathing stoma, Neil—a fan of the procedure and any change that facilitated independence, for that matter—arranged for a former patient of his to visit. We saw firsthand how slick the Mitrofanoff worked. Over time, Mom softened. She hoped I would change my mind through the course of my first year in this new body, but she always trusted Neil. In fact, Neil's advocacy of the stoma was probably the only reason Mom gave in to the idea by late summer.

As soon as I arrived at the Ronald McDonald House, I felt even more strongly that the Mitrofanoff surgery was the right thing for me. As we unpacked in my new room, I looked forward to being in more of a home, yet I appreciated the security of a hospital room only two blocks away. The sofa and TV area of the Ronald McDonald House, cozy and inviting, sent the message that social time was important. As I met my new neighbors, I recalled all the stories Mom had brought to my hospital room about the friendships she had made with other families. I put faces to names and felt confident that I recognized these residents far better than they knew, simply because of Mom's connections in recent weeks.

"Oh, hi! Sure, Mom told me about you ... your daughter ... your son ... your baby." I learned the details of their illnesses, their financial worries, and their emotional struggles simply because my mother was the best listener any of them would ever meet.

I finally understood why Mom made friends with strangers. There was comfort in the shared experience of extreme adversity. These people were battling cancer, paralysis, and other health hardships that left their future unknown. *Hope, love,* and *strength* were common words used around the House, and they were often the topics of informal group discussions as we planned for life beyond Mayo's security net.

Living at the Ronald McDonald House bounced me out of my pity party faster than any other component of my rehabilitation. How could I say "poor me" or "this is so unfair" while observing children, mostly cancer victims, express no anger or resentment as they pushed their IV poles into the TV room. A couch full of pale, hairless children, the youngest being three, laughing out loud at cartoons, finding joy in playing board games with other kids … this brought such perspective to my own condition, I wouldn't dare complain or show a hint of "Why me?" in front of them. Observing these kids, living with these little survivors, was the single most important influence on my post-hospital outlook. My situation wasn't nearly as bad as that of some of my young roommates who would lose their fight with cancer. As I inwardly acknowledged this, I vowed to try harder to achieve a life of gracious appreciation for the future that lay before me. If these kids could be happy in the shadow of probable death, who was I to disparage my fate?

About a week into living at the House, I decided to have the much-feared talk with Travis. He came on a Monday night so we could watch WWF wrestling in the TV room together. After procrastinating most of the night, I found the courage to finally say, "Travis, we're not doing well at all."

He protested, "What are you talking about, Tasha? I love you. We love each other."

I countered with, "I don't know how you can say that. We're not getting along. You are doing things to deliberately get under my skin—"

"What are you talking about? You know it's been hard with wrestling, and my ankle—"

"Really, Travis. You're coming less and less. You don't call, or if you do, you've been drinking. You need your freedom. You don't need to be tied to me."

"Tasha. Stop saying this. We'll be fine. Once you're home—"

"Travis. We should just break up. I'm trying to let you off the hook. Really, we can be friends, and—"

He sat so close to my chair, I could see now that he had started to cry.

More drama. My 9:30 caregiver had arrived. I had found the courage to start this conversation at 9:25! Mom appeared from around the corner, pointing to her watch—her signal that my free time was up. Time was money, and this caregiver was being paid by the hour. I had to wrap this moment up as quickly as possible, or my mom would soon march out here and do it for me. In typical teenage fashion, I mouthed to her, "Just a minute!" With the biggest scowl possible, I conveyed to her that this was important. I flipped back to Travis, who continued to cry.

"Travis, you know we can still do things together; we can still be friends. But we really should break up." Considering I had dreaded this moment for so long, even dealing with Travis's tears, I felt surprisingly poised and strong, like I was doing the right thing.

His head sunk lower in his hands. Then he looked up at me and the most unexpected words came next: "I was going to wait until you got home ... to break up with you."

What? Did I hear him right? He intended to break up with *me*?! Why was he crying if he was plotting to dump me anyway?

Had he planned this all along? Who knew this? Did he discuss this with our other friends? Did everyone in Ellsworth High School know that Tasha Schuh would be dumped as soon as she was strong enough to get out of the hospital?

All my feelings for Travis, all my concern for what a crappy senior year he was having, vanished in a split second. I knew his tears were genuine, but I was furious.

"I think I should leave," he said as he continued to cry. He sobbed, while I surprisingly did not cry at all. I think all my time in rehab, all my prior anxiety over this inevitable breakup, eased the pain of the actual event. I was prepared, and at this point annoyed and hurt.

"What about prom, Tasha? We have to go. But how can we ... if we aren't together anymore?" I handed him a tissue from the TV-room end

119

table just as my mom poked her head around the corner again. Now it was her turn to give the evil look. She glared and pointed toward my room where a caregiver was cashing in, lounging in a comfy chair, waiting for me to call it quits for the night.

"Just give me one more minute, Mom. Travis is leaving." Prom … I hadn't thought this through. "I'm not sure what I think about that," I calmly stated.

He cried some more. "We'll talk. Maybe we can still go to prom, just as friends."

Our relationship was over. This I was sure of. Or was I?

I watched him get into the elevator to leave. I remained strong—and then, it hit me.

I sat in my chair in front of the elevator doors and started to cry. "Wait. Don't go." The doors paused; Travis looked straight into my eyes, and then the elevator slowly closed.

I lost all my composure. We were done, officially broken up. I was done, officially single forever. I cried uncontrollably—not as long as the day Barb tried to discuss this event with me, but just as hard.

I tried to dry my eyes as I entered my room to inform my mom and the caregiver why I had made them wait. Mom was not surprised. She had heard me talk about this breakup so many times. However, I could tell she didn't want to acknowledge what she knew. It was painful for her, too. This was more than saying good-bye to Travis. Her daughter might never have another boyfriend again.

My caregiver, who rose from the extended break that Mom clearly felt was money unearned, quickly expressed her viewpoint. This God-sent African American woman—a mother of five whose children, incidentally, had three different fathers—clearly trumped my experience with men.

"You don't need to be cryin' 'bout no boy! With all you been through, no boy can tear your heart like that. There's plenty of 'em. You'll find one who can treat you like you deserve!" Just like that, her words calmed me. I would feel a painful void without Travis as my boyfriend, but she was right. There were bigger things to cry about. I would try my hardest to avoid cryin' 'bout a boy.

By the next day, however, this woman's comforting words had faded.

I started crying again, much like the night before. The image of never having a boyfriend preoccupied my thoughts.

The movie *Grease*, rereleased in theaters for its twenty-year anniversary, brought friends—fellow cast members—to Rochester that evening for a movie night. These patient classmates spent the first hour of their visit calming me down.

"You don't need him, Tasha."

"Yeah—what's wrong with the single life? Start shopping around. You can have any boy out there!"

One of my friends brought an old boom box with some songs to cheer me up. News travels fast in Ellsworth. I'm sure my friend knew that I needed just the right song for this occasion. "I Will Survive" was blasted in my Ronald McDonald room. They laughed, I cried, and then I laughed, too. It became my anthem. One minute I thought I would die without Travis, the next minute I was singing at the top of my lungs and savoring the single life!

While my friends and I rode around Rochester that night, I gained just a fragment of confidence about this life I had fallen into. For the first time since I was thirteen, I was without a boyfriend, and I planned to keep it that way.

Chapter 12

A Toaster Ride to Prom

EIGHTY-SEVEN DAYS: this is the time it took Al Hines, magician/builder, to erect a wheelchair-accessible home in the middle of winter. His crew broke ground for the Schuhs on February 5. Al Hines Construction cancelled jobs, expedited material and supply orders, and persuaded clients with more lucrative projects to wait—all to accommodate me. So who ever said small-town living is difficult? If the complaint is that everyone knows your business, I couldn't have been more grateful for this.

I set a personal goal of reentering school *before* prom. This put me out of the Ronald MacDonald House by mid-April. I would have to find a transitional home while Al and his staff finalized the new house on Piety Street, plus figure out a way to get around in Ellsworth, a taxi-less town. The first of two benefits in my honor—this one planned by my drama director, Pete Dulak, with his wife, Lynn, and the Sheldon Theater Singers—took place at the Sheldon in February. The money raised purchased my first van with a wheelchair lift. One problem solved. I had a ride home. But now, where to sleep?

Angie was due to visit. I knew she would help me think. Prom signified more than a night out for me. It was part of my overall return to school. I was instructed to choose one class period to attend, which would start even before prom and continue to the end of the school year. I picked American Literature. Rehab required that I spend Wednesdays in

122

Rochester, so with this varied schedule, I needed more than a simple hotel room to cope with all the change.

I had an idea. I wanted Angie's blessing to actually put it into action. "Angie, help me think. Who in Ellsworth already has a wheelchair-accessible house?"

"Well, the Carrs ..." This was the name I knew she'd say. Rose, Jesse Carr's younger sister, had been diagnosed with spinal muscular atrophy at an early age. Jesse's parents had made changes to their home some time ago to accommodate Rose's most difficult days when she needed her wheelchair.

"Of course ... we have to ask," Angie said after some discussion. We both knew this was not some random family who just happened to have wheelchair accommodations. Jesse and I had been friends since grade school, and the accident certainly brought us closer together. Shelly Carr and Jan O'Meara, both interior designers, had recently volunteered to make many decisions regarding the finishing work of our new home.

More than once during my stay in Rochester, Mom the perfectionist had surrendered some decisions to others—proof of small miracles. Having Jan and Shelly select all the fine details for a home Mom wanted just right for me proved that she was putting me first.

I flashed back to a day in February when Mom left me in rehab so she could go meet with these talented women. I remember it vividly, because it was one of the few days Mom left the premises since I had been admitted to the hospital back in November. I returned to my room that afternoon looking for her, expecting Mom to be waiting for me as always. No Mom. I watched the clock. Finally, the elevator door opened and my mother entered my room. I let her have it when she walked in, and she let me have it right back.

"Where were you all day?" I huffed, practically accusing Mom of loafing at a spa or lounging at the mall without a care in the world.

"Excuse me? Where was I all day?" This is the only time in all my rehab days that Mom used an angry tone with me. She had a right to. I was acting like a spoiled teenager. "Do you realize that this was my one and only day to make decisions for a brand new house? I'm talking everything from flooring to bath fixtures to every light in the place ... door handles and carpet … where the electrical outlets should go and how many per room … what kind of wood trim and closet doors … Jan and Shelly did everything, narrowed down every single choice so I could do this in an afternoon. And you are wondering where I've been?"

I had this coming. Well said, Mom.

So after all Shelly Carr's help with our home, after all of Jesse's long drives and heartfelt visits to my hospital room, after all the Carr family had done for us already, could we ask for more? Could we expect a family dealing with their own daughter's serious condition to take in another needy patient?

All of their previous help added up to this moment. We would ask for a few weeks of support from them. I called Jesse to see if she could visit me, "and maybe your mom, too?" If that didn't sound suspicious! No doubt they were already speculating, and by the next morning, Jesse and her mom entered my Rochester room claiming they had a brilliant idea.

"Tasha, we want you to come stay with us!"

We assured them that it would only be until May 1. "Our new home will be ready then."

Jesse and her mom gave us a wonderful gift that day. "You stay as long as you need, Tasha. We are grateful to be able to help." Finally we could start planning the last steps for my return home with one enormous worry off the list.

I looked at my mom, who appeared grateful but not at all relieved. *Now who's stuffing it*, I thought. For here came another irony: as I moved closer to my goal of getting back to school and friends, Mom's confidence was tested. As I looked forward to change, Mom recognized her own new challenges. As she micromanaged the list of duties for me, she realized what little time was left for other family members, the Schuh business, and herself.

I flashed back to the days when I would awaken at two a.m. to find her combing over the grocery-store books. Accounting 101—she balanced every debit and credit to the penny. Again, Mom had that *look*—determination driven by a slight fear of failure.

On April 17, 1998, we loaded the van purchased through fundraiser dollars. But this was not another field trip. I was leaving the Ronald McDonald House forever. The bright white full-sized conversion van, irreverently nicknamed "The Toaster," came with a mechanical wheelchair lift. It could not be modified for me to drive (thank you, God), so the search was already on for a replacement van. Meanwhile, I needed drivers until rehab advanced me to "behind the wheel." I ordered every friend, relative, and therapist to scour the auto ads for a van that could lock my chair into the driver's position.

Yet today I would be grateful for any transportation home. The ride to Ellsworth scared the life out of me, yet I smiled and looked excited. In other words, I was stuffing it for the sake of those who had worked so hard to make this trip happen. With six months of struggle in the rearview mirror, I lacked the courage to look behind or ahead. As the road extended out toward home, I stared at the floor rather than the scenery, rewinding the movie in my head. My feature presentation: Tasha Schuh, leaving nurses, doctors, and therapists—her Rochester family—seventy miles behind.

The sight of Jesse's home stopped my rerun of all that had happened since my accident. *Yes! We are here!* The ramp into the house was at the back entrance. *No big deal, I'll just motor through the grass a short ways.* But the spring weather made the off-road trek a challenge. My heavy chair sunk into the soft, wet ground. Jesse's family helped, and everyone seemed so excited to see me.

"Oops—sorry. I'll be careful on the corners." My chair barely fit through the doorway to Rose Carr's bedroom. Like my early days of trying to navigate a power chair, I hit a few walls, took out the corners of doorways at times, and felt like a klutz again. I wondered if my desire for this to work had distorted my memory of the Carr's setup.

"You're fine, Tasha. You can bang into anything around here. This home is lived-in." The entire Carr family forgave my clumsy turns and stops. Their beautiful home would need a paint job when I moved out.

Ultimately, every hardship that seemed frustrating at the moment provided me with a new lesson on how to adapt. The "accessible" shower had a step to get over? Okay, not one, but two caregivers needed to help with my manual shower chair. Bedroom hallway had a tricky corner? All right, slow down and use the chair controls more precisely. Mom and Angie not always at my beck and call for personal cares? Let Jesse brush your hair; let her feed you breakfast, if you plan to make it to school on time.

Funny how I had worked so hard with Barb and Neil to master certain care tasks before discharge, like feeding myself and doing my own makeup. These became exhausting chores once again. Like a step backward, I had to let others do so much for me. I *wanted* to do everything, but suddenly I didn't have the strength. Barb and Neil helped me accept this at one of my first Wednesday commutes to Rochester therapy.

"Think about it, Tasha, and you'll see why you find all your cares too exhausting to complete on your own—at least for a while," Neil started.

"When you were here full-time, you did your therapy and then we scooted you back into bed because you were a *patient*," Barb continued. "Remember … you napped … you had downtime. Now, if you want that English class and lunch at school, you have to reserve some strength for what it takes to get through a busy day."

"How many hours are you in your chair, Tasha—now that you're back home?" Neil asked.

"I don't know. Twelve hours," I replied.

"Okay. Compare that to the number of hours we had you in your chair, upright, here at the hospital. There's just no comparison."

"Yeah, it's about double," I admitted.

"Plus now you get in and out of your van, you navigate around your school, you find the lunchroom, you have social contact with everyone you see, you listen in class so you get it the first time, you do some social things after school with the Carrs or others who drop by their house to see you. *Then* you finally get out of your chair. You have some full days, girl!" Barb knew my routine, which was also not the same every day.

"This would exhaust anyone!" she added. "I'm tired just thinking about how busy you are, because I know what it takes for you to do all of this."

"I see your point. But I hate that I can't find the strength to …" I paused to think of the one most desired care that I wanted back. " … at least eat on my own again."

"Well, one thing at a time," Neil said. "Let's start with more upper-body strength. It'll come. And remember, this was your nemesis *before* your accident, right? You said as an athlete, your legs could hold out forever, but you had weak arms. So this will take some time. Let's work those biceps, and you'll be using your fork, driving a van ... conducting a philharmonic in no time." Always the coach, Neil got me fired up for more PT.

Angie and Mom also persevered with answers for every one of my concerns. After a few days of settling in at the Carrs', I could finally relax and enjoy time with Jesse. We watched movies, played cards, and had mutual friends over to help pass the time. One night, the conversation led to Sarina. Coincidentally, the same week I left the Ronald McDonald House, Sarina was discharged home from the Red Wing Health Center—a care center for adults. Sarina must have been the youngest patient there.

"Let's go see her," one of my friends suggested.

"I'll call her mom tomorrow. We can meet somewhere," said another friend, offering to arrange things.

I began thinking back to a time when I believed that Sarina had gotten the better end of the deal. *She'll walk right up to me*, I thought as I lay in my hospital bed still shackled to my trache machine. I imagined a visit from my teammate who had recovered from a long rest. Sarina would walk to my bedside, showing pity for her friend who would not walk again.

As we planned our reunion, I stuffed that old memory, sad now that little of it was true. She would approach me upright, yes, but with a cane. The girls warned me that she looked very different. How could I have been so naive as to think that Sarina's TBI and coma were less serious than what I faced? My distorted thinking—a product of my own struggle to recover—couldn't have been further from the truth.

We decided to meet at a local coffee shop. The front steps of this cafe proved too much for my chair. I recall one of my first drives around town, taking inventory as I watched out the window. "Can't go in there, can't go in there, can't get up that walkway, can't park there ..." I noticed every obstacle from small steps to buckled sidewalks, and almost no automatic front doors. Rochester had spoiled me. That town was extremely accommodating to pedestrians on wheels. Ellsworth had a ways to go.

"It's a nice day—let's just sit outside." Jesse had a way of handling things. "I'll get drinks to go."

Just as Jesse was about to order coffee, Sarina arrived. I would not have recognized her. Her hair was extremely short; no doubt medical staff had to cut it because of the head injury. She wore her glasses, and at this point had a temporary patch over one eye. As she walked with her mom, she limped down the sidewalk, her right hand noticeably tight-fisted—the aftermath of the stroke she endured while still in a coma.

I can't describe the sadness I felt at that moment. Sarina had been through so much! I stuffed the guilt I was feeling and told myself, *I am the lucky one.*

I could tell my friends were working hard to start a conversation, but neither of us said much. Sarina struggled to talk, not because she was fighting old memories like me but because of the traumatic brain injury. She was still healing, and I learned from our visit that Sarina was not expected to make a full recovery. She would eventually make great progress, but TBI reminds us that progress is a relative term.

I was ashamed of my thoughts. How could I be jealous of Sarina and all she had lost? We had sustained almost the exact opposite injuries. My mind, still fully functioning, came with a body that had little self-command. Sarina's body, with full use of arms and legs, came with TBI.

After three full months of life support, Sarina slowly awakened. Doctors had declared her medically gone at one point, so her family knew that she was going to be a very different person. They mourned the loss of the old Sarina and welcomed the new Sarina as a blessing to everyone who had prayed for her.

Although parts of our stories were astoundingly similar, considering my eight-day hiatus from life, I couldn't imagine being out cold for three months. The fact that we were having this conversation at all was truly a miracle. We had both come back from a very dark place.

Over coffee, our friends witnessed the serious outcomes of our accidents. They realized how different our lives would be from here on out. As impromptu group therapy, our visit wasn't entirely serious. We laughed … we reminisced … we caught up on gossip. We discovered that Sarina still had a sharp sense of humor. (Some things would, thankfully, not change!) And we found out that both Sarina and I were excited to go back to school.

School couldn't come fast enough for me. The biggest thing I looked forward to was hanging out with kids my own age. I had spent almost six months with adults, all wonderful people. But I missed the other world, the part of the human race that saw adults and their worries as trivial and a waste of time. My friends would bring me back into the loop, right? Within a few days of a modified eleventh-grade schedule, I realized that this transition back to teenager would be a very difficult task.

"Can you believe Mrs. Pavloski? She just piles on the homework."

"Oh, I don't know—I think her class is pretty easy. All you have to do is read the material she assigns," I heard myself saying.

"Yeah, right. Like I'm reading *Huck Finn*. If I can't do her work from the Cliffs Notes, she's too hard."

In the past, I could easily jump onboard with complaints like this. Why was it so hard to agree all of a sudden? I sounded like a parent if I confronted their whining, but I no longer could blindly agree.

Some of this may have stemmed from resentment I carried toward friends who never once came to see me in Rochester. I told myself, *Now, go to school and act thrilled to see everyone—even the kids who ignored your existence for the past six months.* But when faced with this challenge, I just couldn't stuff it.

Here came the test. One of my first days back, R. J., a friend since seventh grade who never once visited me in Rochester, passed me in the hall without even a glance in my direction. Hmmm ... could he have missed my big black wheelchair that filled more than half the width of the hallway? I stopped and yelled, "R. J., are you too good for me now?" It felt right not to stuff it.

He slowly stopped, turned around, and came back. Finally he said, "No, but I don't know what to say to you or what to do."

"How about 'Hi, Tasha' ... or maybe give me a hug? I haven't seen you in six months," I answered.

As he hugged me, I added, "I'm still the same person; I just can't walk."

Ironically, I understood. I didn't want to empathize with kids like R.

J., but I absolutely grasped what he meant. He and so many others believed I had changed as a person. Some thought I was more fragile now. They were afraid of saying something wrong in front of me. Others felt I received special treatment—more accommodations than I deserved.

"Can you believe what little time she has to spend in this building? Attend one class—whoopee! And then she misses Wednesdays for her *therapy* in Rochester. She never takes late points on anything. If she had to operate like the rest of us, she'd never make it." Of course, someone was always willing to report such gossip to me, which warmed my heart even more. Ugh!

In all honesty, it took a long while for some students to adjust to being around me, but it took me even longer to adjust to some of them. Their petty grievances often set me apart from other students. I felt like a parent around some of them, and I couldn't help but be honest when I thought they were being childish.

A table had been reserved for me in the cafeteria, somewhat out of the way, which allowed me to freely wheel up for lunch. I wouldn't have to weave around the maze of other tables or block kids who were on a mission to eat quickly. One girl openly complained that I was treated like "royalty." This time, I stuffed my inclination to say, "And would you like to trade places with me? Please, have my table—and my useless legs, too."

Ironically, Travis spent more time with me *after* our breakup. He was by my side at the second benefit, this one a joint event for Sarina and me. That night, Travis constantly reminded me that prom would all work out. He was extremely affectionate in front of people—no doubt he feared what others would say. Who breaks up with a girl so down on her luck? But I wanted him to quit worrying what others thought. People couldn't possibly know how supportive Travis had been for months. Only a few of our closest friends knew what a true friend Travis had been to me through some of the hardest times.

Sarina with me at our shared benefit.

Travis stood behind me all night, his hands literally on my shoulders for hours. "Travis, you don't have to stay by me. I'm fine," I whispered to him more than once. "Hang out with your friends." But he never left my side the entire evening. I knew deep down that his behavior in public was another sign that he was still trying to protect me. So I stuffed my concerns for now, expecting more to change after prom.

My American Lit and lunch schedule brought normalcy to a life full of medical worries. Unfortunately, Sarina had not yet returned to any classes. Prom would definitely be a highlight night for her, since so many people looked at it as an important step in her recovery. Since both of us were nominated for prom court, Sarina and I knew the majority of our classmates were respectful of our struggles to get back into school.

By now, I owned two wheelchairs. The lighter, manual chair—like Rose Carr's—seemed ideal for the Grand March. I was scheming to avoid the "heavy machinery" look that night. I appeared far less disabled when seated on my low-tech wheels. This meant Travis would have to push me down the aisle, but he agreed that the attention should be on me and not my limitations. After the Grand March, my power chair would allow me

131

the comfort and independence I wished to have at the dance. I didn't need Travis sitting around looking tied down all night like he appeared at the benefit.

For the first time since my accident, I had my hair and nails done professionally. I put my dress on, and with Angie's help, we camouflaged the fact that this fabric was not ideal sit-down material after all. Getting ready for prom always took the entire day—why would this year be any different? I felt like a regular high school girl for the first time in months.

Travis, Mom, Dad, and I pose for prom pictures.

Who knew the paparazzi were invited? My family and friends of all ages arrived before the Grand March to take endless snapshots of me ... then me with Travis ... then me with Sarina ... then me with Jesse ... then me with Travis and our closest couple friends ... then me with Angie ... then me with Ryan ... then me with Grandma Thalacker, Mom, and Dad ... well, you get the idea.

Once the ceremony began, Sarina and I, elegantly dressed in our royal blue gowns, listened as the emcee introduced us with all the candidates for prom king and queen. I couldn't have cared less about the outcome—

another sign that I had matured beyond my years. The important things had already happened: shopping with Angie, my move back to Ellsworth, trusted friendship from Jesse, some semblance of real school life, and finally, the sight of Sarina walking into prom on her own.

I'm sure people thought that either Sarina or I should be named prom queen. At that moment, as the emcee opened the envelope, I hoped that Sarina's was the name announced. She should get this, considering all she had been through.

"And your EHS Prom Queen for 1998 is ..." Not Sarina, not Tasha. "Jesse Carr!" Perfect! Why hadn't I hoped for this? Jesse deserved this honor tonight for all she had unselfishly done to help others this year. Within minutes, her boyfriend was crowned prom king, and the paparazzi were at it again!

The excitement of the night continued at The Bluffs, an area dinner and dance club. The Toaster ride there went as planned. I transferred into my motorized chair and zoomed into the building without much delay. It still amazes me how fast things began to unravel—at least in my mind.

My first point of embarrassment came with supper. I had not anticipated that dinner would be impossible to eat on my own. With Barb's therapeutic support, I could feed myself, as long as I used a fork extension wrapped around my hand. This attachment would be awkward and out-of-place at a formal dinner. So I left it at home. Suddenly, as Travis began feeding me, an embarrassing feeling stole my appetite.

This was not picnic food. Yet I was somehow degrading the entire dining experience by casually allowing Travis to shovel each mouthful in for me. He had helped me eat so many times before. All of my closest friends had either fed me or watched my mom, Angie, or Travis spoon food for me. Why I suddenly felt self-conscious had everything to do with the crowd, the fancy gown, and the decorated dance hall. Although I knew this, I couldn't stop the feeling that I was stuffing back tears of embarrassment. I knew if I complained at all, I ran the risk of ruining everyone's night. I felt a gag tied around my mouth for the rest of the evening. I told myself, *Suck it up and let others enjoy their prom.*

Suddenly, music blared from the speakers. My friends jumped from their chairs.

"Go! Really—I want to watch! Get out there. This is a great song."

My friends did as I commanded. I watched and smiled, but my mind wandered back in time. I felt myself falling. *Crack!* I hit the cement. Like the cloud of worry I saw hovering below the ornate Sheldon Theater ceiling, a new cloud floated into my life on prom night. This cloud brought a distinct kind of worry—not panic and frantic cries for help, but the realization that my life was chronically different. There was no going back to "normal" teenage life. And for that matter, I would never be like my peers again, regardless of my age. I could be surrounded by friends, people showing constant respect and concern, but I would be forever different. Our friendships would never again be the same.

Travis sat off to the side of the dance floor with me. With nothing to say to each other, we quietly watched as friends danced to our favorite songs.

One of my classmates who had always been caring, sweet, and genuine came up to me and said, "If you ever need to talk to somebody, if you ever need to cry, I would love for you to call me. I'm a really good listener, and even though I don't know what you're going through, I would like to help."

"Thank you." *Can we have a counseling session right now? Because I need it, right now!* But I knew we couldn't. I probably would take her up on this offer to talk, to share, to cry on another day. But her timing put the icing on my rotten prom cake. *Could this night get any sadder?* was all I could think. I suddenly wished that a trapdoor would open up and drop me out of this room forever.

Stuff it, I told myself. I knew if I started crying, everyone would feel bad, my friends would try to rescue me, and I would be forced out of this funk. I sat safely on the sidelines with Travis—who looked equally numb, by the way.

We rode the Toaster back to Jesse's house after the dance. Post-prom plans—a drinking party and bonfire—brought slight optimism back to me. We put on our warmest clothes and headed to a classmate's backyard.

I was having a good time! Now this was something I could do—hang out with friends, talking and laughing, beer spilling down my chin as a friend quenched my thirst. But clearly I was out of practice. I had not tasted alcohol in months, and even in moderation, it hit me like a heavy dose of Demerol. Alcohol, truly a depressant, magnified my sadness. I cried myself to sleep that night at Jesse's, careful that no one heard me.

I awoke early the next morning and did what I had come to do best while waiting to start my day—I thought about my life. I analyzed and ruminated over things I could not change. I had built up prom night to an unrealistic fantasy. No wonder I was hit with a huge letdown. I couldn't erase what had passed, but I knew I wanted to prevent such letdowns from happening again.

Here was a new crossroads. Funny how this forked path kept showing up. Once again, I was faced with the realization that I could fall into profound depression over all this change in my life, or I could take everything that had happened to me in the past six months and convert it to something positive. That morning I acknowledged the fact that I was not a person who could survive the first option. If I fell again, even an emotional fall, I would not survive. I had to stop feeling sorry for myself. I felt compelled to make something happy from this new life—this second chance. Instead of letting things happen, like the events of prom night, I would *make* things happen.

My good mood surprised Jesse the morning after prom. No doubt she wondered if I should take up the classmate's offer for some serious counseling. Yet my cheerfulness was genuine. "Hey, can we take a ride by my new house today? I can't wait to get moved in. I know exactly how I want things arranged."

Chapter 13

Tasha's Life:
Instructions Not Included

BUILT IN THREE months—I cannot stress how amazing this was. Twenty-eight hundred square feet … an entire wheelchair-accessible home … constructed in ninety days … miraculous! A close friend of mine, whose devastating accident landed him in a wheelchair, planned the same style of new home. His took ten months to complete. Obviously, he didn't have Al Hines as his builder, and Ellsworth as his community.

Here's small-town inspiration again: in roughly one week, twenty-six years of Schuh family stuff got packed up and moved across town. Dad's ground-breaking date for the new store had been moved forward. But running the current business plus studying blueprints and financial details utterly consumed him. Mom's new position, head caregiver for Tasha Schuh, ate up her days as well. So friends and family packed up boxes, transported everything from toothpicks to deck furniture, and unloaded the Schuhs in record time. The fact that Mom surrendered her right (and talent, I might add) to organize a massive move represented even more proof that God worked in mysterious ways.

The calendar turned to May 1, and I found myself saying good-bye and thank you to all the Carrs. The Toaster took me the few miles to town, where I rolled into our new house right on schedule. One tour of our finished home, and I realized that Mom was a visionary for knowing this was the right move. The doors and hallways were exceptionally wide, with so much turning room. My bedroom and shower had incredible roll-in space, plus room for one or two caregivers. I saw for myself that a great deal of thought and planning went into this place. My parents had toured several wheelchair-accessible homes to get ideas; how they found time, I don't know. So many details had been thought through for me. Funny how emotional ties to the old house faded fast when everything *new* captured my attention. Instantly, it felt like home.

Guilt hit me hard that day as I recalled my anger with Mom for making us move. "This is amazing! You were so right, Mom—this is beautiful." I was loving and praising her for standing up and making the tough decision to sell and build. I hope she felt some pride for all she had done.

The new home was a small part of everything Mom contributed that year, and would contribute in the years to come. If I heard it once, I heard it a hundred times from medical staff—"I wish we could clone your mother." Every hospital person we've met, from the cleaning help to the top-ranked neurosurgeon, has thanked my mother for full involvement with her daughter's health. Mom has bathed me, fed me, transferred me from chair to bed and vice versa, administered meds, cleaned hospital rooms, and wiped my tears. She has managed multiple care conferences, supported me through months of rehab, and at this point had orchestrated the construction of a wheelchair-accessible home. I love my mom, but also, I am immensely proud of her.

One grocery store … the second being built … discharge papers for a medically fragile daughter … limited health-care assistance … insurance red tape … brand new house, one yet to sell … depleted savings account … what more could one family take? How about a wedding!

My brother suddenly announced that he and Nikki were getting married.

"Not next summer, Mom. This summer." August 22, to be exact.

I will never forget the shocked look on my mother's face. She tried everything to convince Ryan to postpone the ceremony. It's not that Mom wasn't thrilled to have Nikki in our family. Quite the contrary, everyone felt Nikki was a godsend for Ryan. He needed to find happiness among the chaos caused by all the recent change in the Schuh family.

"Please, Ryan. Reconsider. A year from now, things will be more settled. I can help you two make so many decisions—the meal, the ceremony, entertainment. This is not good timing for an event that should be the highlight of your lives."

But Ryan refused to compromise. Their minds were made up. He and Nikki would plan everything on their own. "Nikki's parents understand. They will take care of things—the plans, the finances ... they want to do this."

My mom couldn't change their minds. Quite honestly, I think she felt sad that she wasn't involved. Just another event she had to let happen without her input ... another sacrifice.

It was official—the wedding would take place at English Lutheran Church, and since music meant so much to us, Nikki and Ryan wanted something memorable for their service.

"Will you sing at our ceremony?" they asked me.

"What? You know what the doctors said." I couldn't believe they were asking me. Were they being cruel? They heard my doctors plainly state that I would never sing—for an audience, anyway. Paralyzed stomach muscles, multiple intubations, and a tracheotomy had stolen my capacity to project my voice and had compromised my vocal cords.

Ryan explained to me that they didn't care what I sounded like.

"What do you mean, you don't care?" I replied. "Of course you care what your wedding music sounds like. *I* care what it sounds like."

"We aren't asking you because we want to impress people. We're asking you because it will mean so much. We just want you to sing, Tasha. A microphone will give you volume."

I watched both their faces, wondering if Nikki had agreed to this. Finally she said, "Quit worrying about it, Tasha, and just do what you love to do."

Their song choice: "From This Moment On" by Shania Twain and Brian White. I found myself agreeing to try. I was petrified, although I would have Dad harmonizing with me. He was my safety net—Dad could create a melodic mix with bullfrogs and still sound good. At least I was partnered with the best. I pictured myself all dressed up, sitting in my chair, mic in place, my mouth wide open … and nothing coming out. Worst case scenario, Dad would deliver a solo.

But, that's not how I really wanted it to come down. They were right—this is what I loved to do. "Okay, I have to practice—a lot." I worked to gain as much muscle strength, and therefore volume, as I could. I remembered vocal techniques I had learned for the stage. I was suddenly motivated to do even more in therapy so I could prove to myself, and maybe a few doubtful doctors back in Rochester, that I wasn't giving up my voice as graciously as I had given up dance, piano, and volleyball. Between this and the new house, I suddenly became preoccupied with positive goals that were meaningful to me. Ryan and Nikki put me on the spot, and possibly set me up for failure, but I would gain so much from trying.

My family members conducted the majority of my cares during our first month on Piety Street. Angie and Scott moved back to Ellsworth with career plans to assist my parents in the new store. Ryan continued his college classes, worked store hours, planned a wedding, and actually did my makeup from time to time. "I won't tell anyone if you won't" was our secret agreement. Mom, Dad, Ryan, Angie, and Scott all transferred me, put me in my shower chair, dressed me, and answered any request, often before I even asked for help. I was so incredibly blessed with family who couldn't say no to me. They made it seem easy, although I know it wasn't. It was like they'd been doing these things for others all their lives.

During this last month of my junior year, I focused on finishing my American Literature class. I prepared for Ryan's wedding by singing and gaining measurable progress in upper body strength. At times I'm surprised at how easily I gave in to others who wanted to perform cares that challenged my strength each day. Yet as long as I was making progress, I felt driven to persist in this new way of life.

My dad, however, lost his zip about this time. Who could blame him? With so much worry—endless days of work, store expenses, medical bills, losing Mom as a business partner because of her hours with me—he had anxieties none of us shared. Up to this point, Dad camouflaged his concerns better than anyone I know. And although he was thrilled when

I came back to Ellsworth, his smile gradually faded. Years of conditioning brought Dad to the point where he automatically made eye contact and smiled at every person who entered our store. "It's just what you do, bring a little brightness to your customer's day," was Dad's sincere belief when he trained me to work as a cashier after school. Now, the natural, easygoing look that had seemed effortless for him was gone. His smile became mechanical ... deliberate ... out of necessity.

One early morning, Dad came into my room. He sat in my wheelchair beside my bed with a stiff, indifferent look.

"Dad," I said. "I'm moving on. Are you going to come with me?"

The look on his face told me he believed he had been covering. He thought I wasn't on to him. In an instant, his worry faded. I don't think I can take full credit for bumping Dad out of his funk that day, but at least I reassured him that I was not his principal worry. He could knock me off the top of his list, down a notch or two. And I can say that Dad never again made me feel that I was the direct cause of his troubles.

Despite my new home, our family stress continued. Dad's sadness might well have contributed to his decision to stay most nights at our old house. An unofficial separation for my parents was possible since our other house had not yet sold. Mom and Dad both battled depression, the sadness that comes from knowing a marriage has not been good for some time.

"The stress from the accident—it's just too much for their marriage."

"How can a business make it like this? There's too much on their plate."

"Sorry, I can't join you. I'd love to, but I have to help Tasha tonight."

These were some of the most hurtful comments I overheard from family or friends in the months to come. I was to blame. My accident caused all of this grief. As much as I tried to carry this burden from time to time, I eventually learned that many of our problems were just part of the normal course of family life. Did the accident help some family issues rear their ugly heads sooner rather than later? Most definitely. My narrow belief at the time of my parents' separation was that I had caused a laundry list of problems. I would struggle with this belief sporadically over the course of the next few years.

In an attempt to alleviate family stress, caregivers were hired to take over some of my personal cares. Sometime in May, I began to orchestrate a variety of helpers, just as I had at the Ronald McDonald House. As warned, some caregivers were not certified to meet my needs. Others were unwilling participants in the complicated details of caring for a quadriplegic. My family—most often Mom—continued to cover cath and bowel cares, showers, and some chair transfers, as well as other tasks whenever I panicked from the hired help.

"Please, Mom—she can't keep doing my makeup. I will be laughed out of school. I look like a clown!"

This helpful woman, in her mid-sixties, had come early one morning, excited to do my hair and make-up. I showed her my palette of colors, totally trusting her to apply light makeup for my day at school. Nothing big—no grand occasion. What could be easier for a new caregiver? I patiently waited to look in the mirror, making small talk while the woman fixed my face for the very first time.

"Voilà! What do you think?" she stated rhetorically, looking only for praise. Bright blue eye shadow coated my lids. My cheeks radiated rouge that matched the rose-colored lipstick she had applied. I looked like a 1980s Mary Kay beauty consultant desperate to make a sale.

"Just talk to her, Tasha," was Mom's reply. "Tell her what you want. You have to speak up. Be polite but firm. She'll listen."

I somehow found a tactful way to coach this caregiver on new trends in subtle cosmetics. As awkward as it felt, I slowly hinted, and she eventually made adjustments to my makeup.

On one of my Wednesday trips to Rochester, I unloaded my complaints. Again, I pushed to recoup some of my own cares.

"Please, Barb, I want to do my own makeup again."

"Tasha, we've been over this. You get to pick your battles, but you can't do everything. If you choose to do your makeup, something else may have to go for a while." Barb reminded me to be patient.

"No more Heimlich coughing, right?" Neil seemed to change the subject, but I knew where this was going. "Now that's progress! You're hanging with your friends, doing social stuff, right? You weren't doing that a month ago."

Barb jumped in to help. "Don't be so hard on yourself. If others do some things for you, that doesn't mean you aren't gaining ground."

"I want to do this … I want to do that. But at what price?" Neil pressed on. "*All* of this is so new—and more will come. I guarantee it."

"How many weeks of school do you have left? Two? Maybe three?" Barb urged me to take the help a little longer.

"Yes," I sighed. "I guess I can deal with my painted face a little longer. But over the summer, we are getting the extensions for my makeup brushes. I'm going to do this on my own again."

I think Barb and Neil secretly liked my complaints, since it created a new goal for us down the road. This kept me looking forward, and motivated. "Whoa. So eager!" Neil said. "I recall a time when you didn't want to do any of your own cares—remember? This is a big change! Keep it up."

Medical Assistance allowed some of my friends to help with my care. So a few classmates took the opportunity to earn some extra money while helping me in the process. Holly Kenall lived close by and took my early-morning shift. She helped me dress, she fixed my hair, she took over as makeup artist, and she drove me to school. (Yes, my Mary Kay lady in training would be relieved of her duties earlier than expected.)

After prom, social time became a routine of weekend partying where everyone talked of nothing but summer vacation. Travis had enough credits to graduate in March, so he left Ellsworth High School to work for his dad at the end of the third quarter. Although we weren't dating, I felt a need to see him—be around him. Plus, I wanted to hang out with people the way I did before my accident. I tried so hard to fit in as easily as I had last fall.

Of course, the Toaster required a driver, so I searched out friends willing to pull up to a party in the most unfashionable vehicle around. Thankfully, classmates always volunteered to chauffeur me, yet it came with a price—they had to be sober chauffeurs. At that point, I was grateful to be out with all my friends, although not one of them truly knew what I was going through. Ironically, there's a loneliness that comes with dependency. I had constant companionship, but no one to relate to.

A simple phone call quickly changed my pattern of loneliness. I was invited to a wheelchair sports camp. Initially, I did not want to attend.

"Mom, this will be a bunch of old people sitting around, disabled, drooling, sharing their misery with me. How depressing. Why would I want to participate in that?" *I'm fighting to forget my limitations, not dwell on them*, I thought.

But Mom wore me down. She convinced me to go. Stewartville, Minnesota, hosted the event, and people from all over the country were going to be there.

Originally, this was a one-day gig. I fought this trip at first, believing I would meet old people playing bridge, or for the more agile, wheelchair shuffleboard. But Mom was persuasive.

"I'm sorry, Tasha, you are going! At least try one day. If you don't like it, that's fine. I won't make you go back."

"Ugh! Okay. But Sarah, you have to come along." Sarah Sans spent most of her summer days with me. My sun-loving buddy was willing and available to help Mom transport me to and from Stewartville.

A week prior, we looked at the camp schedule, which actually started on a Friday in mid-June and ran through the following Thursday. I picked the one day out of the week that offered an activity both Sarah and I found inviting—boating. That fell on Monday.

As soon as I arrived, every stereotype of people in wheelchairs was thrown out the window. Sarah accompanied me as I rolled up a ramp onto a gigantic pontoon boat for a ride around a nearby lake. From the boat, I watched disabled water skiers, canoers, swimmers, and rowers.

When we returned to camp from the boat ride, we saw so many activities going on around us. I marveled at the athletes playing basketball and softball. All afternoon, the staff invited me to try one of these activities—horseback riding, ultralight flying, bowling and others, but I was content to watch. My comfort level advanced with the day.

I was captivated by these people who, despite their wheelchairs, had hobbies, jobs, goals, and dreams. And I admit, the most shocking revelation of all was that they were young, attractive, and happy. I would spend the rest of my camp days studying their formula for success. Along the way, I would destroy my own misconception that life in a wheelchair would be boring.

Chapter 14

Cute Boys in Wheelchairs

IN LESS THAN twenty-four hours, my definition of success had been transformed. I wanted to be like these people at camp—happy, surrounded by youthful activity in wheelchairs. Hope and joy had instantly replaced loneliness and dependency. After that amazing first day, Mom and Sarah spent the commute home juggling their schedules, since I now insisted on returning for the rest of the week's activities. It's as if a switch was thrown. On Day 2, I couldn't get out of the van fast enough.

"See ya, Mom." If I thought about the burden I caused my mother to prepare and transport me, much of the camp's charm would have been lost. She got up before dawn each morning to make sure I was ready for my commute and a full day away from the convenience of home.

The camp staff definitely saw no boundaries. Even though I was the most physically impaired body there, I was expected to try some of my former activities. One counselor began by taking inventory of what I used to do, what hobbies and sports I had enjoyed.

"Do you swim?" the counselor asked.

"Well, yeah—I did. We had a pool in our backyard my whole time growing up. But I don't know ..." My last swim seemed like a lifetime ago, but in truth, less than a year had passed since we closed the pool at my old house.

I was showing doubt, something the camp staffers were trained to disregard. "I didn't bring the right clothes. There's no way I can get in a pool again …"

That was all they needed to hear, and suddenly everyone was set on doing precisely what I had just stated could not be done. A staff counselor returned to her nearby home, grabbed swim clothes for me and Sarah, and before I had a chance to truly object, I was in the pool!

"Okay, we'll wheel you down the concrete ramp, and you'll feel yourself start to float." I listened and thought, *What then? Will I sink? Will this T-shirt you loaned me float off? There are girls and boys watching my every move.* Just as I was losing my nerve, I felt the manual chair descend down the pool ramp.

As Sarah and other swimmers wrapped flotation noodles all around me, I felt myself drifting into deeper water all on my own. Outside of water skiing, which one counselor offered to teach me, this was the riskiest thing I could ever imagine myself doing at a sports camp.

The experience was far more than a dip in the water. It altered my thinking. I saw what could be accomplished with willingness and the right support.

Sarah swims with me at Wheelchair Camp, summer 1998.

Self-doubt washed off in the pool that day—doubts about every aspect of my future. I knew that I would need to surround myself with helpful encouragement from others, but weren't those voices already available? My family, my therapists, friends like Jesse and Sarah all claimed that I could do anything if I put my mind to it. Immersed in water, I started to believe this was more than a cliché to lift my spirits. I was truly surrounded by loving, caring people who wanted me to accomplish the things I dreamed possible.

That day, the pool gave back what I thought the wheelchair had taken away. More than physical ability, the pool gave back my capacity to dream.

Of course, my favorite dreams involved cute boys. And this camp had plenty of them. On Day 1, I was approached by David—a good-looking guy who surprised me with lots of attention. We started visiting on the pontoon ride, and our conversation continued that night, when I learned he was twenty-nine years old. I was flattered to know that I had caught the eye of a more mature man. He did not seem put-off by my age when I admitted I was only seventeen. Yet by Day 2, David lost interest when he realized he wasn't the only guy vying for my attention.

Jeremy sought me out—a school boy who clearly was the wheelchair basketball star of this camp. In fact, Jeremy was so talented in wheelchair hoops, he flew all over the country competing on a national team. I would find this out and more, since we spent most of the remaining camp days talking while David quietly rejected my invitation to spend time together.

Jeremy inspired everyone. Sure, he had more physical ability than most of the campers. Born with spina bifida, Jeremy's paralysis was limited to his right leg. He *chose* to use a manual wheelchair, since it maintained the upper-body strength he needed for his one real passion, basketball. Jeremy flew from city to city, competing as a highly ranked wheelchair basketball athlete. The fact that this active, successful, good-looking boy picked me out of all the girls at this camp—well, nothing could have been better for my healing self-esteem. We spent the rest of the week with our chairs practically locked together.

With only one other quadriplegic in attendance, I learned that I indeed had the highest level of injury. The irony of hooking up with the most physically capable person at the camp brought even more hope to me. Jeremy found me attractive, which brought an excitement for life that I had not expected.

The fallout of losing Travis still weighed heavy. My confidence was extremely low, especially now, meeting guys who had no prior concept of the old Tasha Schuh. Yet I quickly learned that youth is youth—physical attractiveness remained on the minds of these campers, wheelchairs or not. These boys did not see my enormous chair as a hindrance. And if I entertained the idea that cute boys in wheelchairs had somehow transformed into higher life forms, interested only in a girl's mind ... well, the whistles and catcalls around the pool brought me back to reality.

One of camp's great lessons was that despite paralysis, regardless of limited physical movement, relationships still had the potential for physical contact. Apparently, some things never changed. Jeremy helped me figure all of this out—Jeremy, who wanted to hang out with me because he found me interesting and, despite my ATV-sized wheelchair, very attractive. Jeremy's attention was medicine to my spirit that no psychologist could have provided.

Camp also taught me that my days of shopping for the most provocative bikini, within my parents' discretion, were over. Unlike some of the girls who wheeled around the pool in their swimsuits, I would never be comfortable in skimpy swimwear again. For a girl who had prided herself on making a boy look twice, this was a huge adjustment. But camp helped me realize that in addition to the physical excitement that comes with youth, other aspects of who I am could make boys look and listen. And Jeremy did just that. He was kind, attentive, and fun.

It was amazing to watch Jeremy and others compete in sports that I had played before my accident. This could have depressed me, but ironically, it inspired me. I might have greater limitations than all the others at camp, but if they could participate at the level they did, I could find a level of activity that was my optimum too. I was already planning to return to camp the following year to show off accomplishments that would please everyone.

Jeremy and I spent the second night of camp talking down by the waterfront. We completely lost track of time. People couldn't find us, and we were oblivious to their worries. Mom was near panic when we finally wheeled up the path from the beach.

"There you are! Really, Tasha, I was ready to send out a search party. Do you know how long it's been since anyone can remember seeing you two?"

"I'm not sure," I said, grinning from ear to ear.

"Three, maybe four hours. It's midnight, and we still have to drive home!"

"A search would not be easy, Tasha," one of the counselors stated. "We're talking two hundred acres or more. Please let people know when you plan to go off on your own for a while."

"Sorry" both Jeremy and I replied, in a most insincere tone. The smirk on our faces said *no regrets*. "See you tomorrow, Jeremy."

To everyone there, we seemed like a couple already, and I liked the implication. In fact, I knew that night I wanted to spend the rest of the week getting to know Jeremy even better.

As the days went on, we talked nonstop and found out that we had so much in common. He filled me with hope and encouragement. But to be fair, everyone at this camp contributed to these positive feelings. Still, Jeremy's attention and fearless attitude had a profound influence on me. I left camp at the end of the weekend with enthusiasm for whatever obstacles life had to bring.

The only downside to camp was that it had to end. Although Jeremy was from Texas, we agreed to keep in touch. Phone calls were fine, but we wanted to talk every day, which was not within my family's long-distance budget. I needed a crash course in e-mail, and I got it from a very technology-savvy employee of my dad's. Gary Moldenhauer, a quiet classmate who had started at my parents' store right after my accident, seemed more in-tune with computers than people.

"Tasha, Gary can hook you up," said Holly. When she wasn't working for me, my friend Holly worked with Gary at the store and saw firsthand how he solved every technology problem that arose at work. "I'll ask, and I'm sure he'll be happy to set up e-mail, teach you to use it, teach you Yahoo Messenger—anything at all you want to learn. You can talk to Jeremy every day if you want!"

That's exactly what happened. And within two weeks of daily computer talk, Jeremy and I declared ourselves boyfriend and girlfriend. We didn't care who thought it ridiculous to "date" when we lived thousands of miles apart. We felt closer than most teenaged couples because we talked about everything. One thing I have discovered from people who endure the kind of challenges that we have is that you cut through the small talk immediately. The closeness most people develop over time seems almost instant with spinal cord injured people. We shared triumphs and falls, accomplishments and failures—but honestly, with Jeremy, it was mostly positive. This guy had confidence!

We stayed in constant electronic contact that year thanks to my aunt and uncle, who purchased a new computer for me. Technology was a new realm of study, especially in my little town. But with Gary Moldenhauer's help, and my motivation to keep in touch with Jeremy, I picked it up quickly.

I spent the last half of my summer getting as much sun as possible and learning my duet for Ryan and Nikki's wedding. Although we no longer had a pool in our backyard, one thing had not changed—I still worshipped the sun. I always found willing friends to lay out on my new deck to darken our tans and, in my case, warm up my body. Circulation problems, one of the many changes brought on by my accident, left me cold and shivering even on summer days. Direct sunlight warmed my body and brought back memories of basking in the sun around our pool. I could no longer dive in to cool off—nor would I feel compelled to, since I never seemed to overheat.

My internal air-conditioning actually helped with one post-hospital concern: my trache scar. Doctors had warned me that direct sunlight would make the scar more pronounced. Since I could shiver with goose bumps in eighty-degree weather, scarves and turtlenecks not only kept me warm, they protected my skin for that first summer while the scar was healing.

When the hot, humid day of August 22 rolled around, my dad and I sang beautifully for Ryan and Nikki's wedding. This accomplishment, something that my doctors said could never happen, filled me with gratitude for those who cheered me in this direction. Ryan and Nikki felt joy in knowing they had made the right decision to ask and believe in me.

My nerves were my biggest obstacle that day, performing with Dad for all my family to hear and see. But people were full of compliments, and once the ceremony ended and the party began, I could relax and glow in their praise.

That was one mission accomplished, but I still wrangled with my nerves most of that day. Frankly, I wasn't comfortable trying to have fun at a wedding in a wheelchair. Memories of an awkward prom night filled my mind. Yet hadn't I conquered these insecurities at camp? Shouldn't Jeremy's confidence in me, along with my own bold decision to sing again, make the dinner-dance seem a minor detail of the night?

My high school friend Brooke rescued me. I didn't have to be a withering wallflower again. "You are going to dance with us."

"What? I can't ... Go—I'll watch." But Brooke wouldn't let me retreat back to the melancholy prom girl. She sat on my lap, and Jesse, Stevie, and others surrounded me with our own little dance party.

Like the counselors who whisked me into the camp pool, Brooke soon had me waving my arms and shimmying my chair. Despite some incredulous looks, which I brushed off, I ended up having the time of my life as my friends helped me figure out the art of dancing in a wheelchair.

My friends get me out on the dance floor the night of my brother's wedding.

Ryan and Nikki's wedding put the finishing touches on my first summer as the new Tasha Schuh. I now faced my senior year. Since I had so many elective credits, mostly due to music and theater, I only needed three and a half more credits to graduate. So I was allowed to skip the first block of school each day. They gave me a work-release pass, although I no longer had a job at my parents' store. This allowed me to get the extra sleep my doctors said I still needed to continue to heal. I slept later into the morning and, despite the time-consuming cares that were part of being the new Tasha Schuh, I still arrived at school by ten a.m. every day.

My graduation requirements included American Government, with a teacher who intimidated me so much, I scored 100 percent on all of his exams. Algebra II, a college-prep class, brought some rigor to my studies, and Mrs. Rumpel, the instructor, was compassionate yet demanding— something I grew to appreciate once the course was conquered. I elected to return to choir, which included vocal jazz as well as the a cappella group, so my fourth and final block of the day was filled.

Choir posed a peculiar problem, since our school was in the midst of construction. Ultimately, grades nine through twelve would join together under one roof, but while the building addition was in progress, the old junior high—the North Campus—provided temporary classrooms for overflow. EHS Choir, held in an old North Campus gymnasium, made transition between classes quite challenging for me. Should I motor up the street one block to attend choir? Or should the school provide some sort of transportation? Had I been more experienced at navigating my high-tech chair, I think I would have insisted on zooming to choir on my own. But considering our school was indeed a hardhat zone, my principal insisted that I take school transportation to and from North Campus.

The spring semester would bring other classes—chemistry, which I was advised to repeat, despite the fact that I had taken almost half of the course in the months prior to my accident—and psychology, a class I loved and chose for my college major. In addition, I took an independent study for my adaptive phy-ed credit. I spent one quarter tackling the manual wheelchair, which I believed would give me a less debilitating look. But as Barb and Neil reminded me, "You pick and choose your battles. Pick a task toward independence that will enhance your quality of living, not degrade it." The power chair proved to be a necessary vehicle to save my physical energy for more intellectual goals in life. Of course, the manual-chair lesson had to be learned the hard way; one quarter of independent study taught me to appreciate technology even more.

My school hired an aide to accompany me from class to class, mostly to take notes, but also to help me with written homework. I literally used every minute of the day to complete paperwork so I wouldn't have to worry about it at home. My parents did not have a spare minute to write out algebra problems for me.

With three full blocks of school every day and continued therapy runs to Rochester on Wednesdays, I constantly encountered new obstacles. Funny how some challenges were never anticipated during my hospital stay. Once at school and even in the new house, I confronted tasks—anything from reading a book to using a TV remote to operating my chair on a grassy hill verses a gravel driveway—that required techniques I hadn't learned, or that needed tweaking.

Upon hospital discharge, I had previewed different splints that could help me accomplish the tasks of eating and writing. Of course, my teenage mind rejected these tools because they were ugly. "People will stare at me." The tenodesis splint was the most functional of all splints for someone with my limited hand movement, but even Barb's artistic talent could not transform it into something aesthetically acceptable to me.

Then I met Holt, a Minnesota hockey player who experienced a spinal-cord injury in the heat of a game. Holt Bennington suffered a similar level of injury about two months after I did. I had seen him on TV, and my aunt knew his aunt. When I got together with relatives for Easter dinner that spring, my aunt told me some of Holt's story and suggested I call him.

One phone call and I was convinced that Holt was some cocky kid who still believed he was invincible. When he said we should meet, I feared his cockiness would completely alienate me from making a connection. Still, with my mom's encouragement, I decided to visit Holt. Who knows, maybe I could offer him a taste of reality. I had been at this rehab stage a few months longer than he. I decided to meet him at the Courage Center in Minneapolis, Minnesota, where he spent ten months of rehab before moving into his own new wheelchair-accessible home.

His brashness bothered me immediately, but I saw that he was using the Tenodesis splints. I watched as he did things with his hands despite the fact that, because of his injury, he had no more movement than I did.

"How did you learn to use your hands like that?" I asked, half curious, half offended that he had made such progress with fine-motor skills already.

"What? It's the Teno. Where's yours? Aren't they amazing? I wouldn't do half the stuff I'm doing without them."

"I don't use a Teno. They're so ugly," I admitted to Holt.

"What? How do you do what you need to in a day? How can you get around, do stuff for yourself without one? You gotta get a Teno, Tasha."

His know-it-all tone irritated me only until I saw him lift his water bottle on his own to take a drink. I quickly gave in and asked all about the Teno.

Visiting my good friend Holt Bennington at the Courage Center.

Holt became my dear friend, partly because of his generous desire to help me, partly because, like Jeremy, his confidence was contagious. Holt helped me so much. Out of his stubborn determination came daily progress that put my improvements to shame. Holt showed me how to use my splint, which motivated me to learn and share my progress with him later. After that first day with Holt, I had a splint made for my right arm and asked Holt to be my trainer for my ugly new piece of equipment.

More than anyone, Holt motivated me to use the Tenodesis splint; however, I continued to complain about the looks of it—all metal with multiple joints, straight out of *The Terminator.* "People will see me coming a mile away! Metallic Girl will crush them if they try a simple handshake greeting. I can't wear this in public!"

"Well, use it at home at least," was Holt's advice. Mr. Hockey didn't worry much about public opinion. He called me once to say that he had fallen out of his chair on a rolling start.

"Are you okay?" I asked, all worried about a possible new injury.

"I'm fine. I just wanted to see what it would feel like, wiping out in forward motion," was his calm response.

"You fell out of your chair on purpose? What, are you crazy?" I scolded him ... but I also laughed at the utter fearlessness of it.

"Yeah, it was cool. I rolled—just like the old days on the ice. No worries. I don't think I can do any more damage." The stunt was done; Holt knew what it felt like. He checked off one more fear instilled by doctors and therapists who devoted their lives to teaching the very preventative skills needed to avoid the spill Holt voluntarily took.

I agreed with Holt's advice to start with the Teno at home. Of course, nothing ever comes one-size-fits-all, so my Teno had to be custom-made. I met with someone from the Prosthetic Laboratories of Rochester to learn all I could about my new gadget.

About this time, I also visited the Center for Independent Living in Menomonie, Wisconsin, to ask about possible obstacles that the Teno might help me overcome. The Teno was not their area of expertise. However, they had a typing aid with a rubber pointer on the end that hit the keys just right, as well as some other small-motor tools. I would eventually type my own college papers with this tool. This was about the time that I began to use a rubber bubble pad of buttons to operate my wheelchair so I wouldn't have to wear the Teno for simple chair movement.

*My Tenodesis gives me small-motor skills since it creates
a pinch between my thumb and first two fingers.*

With the Teno, I learned to pick things up, since the splint gave me a small-motor pinch between my first two fingers and thumb. I could eat with far more ease on my own, although eating with the Teno at school was not something I relished. Wearing the Teno and using it in public would be far worse than having someone feed me, right? Jesse coached me on this point.

"Tasha, I just think that if you come to the cafeteria with the Teno already on, you will be less noticeable than if I continue to feed you."

"I'll feel like a freak show." I was honest about not wanting to draw any more stares from the underclassmen who did not know me, and who lacked the tact to mind their own business.

"So you're more concerned about some little kids who haven't a clue what you've been through than you are for meeting your own goals? Hmmm ..."

Rats! Jesse was making so much sense.

"Lunch will taste better off your own fork, I guarantee it." Jesse's final point.

I couldn't argue with her. Jesse helped me focus on what mattered. The next day, I put the splint on, set my fears aside, and fed myself, and I haven't stopped using my Teno at home or in public since.

Chapter 15

The Loneliness of Dependency

"Well, Tasha, if you absolutely have to do this—and Neil approves—I guess we'll be scheduling your next surgery." If my mom had her way, I would never go under the knife again. Mom's memories of watching my fever spike to 108 degrees, being instructed to say her good-byes, being asked to leave the hospital room while staff performed heroic measures to save me from flatlining—all of these things built a defense within Mom to fight any inessential medical procedure. Yet here I was, consulting with Neil regarding the bladder surgery I'd had on my radar since discharge last spring.

By fall, when I was nearing my one-year anniversary—the minimum time frame before this surgical procedure could be approved—I was obsessed with changing this one aspect of my daily care. I did not want to depend on a catheter caregiver every six hours for the rest of my life. I can't explain the pure frustration of being tied to a cath assistant, knowing that wherever I went, I had a window of four to six hours max before I needed to participate in cath cares once again. Whether I was at the mall, watching a ballgame, finishing schoolwork, or partying with friends, this tedious task halted a good time in its tracks, because it could never be done hastily. I had to transfer from my chair into bed, get undressed, allow the cath nurse to do her duty, get back into my clothes, transfer back into my chair ... blah, blah, blah.

The current cath expert happened to be my mother. And although I was immensely grateful for her constant willingness to complete this ritual, I did not intend to drag Mom to my college dorm for four years. Certainly a different kind of umbilical cord, this tie with my mother had to be cut. The Mitrofanoff surgery, also called a vesicostomy, would reroute my urinary tract. Using my appendix as part of the plumbing system, my bladder could empty via my belly button through a properly placed catheter. Although I lacked the fine-motor skills to insert this catheter four times a day on my own, I intended to change that. In time, I fully expected that, armed with my Tenodesis, I would take charge of my own cath cares.

Barely into my senior year, I returned to Rochester for this serious procedure and spent two and a half weeks in the hospital. I endured the surgery, learned the how-to details for this new bodily function, and studied up on autonomic dysreflexia. With trepidation, I watched for the typical signs of the dysreflexia alarm system—my sixth sense and my guide for avoiding disaster.

With the vesicostomy complete, slow but positive change steered my life through my senior year. I should have been basking in self-confidence. On the contrary, I worried about everything. I feared life would become a series of failures, a string of botched decisions, all seemingly more complicated because of my condition called quadriplegia. I worried about my future, my grades, my ability to maintain a long-distance relationship, and worst of all, my what-ifs.

I heard the what-ifs constantly, whispering spirits ordained to fill my silence with doubts. When I appeared lost in a good book, I was playing the what-if game. Pretending to answer e-mails from friends, I played the what-if game.

Triggering reruns of my life, the what-if game cued up past decisions, now in syndication for constant review ... always leading to the accident at the Sheldon Theater. The what-ifs forced me to search out all the wrong turns I had taken. And no matter how long I played the what-if game, responsibility always fell on the same player: me.

What if I hadn't been in the show? What if I had turned down the part of chorus girl? I should have been offended when Mr. Dulak demoted me from Grease star to minor player ... walk away from the part, and this doesn't happen. Why was I so compliant? Why was I so easily pleased with my Oz role?

What if I had gone out for basketball instead? What if I had gotten in a varsity game and proven myself? Surely I would have stuck with the team and missed tryouts for Oz altogether! What if I had never taken that step backward? What if someone had caught me before I fell?

The what-ifs presented an endless mind game with no answers and no winner. These questions cloaked my accomplishments. Every triumph I had that year, from beating septic shock to losing the trache, to leaving a hospital bed and learning to navigate the real world from a Swedish high-tech chair—all were tarnished by the game and the regrets it carried.

I was facing a new paralysis that threatened my progress if I didn't stop playing what-if. Talks with Jeremy or Holt helped, but both fought their own demons of regret. Two or three disabled people sliding into the depths of self-pity only magnified the problem.

I calmly covered my addiction to the game. Even my friends would say, "Wow, you're quiet today." But none of them seemed to suspect how low I was—how beat-up I felt from playing and losing the what-if game.

"Aw, I'm just tired. So much homework. I'm drained by the end of the day." Everyone bought it.

Everyone but my mom. I could not hide the what-if game from her. Mom knew that something had to stop this pattern of negative self-thought, or my addiction to it would paralyze me even more than my accident had. One evening she interrupted yet another round of the what-if game and handed me a tattered yellow sheet of notebook paper. Random names and phone numbers covered the page, with no apparent rhyme or reason to their order. As she handed it to me, I asked, "What is this for?"

She calmly noted, "It's a list of numbers that people wrote down for you ... while you were sleeping ... while you were in your coma. I didn't know where or how to keep things. I was such a mess. But for some reason I kept having them write things on the same piece of paper. Every one of these visitors said to call, day or night, if you ever needed something—anything. I think it's time. Take someone up on the offer."

I was touched. I needed the reminder. So many people had reached out to me when I was sick and in the hospital. I recognized names—the doctor who cried at the end of my bed the day I woke up … the family from overseas whose nation paid for the Mayo meditation room … the two Ellsworth women who prayed for me, then *with* me, and tried so hard to convince me that God had blessed, not abandoned me. At this moment, with Mom's help, I acknowledged that random offers for support, given months earlier, still held. All I needed to do was ask.

One name suddenly jumped off the paper. Darcy Pohland.

"The news reporter? Really? Darcy Pohland said to call her, whenever?" Her name, in cursive, scrawled across the top of the page along with detailed contact information, struck me as odd. Wouldn't she find the story of Tasha Schuh, almost a year after her accident, old news?

"She left more than her WCCO number, Tasha. That's her home phone too. People care. They want to know how you are doing. They want to help if you need it." Mom paused, but only long enough to grab the phone for me. "Darcy cares—you are more than a story to her. Call her."

Someone had told me—maybe Mom, maybe Angie—that Darcy Pohland had done a news piece about my accident. "She's a quadriplegic too," I recalled hearing. "She's amazing, wheeling into this hospital like she was on some mission. What a confident woman. She covered what she could about your accident, but you were out of it."

Mom quickly reminded me that Darcy left that day from my intensive-care room with every intention of following up on this story. "I'm telling you, Tasha, it's like she knew you would make it. She knew it was a matter of time. She lifted everybody's spirits that day and told us to contact her when you were feeling better. Like you had a cold—no big deal."

I pushed the phone away. Mom looked disappointed. But before I could set her straight, I rolled to my computer and started to e-mail Darcy Pohland. I'm not sure what came over me, but I shot off a list of questions so fast—well, as fast as could be done with my rubber-ended pointer that allowed me to type one letter at a time. I only hoped she didn't feel like the tables had turned and I was now the reporter looking for a scoop. I finished typing my last question, let her know how I was doing, hit send, and crossed my fingers that she would reply.

The following morning as I was getting ready for school, the phone rang. Mom answered it and yelled, "Pick up, Tasha. It's for you."

No one ever phoned me in the morning. Teenagers never have a spare minute to make an early call. Plus, friends knew how challenging my morning care was.

Maybe Holly can't drive me to school today, I thought. I pushed the button for speaker phone and said, "Hello?"

An unfamiliar woman's voice replied, "Hello, is this Tasha?"

I answered, "Yes, this is she."

"Hi, Tasha. This is Darcy Pohland. I just read your e-mail from yesterday."

Excited to hear from her so soon, I said, "Oh, hi! Wow, you got back to me quickly. That's so nice of you!"

"Yes, I try to get back to people as soon as I can. And in your case, I was really eager to hear your voice. I'm so happy to know you are home and back in school. I was wondering if it would be okay for me to come and do a follow-up story on you today. And if you would like, we could hang out later, so I can try to answer all those questions you asked me in the e-mail."

Like a good news reporter, Darcy Pohland moved fast when she had an idea. I, on the other hand, hesitantly replied, "Sure ... that sounds good. I would love to get together with you sometime ..."

"Actually, I already called your school and secured a visitor's pass to tag along with you throughout your day. That's the best way for me to report firsthand how well you are adapting to all of this. Plus, I get to spend some quality time with you. How does that sound?"

"Great." I hoped that my voice covered my nervousness. Taken off-guard, I might have sounded ungrateful. But I was trying quickly to process this whole wonderful opportunity. Not only did a major city news station, WCCO of Minneapolis, care to report on my small-town story, but Darcy Pohland, a successful professional who had overcome her own spinal-cord disaster, wanted to "hang out" with me!

Darcy arrived at my school right around lunchtime. This bright-eyed blonde seemed younger than her age—about forty— because she sat so tall and confident in her wheelchair. Her infectious smile drew my friends in as she interviewed a good number of classmates in the cafeteria, then led her camera crew to a classroom for some one-on-one questions. We ended the school day at the North Campus, and once choir was over, the camera crew departed. Darcy followed me to my house, where we both took the time to get to know each other by swapping stories "off the record."

I learned that after her accident, she had attended college at Minnesota State University, Mankato. She learned to drive her van independently, secured her job in journalism, and lived on her own for many years now. I was inspired! More than any of the people I met at camp, Darcy gave me hope, since her level of spinal-cord injury was closer to mine than any other person I had met at this point. Plus, she was a woman. This was the first female quadriplegic I had met. Male quadriplegics outnumber females about four to one. Darcy was living proof that all of her independence was achievable for me.

"Well, fire away with questions. What is most on your mind, girl? I had my swimming accident almost twenty years ago, so there isn't a thing I haven't encountered from this wheelchair. What bugs you the most?" Darcy candidly asked.

"Okay." I started a bit tentatively. I didn't want her to think I was a ball of insecurity, but sometimes the small stuff made life from this sitting position a total chore. "So, how do you handle all the stares? Should I say something? Ignore it? Do you have a favorite line for people who just gawk for no reason other than the wheelchair?"

"Honestly, Tasha, the reason people stare is because you're so beautiful." Darcy said this so matter-of-factly, I didn't know how to react. "Enjoy it. Soak in the attention."

Despite the fact that I disagreed with this answer, in some curious way, she helped me. I began to think more positively whenever I got the "look" from someone, stranger or classmate. Darcy assured me that it was part of being in a wheelchair. "There is no way to avoid it," especially with high hopes of getting around in the world with few restrictions.

"If you let the staring get to you, you will begin to find ways to avoid it. That means staying home, sticking only with people you know who make you feel safe and guarded. If I didn't go out, the quality of my life would be so much less. Goodness, I've reported on the Minnesota Vikings, the Golden Gophers, and lots of local high school athletes. I can't tell you how many comp tickets I've gotten for big games. I love my sports! I don't want to watch them from my living room. I want to experience them. You will find the things you want to experience too. Like singing for meaningful events, participating in college activities. You'll have to roll out into the world of staring people to do this." She talked with such a glowing smile, I felt moved to busy myself even more. I couldn't wait for tomorrow—I would draw stares from people just for practice!

Darcy and I swapped stories for two more hours. After that day, we agreed to keep in touch through e-mail or phone calls. "I know how time flies, so let's make an agreement—no more than six months can go by. If there's a need before that, great!" We rarely let six whole months elapse. We grew closer with every visit, call, and e-mail. She could have easily thought, *This kid has no clue how busy life is for a quadriplegic field reporter.* But she never once showed impatience or annoyance with my need to reach out for her wisdom and friendship. She was always there for me.

Darcy's mentoring got me fired up to make the next big decision: picking my college for Fall 1999. My original plan had always been to attend the University of Wisconsin-River Falls. The campus was only thirteen miles from home. Back before the accident, when Travis and I had planned out our entire lives, I talked of living at home … skipping the dorm fees … working at my parents' grocery store for gas money. I loved my hometown and never wanted to leave. Saving cash by commuting was just a bonus. Sarah helped me reconsider my UW-River Falls plan. She wanted to go there, too, but preferred to live on campus.

"I just think we'll miss some things if we don't try the dorms. If we live together, I can keep helping you as a caregiver." I liked the offer and made a campus visit to work out the extra details that would inevitably come with my unique needs.

I don't recall the name of the admissions rep we met, but when I asked this woman about wheelchair accessibility at the school, she was not very accommodating.

"I noticed that all of the elevators are behind closed doors. I won't be able to open them. What do other students in wheelchairs do?"

"Well, we have what we have. If you don't think it'll work for you, you'll just have to go somewhere else." In hindsight, I wish I had been up on ADA (Americans with Disabilities Act) and accessibility laws. I could have at least advocated for myself. Instead, I left feeling defeated and unwanted, and without a college plan for fall. A new search was on.

I had three choices on my list, all within about seventy-five miles of my home: the University of Wisconsin-Eau Claire, Winona State in Minnesota, and UW-Stout in the city of Menomonie. I visited Winona first, and I completely fell in love with the town and school. Some campus apartments had already been converted into wheelchair-accessible dorms. I asked for a roll-in shower, and people in the housing department promised they would make this happen if I enrolled as a student.

On to UW-Stout. They were in the running until I learned that I would have to live in a standard dorm room. "You aren't the first to come here in a wheelchair. You know, we have accessibility to all of our buildings. We take pride in the ease in navigation along our paved paths designed specifically for chairs like yours." This rep seemed very proud of Stout's accessibility reputation. They were reportedly ahead of most mandates required by colleges through ADA, legislation passed in 1990. Of course, I would learn about these policies over time, but at that moment all I cared about was a private roll-in shower and a dorm room with more space.

"I doubt if I can even turn my wheelchair completely around in one of these rooms. And I have to have a roommate?" With no "single room" option and an unwillingness to modify anything, they instructed me to wheel my shower chair down to the community bathroom. "Students are wonderful here—they will help. Isn't that part of the experience? Aren't you hoping to make lifelong connections here? You'll see girls step up—you'll find out who the helpful ones are."

I didn't understand why I had to be the vehicle for others to discover if they possessed the helping gene. Winona State, with full understanding of my need to be independent in front of my peers, soon offered me a completely remodeled dorm room. "I'll take it!" I canceled my appointment with UW-Eau Claire and set my sights on Winona.

Despite Darcy Pohland's attention and my success at narrowing down a college choice, I still struggled with so many things. I would take two steps forward, but then one step back into my old habit of stuffing it.

With friends, I attempted to mimic life before my accident, party-going and drinking included. I would have moments of a new positive attitude, but then I fought depression by staying busy with the drinkers, believing alcohol would alleviate my sadness. *Laugh and forget*, I thought, *and you'll get through another week.* My motivation to drink had definitely changed, however. Before the accident, I drank socially … to be cool, to fit in with others. After my accident, I medicated to escape the stress of everything from financial fears to roommate worries to Travis sightings.

Hanging out at the usual party spots brought more high school drama than I was equipped to handle. Travis began dating someone else, and my friends kept me informed when the two were seen together. When Travis and I last spoke, we agreed to keep in touch. He had not held up his end of the bargain, perhaps finding it easier to make a complete break from any contact with me. In retrospect, I fully understand. "Out of sight, out of mind" would have been a good strategy for both of us. But small-town living made this impossible. And he was certainly not out of mind for me. Travis had been my best friend through harder things than most couples ever encounter. I could not possibly watch him develop another relationship without being personally hurt by what I saw.

My answer to the pain that came with these failed attempts to recreate last year's social life was to drink more. Quite frankly, my classmates seemed to love it. "All right, Tasha! Pour her another one. We never thought you'd be here after all you've been through—way to go, girl!"

Oddly, I felt I had a new image. "This girl can overcome anything and party with the best of them," was the underlying tone. And I didn't intend to disappoint them. Alcohol became my escape from inner pain, plus a way to be socially accepted … until the next day, that is. What appeared to be a win-win on Saturday night at eleven p.m. was a total failure when Sunday morning's hangover hit.

Of course, I was still dating Jeremy. If he could have attended a party with me, I might have reacted differently when Travis and his new girlfriend arrived. Alone, I was free to notice how Travis looked right through me—pretended I wasn't there. Not even a peek; he was so disciplined to look the other way. Anger, hurt, curiosity … the emotional response depended upon how much I'd had to drink.

Jeremy couldn't rescue me from these awkward and painful parties. Yet he surprised me when he said he was hopping on a plane during Christmas break to see me. I was thrilled. It would be a fast week, but a memorable way to spend the vacation. My girlfriends supported me, too—excited to meet Jeremy, making him feel so welcomed. Brooke, Holly, Sarah, and Jesse made Jeremy's visit a big deal, including us in every group plan.

As senior year progressed, I started declining the invitations to hang out at parties—no, actually people quit asking. I stayed home alone more and more. I feared that I would ruin a good time by strapping others with the "rules" for taking Tasha out. Although I managed to have unlimited access to alcohol, my van driver had to remain absolutely sober. This pattern was getting old for the unlucky driver strapped with my van keys for the night. I'd like to say that I quit wanting to join in on the weekend fun … that some moral sense kicked in … that guilt tugged at me for expecting friends to watch while I partied. But I would be lying if I took credit for this change in my social pattern. On the contrary, friends planned their weekends without me, and I felt horribly left out.

I never called my friends out on this. I never asked, "Where were you Saturday night? Why didn't you call me?" For indeed, these were my friends. I frequently asked myself, what would I do? Would I continue to haul a paralyzed, at times intoxicated, friend around so she could have fun? And would I have remained sober to do the driving? When I say *sober*, I mean absolute sobriety. Drinking and driving has never been an option for me, and I can say adamantly that I have never broken this personal vow.

I can't say that I would be that self-sacrificing friend. In addition, I couldn't challenge any one of my friends on this—they had done so much for me up to this point. I might have the courage to confront a staring stranger, a gossiping acquaintance. But I could not, would not, confront a true friend and run the risk of losing that friendship.

Consequently, Monday mornings at school brought whispers and laughter at all I had missed. I hated the hush-hush around me as others kept their weekend stories exclusive. What they didn't know was that the pain of exclusion was compounded by, "Shhh—there's Tasha."

Over the years, many classmates, for whatever reason, had been shunned from the fun of the "chosen"—the popular students. Throughout my childhood, I had played both roles, sometimes joining the chosen, other times experiencing the pain of exclusion. During the second half of my senior year, I have to say I spent most weekends dealing with the hurt that comes from being left out.

In the spring of that year, Mom heard from the two local women who had prayed so diligently for me. Despite all my progress since their visits back in Rochester, they fervently continued their power of prayer, even after my discharge from rehab. It was Easter season, so both women invited me to a play at their church in River Falls, a nearby community with strong and varied congregations. Of course, I acknowledged the kind gesture, but I really had no intention of going.

"Tasha, this is the least we can do. We have to accept this invitation as our thanks for all their prayers and concern." Mom was right, so I asked Angie to go, too. The church was packed, but Mom and Angie found seats near the aisle where I could wheel in next to them.

The play opened with Jesus carrying the cross down the center aisle. Funny how many times you can hear the Passion of Christ and still be alarmed by the heightened emotions of it all. Suddenly, Satan and his demons appeared, tormenting and accusing Jesus. I was petrified. I hated my seat on the aisle, so close to the devil. Full of fear, I had nowhere to go. Feeling powerless to stop what I knew was His fate, I was frightened for Jesus, and forced to watch until the bitter end.

The story played out a variety of individual lives—some good, some bad, but all pointing to one thing: when face-to-face with death and confronted with final destiny, did these people have solid proof that Jesus had entered their lives?

I found myself grappling with a theological question I had not confronted before. Eternity, whether spent in heaven or hell, was not my choice. Being a "good person" would not save me from eternal suffering. I had to be a believer. My destiny depended upon truly accepting that Jesus suffered and died on the cross to save me. At that moment, I wasn't sure what frightened me more—this revelation or the demons in costume taunting the unbelievers.

I was mesmerized. Never in my wildest dreams did I expect to have this reaction from a local church play. The performance ended, and a man came up onstage to address the audience.

"Come forward, anyone. If you would like to receive Jesus into your lives, please, the time is now. Don't wait."

I feared going up in front of the crowd. I had noticed a few classmates in the audience, and I felt their judgment for even thinking about this offer to publically receive Jesus into my heart.

Then someone read my mind. The daughter of one of the women who had invited us approached me. "Tasha, do you want to go up front?" I shook my head yes.

As I motored toward the front of the church, something amazing took over. I have no memory of the crowd. It was as if the audience did not exist. This sudden, inexplicable feeling came over me and triggered two reactions. First, I felt immense regret for all the poor choices I had made. Selfish insecurities had guided my living and ruled my judgment. Then, almost simultaneously, I felt complete peace. This was a feeling I had been searching for in so many places—in my boyfriend, in my social circle, in my college plans—but I never expected that God would be the one to share this power with me. I intuitively knew that somehow my life had changed, and for good.

Overwhelming emotion engulfed me. My whole life, I'd believed that Jesus was the savior of the world. It was not until now, however, that I believed I needed a savior. It went from the world, to me. I finally knew God—that he was real, that I needed Him, that I should live for Him—and there was no going back. This would not be an overnight transition. But for the very first time I talked with God, had hope in my life, and trusted that He would stay with me.

I feared this change, but Angie was there for me. She had already rededicated her faith and knew it was a just a matter of time before I would experience the same thing. My accident had directed her—once again, goodness born of tragedy. Angie's prayers for my own faith-encounter were answered.

For the first time ever, I truly felt God's presence. With little wavering, I received Jesus Christ into my heart as my Lord and Savior. It happened in a stranger's church that April day, and I will never again be a faithless person. These women who seemed so overboard in their faith—so extreme in their desire to bring Jesus into my life—played a huge role in saving me. I couldn't be more grateful for Nancy Vircks and Redina Bang, two patient, loving women who prayed for the right thing: self-awareness of God's plan for Tasha Schuh.

Chapter 16

Liability Limbo

FLASH BACK TO the day of my accident.

"Are you going to sue?"

This was a frequent question asked of my parents within hours of my arrival to Rochester. Hire a lawyer? The Schuhs' instinctive reply was no. A common stereotype popped into their minds, an image generated by every tragic yet preventable accident: ambulance chaser. Mom and Dad possessed very little experience with lawyers, mostly legal exchanges regarding property, like when they bought their first home and purchased the store. Attorneys helped people conduct business. They did the research. They knew the laws. To my parents, suing to gain money from an unintentional tragic incident was just plain wrong. That is, until the medical bills from my sixteen-foot fall began to pile up.

Suddenly, something else seemed wrong. It seemed wrong that an insurance company expected to cover catastrophic medical events had gaping loopholes. It seemed wrong that emergency-room visits, including ambulance rides and airlifts, were not covered because, "You didn't contact us for preauthorization." It seemed wrong that although my school had insurance, the fact that this play rehearsal occurred in another building made the coverage questionable. It seemed wrong that every party involved with potential funds to pay for my lifesaving needs pointed the finger at someone else.

That's when my parents sought legal help. Every person who sincerely wanted to help us with insurance claims—friends, family, school employees, even local insurance agents—hit a wall of legal mumbo jumbo. This dead end revealed the frightening truth that not only did my folks face the loss of their daughter as they knew her, they would be financially devastated in the process.

"Hello. Yes, I'll hold ... yes, can you help me? I am trying to explain that my daughter's hospital room *should be* covered. I can't find any language in the policy that limits the coverage ... Yes, $1,300 per day ... Of course I know that a standard hospital bed costs far less than this ... $200 a day? I don't doubt that. But, when we agreed to this policy last year, we were sure that major medical would cover ... Okay, I'll hold ... I'm sorry; they are calling my family to Tasha's room for a care conference. I'll have to phone later ... Oh. I'll call first thing in the morning then ... You're closed tomorrow? All right, I'll call Monday. I don't even know what day of the week it is anymore. Thank you."

Mom and Dad had calls like this with the school's insurance as well as their own medical insurance company. No matter who held the receiver on the other line, my parents could count on a couple of common replies: another party was liable, or my parents misinterpreted their own insurance policy. Repetitive arguments with various players left Mom and Dad feeling powerless. They wanted to put their attention and energy into helping me, praying for me, coordinating visitors, keeping the rest of their family and their business afloat. They needed someone to guide them through the technicalities of contracts, premiums, and loopholes.

Relatively protected from legal concerns, I do recall horrible feelings of guilt whenever the subject of unreimbursed bills arose. I also remember a day in rehab when an attorney came to visit. I knew by then that a family friend, a court reporter, had suggested we find an experienced attorney to manage legal action against insurance companies that seemed to be passing the buck on my needs. "I see this all the time in my job. You have a solid case. You just need the right representation," my mom's friend advised.

After my first week in rehab, Mom and Dad agreed to meet with two different law firms. Bill Sieben from Schwebel, Goetz, and Sieben sent a representative to Rochester to assess my long-term needs, to review my unpaid bills, and to analyze other concerns regarding the preventive nature of my accident. There was in no way a desire by my family to point fingers. This was a matter of interpretation of liability, and Bill Sieben's staff promptly defined the need and likely success of legal action. Mom and Dad found immediate relief and confidence from this law firm's approach, and so agreed to pursue a suit.

Fast forward to my senior year, much of which was spent orchestrating litigation that would seek to answer one burning question: which party would provide financial coverage for my accident, as well as support for my future needs?

The legal team started by investigating the venue. The Sheldon Theater presented a waiver, signed by school personnel, indicating that one adult would be present for every ten kids under the Sheldon's roof at any given rehearsal. Unfortunately, this adult-to-student ratio was not honored the night of my accident, which exonerated the Sheldon of any wrongdoing. With one party eliminated, Bill Sieben narrowed the liability issue considerably. The trapdoor's construction firm was next to be dismissed, since all parts had been properly assembled. Logically, it was up to the theater personnel to use the door as intended.

My parents discovered over the course of many months that lawyers are gifted interpreters of contract language. It wasn't long before Mom and Dad learned how naively they had accepted their own medical insurance policy—which was indeed weak and full of perfectly legal loopholes. With my parents' insurance company off the hook, Mr. Sieben and his staff determined that the most likely party regarding liability was the school's insurance company.

My parents did their best to convey to their friend Pete Dulak, my teacher and theater director, that this was not a lawsuit to place blame. This was a suit to pursue financial coverage from the source of obligation. This would prove to be a most difficult road since friends, classmates, and a wonderful teaching staff were involved. But irony would prevail once again. Because of the closeness of the people brought together by the suit, all those asked to give depositions spoke the truth. They managed to salvage some good from all the physical, mental, and emotional pain that an accident like this caused for more than just the victim.

A series of surgical procedures, a nearly six-month hospital stay, a $1,300-a-day room-and-board charge, specialists with separate billing, daily caregivers for current and future needs, cath supplies and other medical equipment, a custom-made motorized wheelchair, a specialized van requiring costly conversion if I intended to drive, countless therapy sessions involving miles and months of commuting, gadgets and gizmos like the Teno and my touch pads ... everything cost so much! It's no wonder that every party involved sought thorough depositions to solve the financial aspects of my case. But again, isn't this why insurance exists?

My own deposition, scheduled for a hotel conference room in Red Wing, Minnesota, took place the June before my senior year. Mom, Angie, Bill Sieben, and eight other attorneys were present while my every word was scrutinized by all. Multiple parties still sought exoneration at this point, including the Sheldon Theater and the trapdoor designers. My school's insurance company, led by an attorney who reminded me of Jon Voight's role as nasty lawyer in *The Rainmaker*, utterly intimidated me. But Bill Sieben and his staff had prepared me for tricky, repetitive questioning—attempts to find flaws in my recollection of that night at the Sheldon.

"Who was standing behind you? Who was in front of you? Why was your back to the trapdoor? Where did you think you were going? Why were you in the other student's way? Why would you move just because a student said to? Who was that student anyway? How close are you? Why did you step backward? Why not sideways? Why not forward? How big was that hole? And you're telling us you didn't see it?" Seven and a half hours of recurring questions. I felt trapped in an endless cycle of cross-examination. Yet I thought, *Tell the truth. Answer honestly every single time, and you won't be tricked. A snare won't work if there's nothing to catch.*

Although Mom and Angie were permitted in the room for this session, neither of them could answer for me. Pregnant with Isabel, her first of three daughters, Angie shared Mom's maternal instinct to protect me, yet she knew I had to endure the questioning on my own. My what-ifs came racing back again, the most powerful being, *What if I could have prevented this disaster?* Of course, that is precisely what my school's lawyer tried to prove. That I knew what I was doing. That I was to blame for my step backward. That I willed this to happen.

In that room full of lawyers dissecting my every word, I wanted to say, "Had I known that I was on the brink of disaster, I would have taken impeccable notes for you. But I wasn't a third-party observer. I was living in the moment. I didn't see the high school student tumble and fall through the hole. I was busy experiencing it. I didn't watch the girl as she randomly moved around the stage, as she cluelessly tried to figure out her new stage directions. I was lost in her confused thoughts. It's amazing I have any recollection of the event—that I have conscious memory of something so worthy of blacking-out." But confronted by this team of lawyers, I knew that if I pled poor memory, traumatized emotions, weeks in a coma, stressful rehabilitation, loss of so much of myself, no excuse would dismiss me from this deposition.

"Okay, Tasha, let's go over it again." Seven and a half hours later, I was exhausted and drained. I had nothing more to share. We went home, and I was physically sick for the rest of the night.

Despite that early deposition, almost a year—my senior year—would lapse under the shadow of the lawsuit. Meanwhile, bill collectors hounded my parents while they struggled to sell our first home and focused on saving the store.

My expensive wheelchair, a Swedish custom-made vehicle, had been prescribed by my Mayo doctor. The medical supply company initiated the order without preauthorization—another violation of our medical insurance. Off the hook again, the insurance company as well as Medicaid washed their hands of this expense. To top things off, I was having issues with my chair. I had so many technical problems at first, but the manufacturer would not stand by its warranty without payment. Around the time of my one-year anniversary, the company called and said that we had two weeks to pay or they would repossess the chair. Once money was available, a new chair could be issued, but it would take two months to deliver from Sweden.

This is when I took action for the first time on my own. In a panic, I called Bill Sieben's office and asked if there was anything they could do to clarify that all payments were pending due to the lawsuit. Bill Sieben composed a contract for the chair manufacturer in which they agreed that this bill would be the first item paid from any settlement. Thanks to Bill,

I kept my chair, sought the repairs and adjustments, and accepted it as my means of mobility for about six years.

I know there was no ill intent—no wish for a student to get hurt. But negligence resulted from technical changes made in the theater that evening, under the duress of staging a production that was not ready for opening night.

Besides the waiver violation that had our student-to-teacher ratio at the Sheldon far beyond what was agreed upon, the most convincing evidence that my school's insurance was liable came from changes that occurred just twenty minutes before our practice.

The decision to run our new scene changes with the lights down was one incriminating factor. The lights had been on when this scene had taken six minutes to orchestrate the night before. Now that we were attempting to revise our moves to within thirty seconds, it was suddenly pitch-black.

Prior to that evening's rehearsal, a platform stood underneath the trapdoor. Clearly, someone involved had considered the potential for disaster. The revolving bridge, a quintessential showpiece for that fateful scene, hooked into a pipe that caused distracting noise when it turned and rubbed against the platform. That evening, the platform was ordered removed, just twenty minutes prior to all of our scene changes. The decision to remove the "safety net" platform was the final implicating evidence that human error had occurred.

I was so angry when this information emerged from the depositions. If someone had anticipated the potential for a fall through the trapdoor, why would removing this safeguard just minutes before a complicated re-blocking make any sense at all? My step backward proved that the absence of the platform endangered every single student onstage that night. It would take years for me to accept my role as the chosen one. Over time, my anger would fade. I would learn that human error happens for a reason much larger than most of us can comprehend. But at that moment, I admit, the revelation that a platform might have stopped my fall brought all the what-ifs back to torment me.

My senior year came to an end with the lawsuit pending. Mr. Dulak, now my vocal jazz director, gave me ample opportunity to share my voice again. I had two solos within the vocal jazz performances. However, the most memorable part of our spring pop concert for me was when I sang Sarah McLachlan's "Angel." Truly, angels had lifted me from the darkest of places to sing again. Despite all of the worries that came with my new life, I wanted everyone to know that I felt blessed—saved—and we could rise above this sadness. What better way to express this than through music? The girl who had been told she would never sing again jumped at the opportunity.

By the end of May 1999, I had earned the rest of my credits required for graduation. At the ceremony, Sarina sat next to my chair, which was snug against the bottom bleacher of a packed gym. From classroom memories to high school athletics to our final moments as the class of '99—we experienced a journey no one could have predicted. I was glad Sarina was by my side that night.

Lawsuit pending, bills still unpaid, tuition and dorm life just around the corner, friends leaving for other colleges, shaky times with Jeremy as my long-distance boyfriend—I feared my future more than ever. However, my fears would transform into determination on graduation-party day.

My family was blown away by the number of people who came. "We have hundreds of invitations out," Mom admitted, "but you know how these things go. There's no way everyone can come." Yet they did.

Over and over, I was asked the typical graduate's question: "Well, Tasha, what plans do you have now that high school is over?" I'm sure this meant, "What plans do you have now that your education has abruptly ended? No more school for you."

"Well, I'm all set to go to Winona State University. I move in August."

Jaws dropped and faces contorted. Some tried to fake it with words like, "Really? That's wonderful!" But their body language said, "What? Are you crazy? Be realistic." *College is not possible from a wheelchair,* was the message. This fueled my fire. I intended to prove them all wrong.

Of course, some who came to my graduation party had full faith in me. A woman bent over to whisper in my ear, "He never does this." It was

Neil's wife. They had driven all the way from Zumbrota, Minnesota, for the afternoon. Neil liked to keep in touch with his patients, but he rarely went out and about to them. Neil and his wife made me feel so good to know that I was an exception to the rule. Gayle, Val, and Barb traveled all the way from Rochester too. These were the people who believed me when I said, "I'm so ready for college!"

Cleanup was easy since not one piece of food remained from my party. With high school behind me, I had the summer to plan for my move to Winona while both of my grandmothers tried to talk "sense" into my mom. "She can't do this. She can't go all the way to Winona for school! You know who will be running there all of the time? You! Now, talk some sense into her before she fails." However, both Mom and Dad supported me, and our plans were underway.

In June, Jeremy and I had a mutual breaking-up moment—another sign of my maturity and independence. Without drama, we both agreed to move forward with our lives and to end the long-distance correspondence. It was time to meet different people and start new relationships at college, or in his case, through his wheelchair-basketball ventures.

June also meant Year 2 of wheelchair camp. Once again, my time in Stewartville would be shortened. This was not because I postponed my start of camp, like last year. This time I arrived on Day 1 but knew the week would stop short because of a settlement meeting scheduled for Wednesday. Back in Red Wing—the same hotel room, but considerably fewer lawyers this time—Bill Sieben met in another room, conferred, and then popped into our room periodically to convey an offer. Mom and Dad both showed complete trust in Bill when he came back two different times saying, "This is far from our needs analysis. It's just not enough."

To forecast the cost of this lifestyle, acknowledging that my needs would be greater as a quad patient, Bill Sieben hired a paraplegic to help calculate my lifetime expenses. My earning potential was limited, at least until I earned my college degree. I couldn't do the typical service jobs to pay my way through college. No flipping burgers or babysitting. No waiting tables for big tips. Hence, my college expenses were a part of the formula.

This formula also emphasized my age. At eighteen, my life expectancy was pretty much the same as the average human life span—about seventy years. However, if I expected to live that long, I faced a lifetime of unusual expenses. All had to be calculated and adjusted for inflation. For example, the rate for reliable caregivers, about $2,000 per month, would prove to be my greatest, yet most valued, expense.

Gadgets and vehicles, like my high-tech wheelchair, enhanced my mobility and independence. Chair updates and maintenance became a part of the equation. In addition, my van cost $100,000, the gas and brake system alone making up almost half of that price.

The formula continued by presenting the price of yearly physicals, far more costly than most checkups. X-rays and CT scans, ultrasounds and other technology are required to thoroughly examine a body that cannot feel pain or symptoms. My longest stretch of "normal" checkups at one point was almost ten years. Yet even when the clinic statements announced my impeccable health, the whole process set my monthly budget back in overwhelming ways.

Despite all of this research and financial forecasting, my settlement would fall short of the medical-expense predictions prepared by Schwebel, Goetz, and Sieben. Needs analysis calculation: $10 to 18 million. My settlement: $5 million.

All during Bill Sieben's fact-finding, I dwelled on this story: I met a guy with a similar case during my first wheelchair-camp visit. A victim of a grain-elevator accident, he settled for $18 million. He was paraplegic, not quadriplegic. He did not have the expensive monthly bill for caregivers, which made his story frighten me even more, because by the time I met him, two years after his settlement, all his money was gone. Sadly, it was mismanaged from the start. I would have to learn from his mistakes, just as I would have to learn to manage the anxiety that comes with a fixed income.

"Tasha, I think we should agree to this offer. I've seen cases like this go back and forth over a dollar figure. Quite honestly, the longer it drags out, the more difficult it is to find an objective jury. Unfortunately, if jurors think someone's holding out for more money, they lose empathy for the case and often rule against the accident victim. You could get nothing."

My family knew the total cost of bills piled up from the past year and a half. What we couldn't predict were the unknowns. The price of future health needs, the cost of lifestyle improvements, and—since I would never get myself in or out of bed—the expense of caregivers. These unpredictable factors brought about a whole new level of what-ifs. However, Bill Sieben's sound advice had served us well up to that point. My parents agreed. Thank God, there would be no jury trial.

I cannot express the relief my entire family felt when the settlement came to a close that day. I called Angie on my ride home from Red Wing.

"Well, are you satisfied? Did you settle for what you think you need?"

This is how naive I was. I did not even tell Angie the dollar amount. "Well, it's over. We're just going to keep this private, okay? If I don't tell you and Scott, you don't have to worry about answering questions or explaining for me. Are you fine with that?"

"Sure. That makes sense. I just pray that your needs are covered. That's my only concern."

I think I was at the kitchen table eating supper, just hours after thanking Bill Sieben, when I saw my picture on the evening news. "Tasha Schuh, represented by Schwebel, Goetz, and Sieben, settled a personal injury case today for $5 million ..."

What? Did I hear this right? My settlement, an undisclosed amount of money I refused to even share with my closest ally, my sister, was announced for all the world to see? How could this be? How did they know? Why do they care?

Apparently, this type of settlement is public record. Mom was upset but seemed to understand that part of the responsibility of managing this financial agreement was dealing with public opinion. The *Red Wing Republican Eagle* called within minutes of the TV newscast ... to congratulate me.

"Congratulations? Excuse me. This is *not* the lottery!" I heard Mom say to a reporter from the *Eagle*. "Tasha would give it all back in a heartbeat just to walk again." This at least changed the direction of the conversation. Mom knew the reporter would go ahead with this story regardless of our cooperation. So she reluctantly decided to answer the woman's questions.

As consolation, Mom felt as if she changed the tone of the report to a more sensible one.

Indeed, over the years, so many people have had unique reactions to the financial settlement provided by insurance money ... money from a policy taken out by our school for precisely such a case. Isn't this why premiums are paid? If the unthinkable happens, financial support is in place, right? Yet so many people reacted as if I *won* something, as if I hit the jackpot—that this money was a great trade-off for losing control of my body forever.

The phone rang again. This time it was my sister. "Tasha, what is going on? I just heard about your settlement on TV. What business is it of anyone's? Do people have any idea what bills you have piled up?" Indeed, $5 million was not going into the bank. We hadn't even calculated the left-over balance after 25 percent was paid to the law firm and other pretrial legal expenses were met. Of course, my chair had to be paid first, as stated in the contract with the Swedish company. Mayo and Saint Marys Hospital were still waiting for compensation after more than five months of care. The money left over was anybody's guess at this point, but it would be far from the $5 million figure plastered all over the news.

Despite the fact that today I usually juggle two or three jobs so I can live off of what I earn, I continue to face all kinds of questions about my finances. I have in fact made decisions to buy property—my home here in Ellsworth as well as a vacation rental home in Northern Wisconsin, which provides income along with a well-deserved retreat for my hardworking, supportive family. Most people don't know that I went years without insurance. I qualified for COBRA for a while, was covered under my mom's policy for a stretch, and paid medical expenses out of my settlement until I could find coverage—a health insurance risk-sharing plan—that would take me once I proved multiple denials from other insurance companies.

Like everyone, I make choices regarding my spending. My home, my vehicle—I feel compelled to put money into these things. These items bring me security, mobility, and pride in my independence. At other times, I can be the most frugal tightwad, looking for coupons and watching my monthly budget like Ebenezer Scrooge.

A few years ago, while speaking at an area Wisconsin high school, I took questions from the audience. "How much did you get? My dad says you're rich!" I was dumbfounded to discover my settlement money was the focus of such discussion. I actually had a caregiver working for me say numerous times, "Tasha, I wish I were you. You have so much."

Another caregiver confessed that her boyfriend once dodged a fight in a local bar over me.

"What? He was arguing about me? Why would I possibly be the subject of bar talk in downtown Ellsworth?"

"He defended you. Some guy was saying you have it made with the government paying all your bills. Don't worry, he set the record straight. After the lawsuit, no Medical Assistance, no Social Security, right? They acted like you had your house built with tax dollars. Some people!"

Besides limited support from the Department of Vocational Rehabilitation and Wisconsin Medical Assistance, which ended once the settlement came through in late August 1999, I have not relied on an entitlement program. If this confuses people, there is nothing I can do about that. I just feel for others in my situation who are affected by public opinion not only because they look different—appear disabled—but also because they are sometimes judged harshly as a burden to their taxpaying neighbors. Clearly, not all disabled Americans draw from Social Security. And if they do need an entitlement program, then I say hooray for that. I am thankful for the temporary help I received so I can now be a taxpaying supporter of accident victims unable to care for themselves.

One way or another, spinal-cord-injured people will confront the financial challenges that come with their situations. The focus *should* be on getting healthy. Their energy *should* go into adapting to change. But more often, the primary concern becomes financial survival. Whether we're criticized for a legal settlement or assumed to be a burden to taxpayers, financial misunderstanding often accompanies this challenge.

Chapter 17

Driving Miss Tasha

PACK BELONGINGS—CHECK. COORDINATE caregivers—check. Plan daily class schedule—check. Confirm the status of my dorm room, made Tasha-accessible by Winona State—check. My college move entailed "extras" I longed to do without. However, I focused so hard on starting my school year without delay that every obstacle was transformed into an exciting challenge. My attitude was, *Put up the hurdles and I will jump them.*

I faced one symbolic hurdle all summer long as we forged ahead with my Winona move: a conflict regarding how to pay caregivers. I fought comments like, "You know, if you attend a Wisconsin college, Wisconsin Medical Assistance will pay your caregivers." The Department of Vocational Rehabilitation made this clear more than once. "You should really go to Stout." But I had to hang in there. I was meant to go to Winona State!

Since the settlement guaranteed I would no longer qualify for Medical Assistance anyway, I would just have to pay my caregivers on my own. I called the private Winona care agency and asked if we could quit pursuing Wisconsin Medical Assistance. I would pay the agency for morning cares out-of-pocket. They agreed—so as of Friday afternoon, three days before I moved to Winona, agreement was established to bypass any state funding.

Other things fell into place too. Brooke Hines, a wonderful friend I grew even closer to after my accident, wanted to room with me at Winona. This caring, patient classmate would not only make a fabulous roommate and friend, I could pay her directly as a caregiver and reduce the hours needed by the agency.

Despite all the work to start freshman classes at Winona on time, many people said I should postpone my move. If I stayed at the Courage Center, famous for its ten-month rehabilitation program, I would emerge a more independent person, with a driver's license to boot. But I feared this path. If I chose the Courage Center just to learn to drive again, my ambition for college might fade. I might never attend Winona. I felt the need to experience college when my friends did, even though most had different campus choices.

Driving was essential, a symbol of mobility and independence. Yet the equipment required for my van was super-expensive. Another drawback was that I lacked the arm strength and endurance to pass a driving test. Still the weakest parts of my functioning body, my arms had a ways to go. So I lifted more weights, increased my stretching and exercises, and waited for a call from Courage Center. I intended to get my driving lessons while attending college—another decision that brought criticism. I was quickly becoming the girl who bit off more than she could chew. Once again, my critics fueled my determination. My new goals: I would learn to drive, earn good grades, and adapt to independent living. If any of the public doubts were attempts at reverse psychology, I must say, the technique worked beautifully on me.

Brooke was one of the reasons my goals that year were achievable. She stayed by my side during freshman orientation week, although I knew she was eager to meet new people. We fortunately took many of the same classes, so she took notes for me throughout the first semester in all but one course. Brooke definitely made my transition into college life easier.

Since I declined full-time residence at the Courage Center, I was put on a long waiting list for driving lessons. Brooke and others continued to drive me around. I was grateful for every chauffeur who hopped in my van, but I won't lie, I was becoming very impatient with this arrangement. I obsessed over a Courage Center phone call that would announce a driving slot ready and waiting for me. I qualified for two lessons, after which I could practice on my own.

Imagine sitting in your own van while careless drivers risked your safety and property with you along for the ride. One friend looked shocked when I yelled, "Hey, you're going eighty! Can we please slow down?"

This was met with, "Jeez, Tasha, you're such a backseat driver! Do you have to sound like my mother?"

Another time I watched as my driver weaved in and out of highway traffic, and then laid on the brakes after suddenly discovering a stop-and-go light behind the cars and trucks she had just passed.

"Whoa! Sorry, Tasha. Hope you didn't feel that whiplash."

Well, not really—lucky I'm paralyzed! was what I wanted to say. *With you driving, maybe we can lose the final nerve endings in my neck.* But I held my tongue—most of the time. How could I snap at people so willing to give of their time to transport me around?

The bottom line: I did *not* want to be the passenger any longer! Reminded daily of my limits, I wanted the Courage Center to call and put an end to this dependency. I also didn't want "driving Miss Tasha" to transform into a dreaded duty, just as I was making a few new friends. I waited and waited for the call that my driving lessons could start soon.

Since Brooke was so present for me in the classroom, I only needed one other student for help—a volunteer assigned to take notes in just one class. My professors also helped by having me take tests in the Disability Resource Center, where a special table accommodated the height of my wheelchair. If I had a multiple-choice test, I would circle the answers on the test itself. Someone would transfer my answers over to a Scantron form, the computer score sheet used for standardized tests. Also in the Disability Resource Center, I was allowed to dictate my answers for an essay test. My responses were written word-for-word by a volunteer writer.

Throughout my first semester of school, I realized many things. First off, Winona State was indeed a great place for me. Everyone was so supportive. In addition to the school's willingness to replace the bathtub with a roll-in shower, other expensive apartment changes and unique campus supports made it possible for a student like me to be successful. That is, if she was ready for the academic rigor of college content.

Like most college freshmen, I found out the hard way I was unprepared. Not because of the difficulties brought on by independent living, but because my time management was not that of a college student. Brooke and I would attend classes for maybe three hours on a given day. And like typical freshmen, we viewed the rest of the day as free time.

Woo-hoo! A kid could get used to these hours! Yeah, done listening to professors by noon … what should we do now?

Time to watch soap operas, or a movie, followed by a three-hour nap. We stayed up late talking or visiting others in the dorm. We ignored this thing called a syllabus that outlined our course reading, scheduled our composition deadlines, and warned us of quiz and test dates. Once we figured out that each syllabus served as our guide for the whole semester, the damage was already done.

At the time, this seemed so unfair. I attended class every day. I wasn't just sleeping in and blowing off the lectures. But after I bombed a few quizzes, I changed my attitude and adjusted my approach. I miraculously pulled off a B average by the end of Semester I, and vowed to change my ways as Semester II started. All that "free time" was redefined, and each grading period ended with a little less panic.

Of course, meeting new friends—people *not* intimidated by my disability—was a huge goal that year. I met students who were curious, kindhearted, and genuinely impressed with my ambition to do what other eighteen-year-olds did. But developing the depth of friendship I longed for was tricky. I knew it would be, but I feared my patience would wear thin. So I was truly grateful when I discovered Forrest living next to me on campus. Coincidentally, I had met Forrest at my first wheelchair camp. He and Brian, his roommate, became my only new friends at the start of my freshman year. We ate meals together, hung out on weekends, and counted on each other for whatever came up. Forrest, my neighbor for five years, eventually showed interest in my faith pursuits—something that came much later in my freshman year. Ultimately, our friendship ran deep, but as a new freshman, I was seriously hoping to expand my social circle. Figuring out *how* would take most of my first year of college.

By October, I finally received that call for an opening at the Courage Center. The outpatient program had a driving slot available. I would receive two driving lessons as promised from a trained instructor—someone experienced with adaptive vans.

Way back when I was first discharged from Mayo's rehab, my family knew that the Toaster could not be modified to accommodate me as the driver. Therefore, a couple of months before I started college, we purchased a 1997 Dodge Caravan with only 21,000 miles on it. It came equipped with an automatic sliding door and drop-down ramp, and we made arrangements for the required gas- and brake-system conversion plus a lockdown mechanism to hold my chair in place. The sale of the Toaster and a little help from the Department of Vocational Rehabilitation paid for the new modifications.

Of course, *feeling* ready and *being* ready to drive were two very different things. That first driver's license I received about six months prior to my accident seemed like a gift compared to the roadblocks I now faced to master this adapted van. Instead of driving a vehicle with a typical foot feed for gas and brake, I suddenly had an electronic system operated by my impaired hands and arms. My right hand and arm, with significantly more strength, tackled the steering wheel. My left hand and arm would control the gas and brake.

This modified gas and brake system required my left hand to slide into what is called a Tri-Pin—three metal upright, foam-wrapped pins hooked to a lever system. The lever system, surrounded by a small metal box, kept my hand from slipping out. The pins enabled me to either pull back a lever to give the van some gas or push forward to engage the brake.

The interior of my van shows the expensive conversion that allows me to drive.

Here we go: Lesson #1, Courage Center, Golden Valley, Minnesota. My instructor drove me in my *new* van to a nearby church parking lot. The driver's seat was pulled out so I could lock my chair in behind the wheel. The concept of the new gas and brake system was pretty simple. The trick, however, was to determine how fast to pull back for gas and how fast or slow to push forward for braking. I could stop on a dime regardless of my speed, which might dangerously send a passenger through the windshield. The controls were so touchy, I feared I lacked the dexterity to operate such a sensitive system. My arms weren't all that strong yet; suddenly, I wished I had worked even harder at my strengthening exercises. A new set of what-ifs clouded my judgment.

My instructor sensed my frustrations and was kind, despite the jerky ride I had given him. "Don't worry so much. You just need practice."

What I lacked in confidence, my dad made up for. Dad is the reason I learned to drive so quickly.

Just after that first driving lesson, I went home for the weekend. With my van parked in the garage, I sat sulking in defeat, knowing Dad intended to take me practice driving. "I don't think I can do this," I said, near tears.

"You won't get better sitting in here. Let's see where you're at." Dad was determined, and he knew I had to get more accustomed to driving with my hands. Every spare second he had, Dad offered to help me. We started on back roads, far away from any other vehicles. I graduated to our small town, where approaching a stop sign was my biggest fear. Eventually, I tackled stop-and-go lights where the anxiety of an anticipated red light almost paralyzed me, no pun intended.

Dad would bravely get in my vehicle, knowing his life was probably in danger. He was fearless, and not a bit embarrassed when I was passed by little old ladies who must have wondered why a college girl was driving so slowly.

We spent most of our time practicing starts and stops. If Dad suffered mild whiplash, he never complained. Once, he needed to move my van from inside our garage and chose to do so using my hand-operated system. "Stay where you are, Tasha. I'll get it."

He came back looking as if he had aged from the adventure. "Whoa! That was fun? Now I see what you're dealing with. I just jerked my way back forty feet. Lucky I didn't take the garage wall out!" We all laughed, but I was actually glad that someone finally understood the touchy system I had to master.

Mom did so many things to support me, but teaching me to drive was not her forte. She lacked Dad's patience. She simply reacted, "You are going too fast. Speed up. Slow down. Pay attention, Tasha. You're gonna crash if you don't ..." These are not confidence-boosting words. Sorry, Mom, but in those early months, I didn't want to ride anywhere with you.

Dad's patience, on the other hand, was a godsend. Within two weeks, he totally lifted my confidence right before my second and last driving lesson at the Courage Center.

Despite Dad's help, I was so nervous for this session. I would be learning the Digitone System that enabled me to operate the rest of my van—left blinker, right blinker, windshield wipers, cruise control, etc.—without removing my hands from the steering wheel or the gas/brake system. I couldn't even fathom how this would work with my hands already committed to two places.

Step 1: When I moved my left wrist to the left, toward the driver's window, the system began a series of beeping in the tone of do-re-mi-fa-sol-la-ti-do.

"Every beep has a different function," my instructor explained. "If you want to put on your left blinker, let it beep once, let go, and your left blinker will go on."

Wow! If that was *do* in my do-re-mi series, I had a lot to memorize and practice.

"If you want your windshield wipers to function," my instructor went on, "you will have to hold your wrist to the left until it beeps three times—do, re, mi—let go, and your wipers will start."

First beep: left blinker. Second beep: right blinker. Third beep: windshield wipers. Fourth beep: windshield-wiper fluid. Fifth beep: cruise control, on. Sixth beep: cruise control, set. Seventh beep: bright lights. Eighth beep: horn is sounded.

Wait a minute—I had to wait for eight counts on the Digitone System just to sound my horn? Clearly, some horrible drivers were going to luck out. I would not have the patience to wait for the eighth Digitone sound, so why bother with the horn? With a delay like that, road rage would be pointless, declaring the horn obsolete.

Obviously, the system had an order of priority, and the horn fell low on the list. In fact, the entire system was an exercise in mental focus and self-control. I know plenty of drivers who would benefit from this system, which essentially makes every driving maneuver a deliberate and preplanned move.

Brooke, Brian, and Forrest love to remind me of one memorable night when all four of us went to a movie in Winona. I don't recall a thing about the theater, but as I drove us home, I had a little trouble with a stop-and-go light.

I coasted uneventfully through a green light, the first of two consecutive lights. Brooke warned me that the next light would probably be yellow. "Start slowing down, Tasha," Brooke stated. "You know how these lights are synced. Pretty hard to make them both."

I was caught up in the guys' conversation going on behind me, so I did not hear Brooke's advice. I continued to drive as the light turned yellow. I remember thinking, *no sudden stops.* Forrest wasn't strapped down in his wheelchair behind me; I didn't want him to flip over. In a split second, I chose to put on more gas, and by the time I got through the second light, it was red.

"Better pull over. There's a cop behind us." I thought they were only teasing, since Brooke and Brian laughed as they said this.

"Right. Very funny, guys."

But in a more serious tone, Brooke added, "I'm not kidding, Tasha. Better pull over before he calls backup." Everyone burst out laughing again with visions of me being part of a high-speed chase.

I had never learned how to pull over—not even Dad thought to teach me how—so my van jerked back and forth as I slowly pulled to the side of the road. By this time, we were directly in front of Winona's campus housing. All of my neighbors just happened to be sitting outside the dorms that day, laughing at me as we pulled up. Brooke, Brian, and Forrest continued to laugh hysterically. Everyone found this to be so funny, although I feared the police officer would not have the same reaction.

Unable to roll down my own window, I had to have Brooke reach over to do it for me so I could finally talk to the officer.

"Are you aware that you drove through a red light?" he asked, just after requesting to see my license.

"I'm so sorry. With this sensitive braking system, I didn't think I would be able to stop, so I proceeded with caution." My friends spit out laughter again. They were not helping.

After looking at my van's conversion, the officer decided to let me go with just a warning. This was one consolation for an event that pegged me as the campus motor-head who could sweet-talk her way out of a ticket.

In all honesty, driving became a long work in progress. Once I made the effort to continually practice and polish my skills, I mastered the system and became a confident driver in the country as well as the Twin Cities. Once I had my license, I road-tripped from Winona to Ellsworth every other weekend just to gain practice and experience.

Chapter 18

Would the Real Tasha Schuh Please Stand Up?

AFTER BROOKE AND I figured out the science of the syllabus, I earned all As in my classes. Eventually, I fell in love with the night class. I was most alert in the evenings. Plus, mornings could be devoted to the rigor of getting ready for the day. By the second semester, I wanted to take some pressure off of Brooke. She had double duty, helping me in class in addition to all her own school work. I worried about the toll it would take on her over time. As the year went on, I saw another reason why I had to strive toward even more independence.

Psychology, my declared major, entailed much more math and science than I had originally expected. I wondered how I could consider this a helping profession yet be so self-absorbed in the rigor of the field. Then I learned I would need a doctorate at some point if I truly intended to practice this career at its most significant level. Of course, I was capable of accomplishing anything in my education if I put my mind to it, but I questioned if I loved the major enough to put forward the necessary time and effort. The more I pursued my psychology major, the more dissatisfied I became with the program.

A mixture of discontent and guilt consumed me. Although I felt God everywhere, I believed I wasn't living His plan. Some of it stemmed from my misguided major. But much of it grew from my poorly managed personal life. I was still trying to fit in, still trying to win people over, still drinking on the weekends—saying yes to parties when what I really wanted was a social life that God would approve of. Besides praying, which frankly seemed like solitary confinement to me, I just couldn't figure out a way to bring God wholly into my life.

God indeed works in mysterious ways. About this time I received a call—an invitation from Nancy Vircks to hear a guest speaker in a small rural church near Ellsworth. I was torn. This happened to be my weekend to stay on campus, something I did twice a month. I compromised. I planned to attend the Friday-night session at church and then drive back to Winona on Saturday morning. The best of both worlds: I could squeeze in a little God time and still party with my friends Saturday night.

But after Friday night's session, I changed my plans in order to take in every single moment with the weekend's keynote speaker. Here was a man who, born into the Mafia, raised with little to no chance of meeting Christ, miraculously walked away from a life of sin to save himself and others who were now moved by his story of resilience. I was so inspired. I had to cancel my plans for fun in Winona in order to learn of this man's complete transformation because of his decision to listen to God.

I admit, I feared how my friends would react when they heard why I had cancelled on them ... to stay voluntarily in church all weekend? I would in no way deny what had happened to me over the course of these few days. But if friends asked about my weekend, I wanted to do more than just satisfy them with an answer. I wanted to declare this huge change that my sister, my parents, and I had experienced that weekend. A transformation had occurred, and people needed to know there was no going back now. One thing that I was certain of, however, was my need to get involved in this new way of life so I could grow with Christ.

On Sunday, I drove back to campus with an Ellsworth friend and fellow grad, Trevor Johnson. In fact, now that I had my license, Trevor often rode to and from Winona with me. I knew he had attended many campus church events, so I thought, *Here's my chance to assert myself. Talk with Trevor. He'll get it.* That's when I learned Trevor and I had more in common than I ever knew. In fact, Trevor led me right into an on-campus Christian ministry known as InterVarsity.

"Do you think I could come to your next InterVarsity meeting or event?" I asked. Trevor was more than excited to hear that I wanted to check out InterVarsity with him.

The closer I got to campus, the more I felt the need to inform, or should I say warn, Brooke of what had changed in me over the weekend. This wave of Christian awareness swept me in a new direction. Equipped with my first cell phone, I called Brooke from the van. She needed to hear this before I wheeled into the apartment. I should alert her that I was a very different person. But my forewarning frightened her at first … as if I had joined a cult over the weekend.

"I knew you were going to some church thing," Brooke said. "That's fine, Tasha. But you are scaring me. You sound like you are dropping everything important for this."

I promised her I would clarify the whole thing as soon as I got back into the apartment. "I have not joined a cult. I promise. But I am not the same person either."

Brooke and I talked and talked, and she patiently understood that I had set new goals for myself. These goals, unlike those that came with my accident recovery, were neither academic nor geared toward making me physically independent. These goals fed my soul. And one thing was certain—they had priority position in my life.

Over time, I would see that my desire to live a life for Christ was contagious. Friends like Brooke and Forrest would ask to join me at church on Sundays or "try things out" at InterVarsity events. But before I could lead others in this direction, I had so much work to do on myself. Within a few days of my drive back with Trevor, I outlined goals for myself—not a list of do's and don'ts, but rather a way to better my life as a whole.

Goal #1: I would stop swearing. Like so many college students, freedom of expression meant I could say words that had been prohibited in my school and forbidden in my home, but were not policed by anyone in campus housing. To use an old-fashioned saying, I could "swear like a sailor." I don't mean to imply that it was okay for a boy to swear. In fact, I don't wish to pass judgment on anyone, regardless of gender, for such word choice. But clearly, for me, I was choosing to swear at this point in my life in order to fit in with the boys. I truly liked the attention this brought, especially since I feared no punishment for it. This bad habit snowballed over time, so I knew it would take Brooke and others to help me break it.

"It's not a big deal, Tasha," Brooke stated, although it was never her bad habit.

"I think it is, Brooke. You never swear. I need to have the self-discipline to stop this now, and for good." I decided it was one step in my new direction of self-improvement.

Goal #2: I would stop participating in the drinking scene. This would also be a challenge since social time was synonymous with partying. Trevor guaranteed me that fun could exist without alcohol, but my mind saw only bland people bored out of their minds, watching the clock on the weekends. Yet Trevor was fun and creative, so there was hope. I predicted that involvement in InterVarsity would be key to this goal.

Goal #3: I vowed not to date anyone until I felt that I had a solid foundation set for myself. This meant I had to figure out who I was and what I believed. I was beginning to acknowledge that my identity as a teenage girl was contingent upon whom I was dating. In the past, I wanted people to ask, "So, who's Tasha Schuh with now? Oh, she's the girl who dates the State wrestler, the lead in the musical, the lead singer of that band ..." I had to turn this around and take pride in hearing, "You know, Tasha Schuh. She's accomplished so much after overcoming that horrible accident." I would start my identity-building list by succeeding at Winona State. Dating could wait until I felt pride in introducing unescorted, single me.

Tuesday evenings were now spent at InterVarsity worship night. The music and fellowship messages were more relevant to my life than what I heard growing up in church. Perhaps the worship was indeed more effective—perhaps I was ready and listening for the first time in my life. But certainly, I looked forward to InterVarsity nights and every other weekend at Abundant Life, the church I now belonged to, where I saw that memorable play.

As committed as I seemed to a life serving Christ, I still feared the loss of the party scene. This would prove to be the hardest of my three goals. Why didn't I embrace this change? No more hangovers; no worries about a sober driver, since it could be *me* every time. Why wasn't I empowered to take on this goal and prove that God's plan was a perfect fit for me?

I had to face facts. My entire social circle spent their weekends at one form of party or another. I was honestly afraid of being left alone—of being ostracized if I declared alcohol my enemy. I believed that I had to participate if I expected to be included in campus life. Fear kept me from meeting my goal. I continued my pattern of self-destruction until, of course, I *had* to stop.

Alcohol does not mix well with most medications, but especially with a muscle relaxant called Baclofen. Baclofen calmed my leg spasms, those jumpy episodes that interfered with my busy daytime schedule and hit me in the night, disrupting my much-needed sleep. When I drank, generally beer, I learned my limit the hard way. While I heaved helplessly, the unpleasant job of holding Tasha's long hair while she puked went to the nearest person. Over time, I determined that if I consumed only four or five beers throughout the course of an entire night, I could avoid the heaving portion of the party. I quickly formulated an acceptable recipe for a quadriplegic's chemical balancing act of drinking and drugs.

Nocturnal by nature, I could outlast most partiers. With Brooke or my hired caregiver helping me to bed around two a.m., I would zonk out immediately. Like clockwork, I could count on two hours of deep, uninterrupted sleep. No leg spasms. And I lacked the normal drinker's urge to empty the bladder, so I should have slept like a baby, right? But I didn't.

As if an alarm sounded, I would awaken in the middle of the night, alert and staring at the ceiling. What could I do? Where could I go? I was stuck, wide awake, in bed until my morning caregiver—usually instructed to let me sleep in—arrived. To add insult to insomnia, my legs would often take me for a ride. My Baclofen seemed powerless after my two-hour nap. My legs would shake involuntarily with spasms that lasted until dawn, or until the alcohol completely left my system.

During the day, my leg spasms sometimes broke my focus so much that I couldn't study or accomplish anything. Of course, I knew I couldn't inquire about changing the Baclofen dosage. Clearly, the alcohol played a part in all of this. I guess it was good that I did not want to lie to my doctors about my extracurricular drinking. Yet my formula for combining two chemicals was failing. I continued to try to find the right balance.

I fought the drinking battle until one night, as I felt my legs crawling out of my own skin, a surrendering came over me. I heard a new voice chime in. It wasn't my usual voice of denial. Nor was it me, recalculating the right mix, like a pharmacist working closely with the bartender, an alchemist searching out the right elixir so the girl in the wheelchair could relax with a drink.

This time I believe I heard God. And He was full of painful and poignant questions: "So how long are you going to punish yourself? Are you miserable enough yet? Why can't you see, life can be wonderful without this? Are you ready to stop?"

"Yes. You're right. I'm done." This was one of the shortest and most important conversations I have had with God.

By surrendering to Him, I felt loss for some of my deepest friendships. In my decision to stay sober, I no longer spent time at parties with Forrest, Brian, and Brooke. I immersed myself in InterVarsity and hoped that I would meet some new friends there. I realized I had not met new people outside of Forrest, Brian, acquaintances of theirs, and a few volunteer students who took notes for me. This far into my freshman year, I felt as if I was starting my search for new college friends all on my own.

It was hard for me to just roll down the walkway in search of new people. For one thing, because of my spinal-cord injury, my body temperature was always compromised. I was a freeze-baby and did not want to go outside any more than I had to. It was not feasible for me to roam around looking for opportunities to meet new people. Out of necessity, I ventured out of my room for lectures, labs, and meals. Oddly enough, people would not come to my apartment, knock on the door, and ask me to be their friend.

Seriously, I knew I had to schedule activities in order to meet others. I felt the need to be proactive—reach out—take the responsibility to attend events where people with Christian values could be found and friendships pursued. I felt like a Christian stalker, but I knew I had to initiate my own social life. It would not come looking for me, and in a college setting, certainly not in sober fashion.

The school year was drawing to a close as I slowly made new connections. I was actually excited for my sophomore year, when some months earlier I had dreamed of transferring to a fictitious college where friends were made instantly.

It helped that I met Ryan at InterVarsity the spring of my freshman year. Ryan, a guy obsessed with football who dreamed of teaching and coaching one day, seemed so set on leading young athletes down a Christian path. Finishing his junior year, he was already established in his Christian values. I envied his overt conviction. I knew immediately I wanted to be around this guy and people like him. I was hungry for it. But this would not be easy. How could I pursue friendship with Ryan and still remain true to my third and final goal?

The beauty of InterVarsity was that we assumed certain values were pre-aligned, so we could cut right to the Christian chase. Ryan had this way of making me feel I could be completely honest with him. So I told him that I worried about going back to my old ways—that I feared I would start attending parties out of loneliness. On his first meeting with me, Ryan listened while I poured my heart and ideas out to him. I had a plan to prevent my return to the party scene. I just needed some support to get it going.

"I want to host a Bible study at my apartment. I want people to come here so that I can learn and grow without having to leave my warm room."

Just when I thought I had chased this new friend away forever, Ryan spoke the unexpected. "That's so odd."

Oh, no. I'm in trouble.

"Sorry—I mean, that's so ironic. Amy—this girl from InterVarsity— and I were just chosen as small-group leaders for next school year. We've been racking our brains trying to figure out where we could host a Bible study next fall."

My idea would become a reality. Ryan, Amy, and I were meant to be partners in this plot to keep me from stumbling back to unhealthy ways.

We would start a party atmosphere around the most worthy of topics—the Bible.

Summer break abruptly stopped our Bible-study plans. Yet Ryan and I both felt confident that our strategy was sound. I'd have an apartment full of college kids by fall semester.

Unexpectedly, I developed a skin sore on my right thigh just as I was about to move home to Ellsworth in late May. Rather small in diameter, it still scared the living daylights out of me, since I recalled all of the horror stories from rehab about skin problems. This could not be ignored.

I rushed to Rochester, where doctors placed me on bed rest at my parents' home. All of June, I left bed only for lunch and to spend a few hours each day sitting on the deck to tan under the healing powers of the warm Wisconsin sun. July came and went, and my sore was still not completely healed. August started with a load of anxiety, as I knew I couldn't go back to Winona and lie in bed all day once fall classes were underway.

Through my checkups, it was determined that I had grown four inches since my accident. Well over six feet tall, my body had become a long wet noodle. Since I had little meat on my bones and no torso muscles, the vertebrae in my back slowly began to curve with scoliosis. This spinal curve caused an imbalance by putting more pressure on one side of my body, which in turn led to a breakdown in my skin. This explained why my skin wasn't healing as quickly as expected. X-rays revealed a forty-five-degree curve in my back. I possessed the classic *S* for scoliosis, which the doctor felt was severe enough to postpone my sophomore year of college.

"You will need to take six months off to have the surgery. We'll place rods in your back, and we'll wire your vertebrae from neck to pelvic bone." The doctor's explanation was more than confusing—it was devastating to think I would not go back to Winona on time to start my sophomore year.

I thought things were turning around for me. I was totally geared up for our Bible study at my apartment. If I didn't host this fall, who would? I kept wondering how this could be God's plan. I cried and prayed and cried some more. I went to church that weekend and asked the pastor if he could pray for me.

While I was relaying my prayer request to the pastor, a woman standing nearby overheard our conversation. When the pastor finished a personal prayer for me, this woman told me of a gel she believed could help heal my sore. By now, the sore was getting smaller, but there were only two weeks before school started. I needed to heal completely and then prove somehow to my doctors that my scoliosis surgery was unnecessary. I gladly accepted a tube of this ointment, desperate to plead my case that scoliosis would not jeopardize my health this school year.

I went home, put the gel on and around the sore … and miraculously, three days later, the sore was completely closed and healed! My next Rochester appointment rolled around, and Neil met me in the waiting room. I'm sure he was prepared to pep-talk me out of a depressed state, knowing the surgery would interfere with my sophomore year at Winona State.

"Hi, Neil!" I excitedly greeted him. "I'm so much better. My sore is gone, and I'm all healed up! Can you believe it?"

Confused by my response, he looked at me in disbelief and then said with a chuckle, "Oh, come on, Tasha. Good one."

"Well, I guess you'll just have to see for yourself," I fired back.

"Okay," Neil replied, still rather confused by my happy disposition. "It would be nice if I stand corrected … let's wheel to the gym. I would like to take a look for myself."

Neil transferred me onto a therapy mat. He took a long look at where my sore once was. When he wasn't able to find it, his jaw literally dropped and he called out, "Holy crap! You weren't kidding me, were you, Tasha? I'll go and get Dr. Christopherson so he can witness this for himself."

Lying there waiting, I thought, *Wow. God sure worked a good one here.* I guessed at what the doctor was going to say. As Dr. Christopherson entered, I thought back to the time when he delivered such harsh news at my care conference that I could hardly breathe. At that moment, I wouldn't have picked him as my primary-care doctor, since I was judging the message, not the messenger. But as I adjusted to the rotation these doctors kept—six weeks of hospital care and then six weeks of clinic work—I grew to trust and love this big man, clearly a football player in his youth and the father of a girl my same age. I appreciated all of the wonderful doctors at Rochester. Yet, at the end of rehabilitation, Dr. Christopherson was my personal pick for ongoing consultation. Today, I rarely call him, but when I do, he calls back as if I have a direct hotline to him. He knows I will not bother him unless his depth of expertise is truly needed. I love the mutual respect that steers our relationship to this day.

Dr. Christopherson took a close look, shook his head, also in a disbelieving manner, and stated, "Wow … that's just totally amazing, Tasha! I'm not sure how you did it, but your skin looks fabulous!"

I couldn't wait any longer to ask, "So this is obviously a good thing, right? And I don't have to have surgery now?"

Dr. Christopherson responded, "Well, Tasha, I guess not, but we'll need to have you make a three-month follow-up appointment so we can follow your progress. Hopefully you can maintain this good healthy skin."

"Okay, I can do that! I will see you guys then."

Within weeks, I was back in Winona, and with a new roommate. Brooke would continue as one of my caregivers, but she planned to move into an upstairs dorm room. A girl named Betsy from California would move into the apartment with me. My classes began, along with the Bible study, and Betsy and I got along immediately. My prayers had been answered on every level.

Although I seemed blessed with healthy skin and a great sophomore school start, some what-ifs began creeping their way into my thinking. What if my next checkup showed the same dreaded S curve? What if my spine actually worsened? What if I got halfway through my semester and had to quit? I didn't want that on my record. What if the surgery was inevitable?

I started to make some phone calls. I contacted other facilities that dealt with spinal-cord injuries and scoliosis. Despite Mayo's great staff and care, I felt compelled to seek a second opinion. My hope was to stay as far away from the operating table as possible.

One day I connected with a man who believed I should try avoiding surgery at all costs. He talked of cases like mine where patients ended up in chronic spine trouble after the scoliosis surgery. He gave me a phone number for Gillette Lifetime, a facility with information regarding alternatives to back surgery.

I called Gillette Lifetime, determined to find my surgery alternative. I made an appointment with Gillette and learned that I should bring my spine X-rays along with me.

As soon as I arrived at Gillette Lifetime, I met with one of the orthotic consultants. We discussed making a mold for a new back brace that could help straighten my spine and hopefully ward off surgery forever. Everything we discussed sounded great except for the fact that I was required to get a prescription from my previous doctor in order to authorize this brace. Once home, I called my Rochester doctor in hopes of getting the prescription for this brace without needing another X-ray. It hadn't been quite three months, but I knew Rochester would order an X-ray at that time to assess for scoliosis again and possibly foil my plan to try this back brace. My scheme was to get the prescription, give it to Gillette, get the mold for the new brace, wear the brace for the remainder of the school year, and totally skip my three-month checkup with Rochester Mayo.

My plan was stopped short. My Rochester doctor said he "wouldn't give me the prescription unless I came in for an updated X-ray." Since I had a forty-five-degree curve in my back, I was pretty certain that the doctor would never write up a prescription to treat it solely with a brace. Rochester intended to do surgery, so at this point all I could do was pray.

I had experienced a miracle three months earlier with my sore. So I set my hopes for the next miracle to show that my spine had not worsened—or perhaps it had improved since the last X-ray. I wanted to give the brace a try, but my medical team at Mayo would not agree if my scoliosis seemed a continued threat.

I asked people at church to pray for me. I felt incredibly hopeful that God would see the best way to handle this obstacle. I couldn't wait to prove the Mayo doctor wrong again!

My Rochester appointment came, and I wheeled myself to X-ray. After some waiting, the doctor walked through the doorway shaking his head. I knew that look. By the time he sat down to give me my results, I knew what he planned to say: "Tasha, I don't know how you keep doing this, but your back has somehow improved over the past three months."

I smiled, listened, and praised God the entire time the doctor explained: "The bend in your back—that forty-five-degree curve—it's now a fifteen-degree curve. This is great news!"

I was determined to acquire the prescription for a new back brace. I would do everything possible to prevent the word *scoliosis* from being stated in my presence ever again.

"Since the curve in my back is better now, can I get the authorization for the back brace? All I need is a prescription, so I can try to avoid the surgery."

The doctor agreed. Without hesitation, he wrote out the prescription for which my congregation and I had prayed.

Dad coined a new nickname for me: Moses. "Here's God again, parting the sea for Tasha—taking care of everything."

Chapter 19

Life, Love, and the Gingerbread Man

I CELEBRATED ALL the way home, and immediately called Gillette to inform them of the prescription. Quickly fitted for a mold to form the new brace, I thanked God for His grace in bringing miracles to my life. I was amazed and grateful to know that God was there for me—that He was real—and I finally believed in the relationship He'd been waiting to have with me all these years.

Within a few weeks, the brace was completed, I was fitted by the orthotic consultant at Gillette, and I discovered the advantages of wearing the brace every day. Essentially a torso wraparound brace, it actually helped me breathe easier. It was comfortable and contributed to my sense of security, and I prayed that it would also do its job on my scoliosis.

In a strange way, I felt totally equipped for school at this point. The brace represented my final tool for success. I had my Teno, allowing me to eat independently. My "pointer," or hand brace with the rubber end, enabled me to type all my written work. Another brace fit a pen or pencil inside a curved tube so I could write with my own weak hand on paper. And of course, I had my most versatile tools for mobility: my wheelchair and van. Armed with the best equipment, supported by reliable caregivers, I made a leap of confidence and began believing that I would succeed in my life, that I could achieve anything if I simply believed in myself.

About this time, I began hoping for a bigger miracle. I consciously acknowledged that God had chosen me as a subject for miracles. So wouldn't the ultimate miracle have me walking again? I couldn't possibly find complete happiness in my current state. If I asked God to guide me, and I listened to His plan, I was certain He would lead me out of this difficult life. I prayed for signs that my chair would become a thing of the past, and I asked God to help me make decisions that would lead in this direction.

As I worked to become as independent as possible, InterVarsity provided many opportunities for me to grow. Not only did I host our Bible study each week, still led by Ryan, but the worship group suddenly had an opening for a singer. I was one of about twenty girls auditioning for a soprano position at the worship-team tryout. Nervous about the competition, I gave it my best shot and ended up landing the one and only soprano position available.

I had never known so much joy and peace. This was the happiest I had been in a long time. God was truly working in my life. I just needed to sit up straight and pay attention to His every lead. When the sign appeared for His plan that would have me walk again, no matter how hard, how risky, I would be ready. With God on my side, there was nothing I couldn't overcome.

Armed with the tools for success, happy with my social activities, I still questioned my major. Brooke also sought to make an academic change that would lead her to a career as a special education teacher. Like Brooke, I asked various professors from that department if this might be the right fit for me, too. Obviously, I would have empathy for children who struggled because of disabilities. Though I declared special education as my major for a short time, the thought of managing energetic kids—hyper and loud like I had been as a child—frightened me into another career search.

I struggled with my major, not because of my grades, but because a career had to be chosen. Then I realized that I had never once asked God about this. I was trying to take the bull by the horns and figure this out on my own. After a semester of special-ed exploration, I finally asked God to show me what it was that I should do.

By now, I had a job on campus—my first since working at my parents' store. I assisted a communication studies professor, Dr. Herold, who was doing research for people with disabilities. He had a mild form of cerebral palsy, and his brother was a quadriplegic with a brain injury, so he had great insight into disability awareness. I decided to consult his expertise one day and see what he thought about my career plans, or lack of them.

"So, Dr. Herold, if I were to switch my major over to your department, what would I be able to do with that?"

He quickly fired back at me saying, "Well, Tasha, the question isn't what you can do with a Communication Studies major; the question is, what do you want to do with your life?"

I sadly responded, "That's exactly the problem, Dr. Herold. I don't know what I want to do. All I know is that I want to help people, somehow."

Matter-of-factly, Dr. Herold replied, "You're making this harder than it is, Tasha; you should be an inspirational speaker."

I sat there completely dumbfounded, trying to find a legitimate reason why I thought that Dr. Herold's idea was absolutely absurd. I hated public speaking. Since my accident, I had done a few speaking engagements, but I was nervous the whole time. My confidence level sat at zero percent. I loved performing in plays and singing in choir, even as a soloist. But my lines or the lyrics were my crutch. Public speaking required a completely different performance style. No script meant no confidence.

Yet at the same time, I experienced the biggest light bulb moment of my life. All my questions seemed answered by Dr. Herold's advice. Deep down I knew that this was exactly what I should do. Despite my fear of public speaking, I realized that the few times I had shared my story with others, listeners were mesmerized, focused, and had more questions for me than I was prepared to handle. I always felt needed and rewarded, that I indeed had something to share. I knew instinctively that my story had influence—that struggle brought inspiration.

The next semester, I switched to Communication Studies, and since that major required a minor, I decided to put my love for music to work. The fall of my junior year brought a brand new focus to my education and my life. The classes were incredibly challenging. Communication Studies entailed much more than public speaking. Since written language is one of the biggest components of communication, I, Tasha Schuh, with impaired hands and arms, would be required to write more than I ever thought possible. Ironic major for a paralyzed woman, but I was beginning to see that irony brought deeper meaning to my life. With God by my side, I thought, *Bring on the twenty-page papers! I am up for this challenge, too.*

At one busy point, I tried speeding up the process with voice-activated computer software, managed through headset and microphone. In theory, as I spoke into the microphone, words would magically appear in my computer document. Clearly, some glitches degraded the quality of this program.

For example, I spoke, "Despite an obsession in keeping up with the news, Americans are reading the daily newspaper less and less each year."

Translation: "This spike lob session in keeping up with anew, Americans arid in the daily newspaper lesson less easier."

I was playing the game "Mad Gab" before it was truly popular, and in the process wasting too much time on a voice-activated gizmo that desperately needed revision. I went back to literally typing one key at a time with my pointer. Despite the arduous process, I never once turned an assignment in late.

With my music minor, the greatest challenge came with the requirement to write my own music. Some students still composed with pencil and paper, but because of my disability, I had no choice but to compose on the computer. Again, the software was in place, but rather new and limiting. For instance, I had to type the word "flat" since the software symbol for this did not exist. Two years of private voice lessons also proved challenging, since I had to sing for at least an hour every day. My stamina improved over time, although memorizing seven songs per semester was grueling. At one point, I actually prepared three songs in English and the other four in a foreign language, and then reversed the order the following semester. The only other requirement for my music minor was that I had to take part in the women's choir—something I loved.

By my junior year, Ryan from Bible study had graduated and taken a full-time teaching position. We would keep in touch, but this changed the makeup of the InterVarsity Bible study. Melissa, a student I connected with in one of my classes, also attended the InterVarsity large group. We developed an instant friendship, sharing so many things, including a decision to try a local church together. I could only attend Abundant Life Church when I was in the Ellsworth area, every other weekend. It meant so much for me to find a local Winona service, especially with my best friend.

At first, I wasn't able to get into this small local church because it was not wheelchair-accessible. Melissa barely mentioned this to the pastor, and soon he was building an accessible ramp with the help of a few church members. The pastor and his wife were such loving, caring people; they hardly knew us, yet they went to all this trouble so I could attend service regularly. Once they heard I had an interest in music, they invited me to sing. In a short time, I began leading the worship team. Such good feelings came from this sense of belonging. I was so grateful for all the new people in my life who impacted me so positively.

Melissa and I soon found ourselves concerned for someone other than me in the Schuh family. The debate over selling or facing foreclosure with the grocery store rested on my parents' shoulders. Over time, the sale of the store became inevitable, as Mom and Dad had fallen behind in payments after my accident. On top of all the financial worries, my parents were not getting along at all. The biggest thing they ever shared, besides their children, was the store. Their marriage had revolved around the business for so long, they no longer knew how to relate to each other without it. They drifted apart and declared an official separation that, eventually, led to divorce.

Melissa and I spent many weekends in Ellsworth, knowing the truth but feeling nothing but love and concern from my parents. Despite their troubled marriage, they were each happy to see us, and Melissa felt like an adopted sister.

Melissa and I shared one other important thing—we both avoided dating like it was a communicable disease. I shared with her my promise to work on *me* first. She told me of her goal to focus only on college while at Winona. Ironically, Melissa would be asking me to be her bridesmaid not long after she left Winona. But for the moment, we vowed to shun the young men who casually asked us, "So, do you want to hang out sometime?"

This didn't, of course, stop us from noticing a cute guy, especially if he paid some attention to one of us.

"He watches you come into class every day," Melissa observed. "Notice how he makes a point to walk out just in time to say hi to you?"

I would shoot back at her. "You know this is leading nowhere. I'm not dating."

"I know. But I still think it's cool." I could read Melissa's mind: *Some guys just don't see your chair.* This made me think back to my very first week at Winona, my freshman year. "Did I ever tell you about Cable Guy?"

"Cable Guy?" Melissa replied in confusion.

Cable Guy proved to be a near miss.

"We're here to hook up the cable." At the start of our freshman year, Brooke and I had barely moved our belongings into the apartment when two cable repairmen came knocking at the door. The construction that made my place totally accessible meant the cable line had to be moved.

I looked as Brooke greeted two men at the door. I saw one guy about my dad's age and another about twenty years old.

"Come on in," Brooke said. After they had messed with the TV for a bit, we thanked them and they both left.

That night, we heard another knock. Brooke opened the door, and there stood the younger cable guy. "Hi. Can I talk to your roommate for a minute?"

Brooke was as confused as me, but she coaxed me out to the door. Her look said, *I don't know? Go see what he wants.*

"Can you come out in the hallway for a minute?" he asked.

"Sure," I said hesitantly. We closed the door behind us.

"The cable is working fine? Good. I just wondered if I could take you out sometime—we could do something together?"

"Oh ... okay ... sure," I lied. I did not see this coming.

As I told Melissa this story, I realized this was probably when I got the idea for my vow to ban dating. The whole time we were talking in the hallway, I was thinking, *No way. I'm not ready* ... yet here I was, exchanging phone numbers, saying I would call him to set up time to meet.

"Cool—I'll call you tomorrow," I told Cable Guy. But I didn't.

The next night, he called me. "You didn't call."

I was so afraid I'd hurt him. "I know. I'm sorry. I'm so busy. I will call you when things settle down." But I didn't.

Melissa took Cable Guy's side for a moment. "What were you afraid of? He sounds so sweet."

"You sound like Brooke. I didn't even have my driver's license at that point! Brooke offered to drive me, but I was so scared." Dating Jeremy from wheelchair camp was one thing. Although he was very able-bodied compared to me, he knew plenty about spinal-cord injuries, had been around girls in wheelchairs enough to know what came with the territory. Men without disabilities intimidated me.

"Tasha, you're so mean!" I heard this more than once as I turned down even more dates after Cable Guy. How could I explain to people that it wasn't Mean Tasha, it was Chicken Tasha who declined to go. I was scared to death of dating as a whole, and I definitely feared rejection.

Melissa listened as I reminisced about another near-miss. "This was so strange, but I admit, I was flattered by this guy. It happened when I was still in high school—my senior year—after my accident, but before I moved to Winona."

A guy from Red Wing—at this point a student at UW-Stout—called me one day to see if he could interview me. "Can I ask you questions about your accident ... for a class I'm taking? I read about you in the Minneapolis paper. Your story's amazing. I have to interview someone who has adapted to a disability. I thought of you right away. Would you mind sharing your story with me for my paper?"

Of course I would share. I was flattered and encouraged that people wanted to know about me ... that they were impressed with my story and that I seemed to be dealing with it in a positive way. I invited him over to my house. He stopped by after school the following afternoon, and we spent a couple of hours talking. He asked great questions, and I loved getting the facts out to people who were genuinely curious. I enjoyed the whole process.

What surprised me was the call I received the very next day.

"Tasha—yeah, it's me. Say, I have to talk with you again. Can I stop over? Would that be okay with you?"

"Sure. I have some homework, but if you come by after seven, that should be fine." He was nice. I didn't mind giving another hour or so to his research.

I have to say, this was the first time I did not see this coming at all.

As he sat across from me, looking much more serious than during his previous visit, I could not have predicted the words he was about to share.

"I've thought a lot about you, Tasha. Not just since yesterday, but ever since your story came out on TV and in the papers. I think I know my purpose in life."

Yikes! Where is this going?

"I moved home today. Out of my dorm. I want to be here if you need anything. I just want to be closer to you."

What?! Are you crazy?! I didn't actually state those words, but I am sure my face said it all.

"I'm sorry. But ..." I don't think I'd given him any impression that I was interested in anything more than his college paper. " ...I have a boyfriend." *Thank God for Jeremy,* I thought. "I'm not dating other people ... I can't spend time with you."

I heard that things were a little rocky for him for a while after meeting me. Oddly enough, I met a girl during my final year at Winona who asked me if I knew this guy from Red Wing. Thankfully, I did not say anything bad. Sure, when it happened, I admit, I was rather spooked by the whole thing. But by now, I had a different perspective on this and any situation where a guy felt an attraction to me. So my response was simply, "Sure, I remember him."

"Wow—what a small world. That's my fiancé!"

Whew! Good! He's moved on ... he's found love in his life. I'm happy for him, and relieved I never openly said a bad word about him.

As odd as it may sound, I truly believe this was God's way of saying, "Tasha, you know you are desirable, right? You should know you are attractive." This and Cable Guy, as well as countless other random meetings with men who wanted my phone number, were truly confidence-builders. I was not yet ready to be there for another person. It was best to postpone a relationship until I felt equipped to give as well as receive. But I thank

God for those little sparks that let me know I deserved happiness in a relationship one day.

I deliberately dodged most of the dates that came my way, as I stuck to my mantra: self-improvement before commitment. But Ryan ... Ryan was different.

By this time, I thought I would marry Ryan. Melissa and many others, including my mom, thought so too—it was just a matter of time. I truly believed there was only one person out there for me, and God would let me know when I was ready to focus on this relationship. Although things turned out much differently than I expected, deep down I always felt worthy of someone like Ryan—someone kind, with the same values, someone who unselfishly cared about me. That's what Ryan taught me.

When he moved off campus, working in his first job after college, Ryan weakened my vow. Maybe I was ready for prime-time dating after all. Maybe I should lighten up a bit on my own self-imposed rules. Although he had graduated, he lived near enough to drive to campus to see me. He knew about my vow, yet he worked to convince me that we could take our friendship to another level. I knew of other girls Ryan had dated. I have to admit, I felt a pang of jealousy every time I heard he was at the movies or out to dinner with so-and-so.

When I finally said, "Yes, let's try this," I was a nervous wreck. I not only felt completely out of practice since my last boyfriend was Jeremy, my senior year in high school, but I also ran the risk of losing a really good friend.

"What if this doesn't work?"

"Then it doesn't work. But let's try a couple dates and see what happens."

Of course I enjoyed Ryan's company; we had so much fun together. But my fear of commitment made me nervous. I literally watched the clock when I was with him, wishing the time away, wondering what might prevent us from becoming any more intimate than our friendship level already had us.

I used my vow as a crutch and told Ryan, "I just can't do this—even though I have done a lot of work on *me*, I'm too busy for this." A heavy school schedule, Bible-study leadership, my minor in music, a chaotic schedule of managing caregivers ... "This isn't a good time. And you do not have to wait for me."

Essentially I said to him, "Date others, please. Just keep coming back!" I was so drawn to him. We dated, stopped, dated again, broke it off again—this went on about three different times.

Every time I told Mom "It isn't the right time," she would give me her favorite line: "You're just too picky. Give it a chance."

Angie, on the other hand, had me completely figured out. "Here we go again, Tasha. I can hear you saying, 'You can't catch me, I'm the Gingerbread Man.'"

Despite this nickname, I *did* want to be caught—eventually. "I will marry Ryan," I told myself. "When the time is right."

Ryan stayed in my life—he even joined my church. And when *I* moved away, he still made every effort to stay in touch. However, I reminded him often he was a free man ... maybe one too many times.

Finally, just when I felt my life had room for a relationship with the man I cared about most, Ryan announced his engagement ... to someone else. Clearly, I'd had my chance.

My last two years in Winona proved that any struggle to gain independence was worth it. I accomplished my mission of living on my own, with caregivers coming in about five to six hours per day. These were Winona State University students who I hired, trained, managed, and paid myself. No agency played middleman.

Punching one key at a time, I finished my final Senior Capstone Project totaling forty pages—a huge feat for me—and I was the first to turn it in that semester. I completed my music minor by performing two of my twenty-eight memorized and rehearsed songs at a concert sponsored by the Winona State Music Department. Although Melissa had returned to her home in Chicago, she visited frequently in my last year on campus, and she remains one of my best friends to this day.

My Ellsworth weekends were filled with laughter and hugs from Isabel while she doted over her new sister. Angie had her second baby, Anna, at the end of April 2002, just weeks before I moved home for the summer with only one semester left in the fall at Winona. That summer, I spent time every week with my nieces to help Angie, but to also feed my kid fix.

Someone once told me, "You know, your parents did it right. They survived all this trauma the best they could. Maybe it was at the expense of their marriage and business. But they hung on to the things that matter most ... the love of their children, their faith in God, and the ability to find happiness in their own lives again." This was a compliment to both Mom and Dad, who certainly balanced it better than anyone else could. But what this person didn't understand was that Mom and Dad's divorce was inevitable. Accident at the Sheldon or not, grocery business kept or sold, my parents' marriage would end. I had come to this truth over time, and therefore I had no guilt. I could no longer blame myself for their breakup.

Love from family, despite Mom and Dad's marital status, has been a constant in my life. One thing I can count on is happy family time. My parents never abandoned that goal, which they continue from different households to this day.

Proud of my college accomplishments, I feared the next step. I had been reading about healing in the Bible. I never lost sight of the miracles God granted me over the course of my years at Winona State, and I fully expected Him to work the ultimate miracle—the one that would have me walking again. I thought for sure this would have happened before leaving my college town. God could see I needed to be healed before I moved on, before I continued my education at the next level. Life would be too hard if I had to face the same obstacles throughout the next step in my journey. In order for me to be truly happy, I needed to walk. God knew this, right?

I envisioned myself walking across the stage to receive my next degree. All the hard work would pay off, and I would be truly happy. It would be some time before I recognized how profoundly happy I had already become. Most of my accomplishments were the direct result of my accident. I was getting closer to God's message but still missing the most important point—my life was intensely rich *because* at one point I had taken a step backward.

As I graduated on my birthday, December 19, 2003, I reminded myself of all the doubters—all the people who believed I had bitten off more than I could chew. Friends and family came for the ceremony, and as I "walked," I was awarded magna cum laude for my high GPA. Graduating with honors was a tribute to God, and I was thankful I had chosen to listen to His plan. I felt pride in this.

There certainly were times when I was torn—when the selfishness of achievement almost overruled a Christian act. Like the night I heard a knock at my door while I struggled to study for a final.

I can ignore that, right? God will understand. I have so much to learn for this test! But I couldn't ignore the knock, and sure enough, it was a friend, depressed and needing an understanding ear. If I failed this test because I helped someone in need, so be it.

The next day, my professor forgot to place the exam in the resource center. I had hours to review while the center's volunteer tracked down the papers I needed.

Another time when I ducked out on a homework assignment in order to comfort a student, a horrible snowstorm hit. "No classes today! Stay home and catch up on your studies."

I am convinced that, because I worked in good faith, God was there for me to safeguard my success. My question now was, did He share my next goal—was I meant to walk again?

Chapter 20

More Amazing Grace

MY GREATEST GRADUATION gift came from the Winona State housing department: I did not have to leave my apartment! Frankly, moving back to Ellsworth in the middle of winter did not appeal to me. Job-hunting seemed premature—I still had so much to learn. Because I graduated in December, Winona State permitted me to stay in my campus housing through spring if I agreed to enroll in at least a one-credit course. My student caregivers were thankful for the ongoing work, since none of them had graduated that winter. So it was easy for me to stay on campus. I was extremely thankful for the extra time, and I spent those days at Winona researching other schools while praying that God would show me the next step.

After much soul-searching, the topic I felt most hungry to study was theology. This would complement my career in public speaking. I had hoped to do it through Living Word, a church in Brooklyn Park, Minnesota.

When the spring semester in Winona ended, I said my good-byes to so many campus students and staff who supported me along the way. I moved in with Mom and scheduled a visit to Maranatha College. As soon as I arrived on campus in Brooklyn Park, I knew instantly this was the next step in my journey.

This would be very different from Winona State. First of all, I would need to bring someone with me—someone who could double as a caregiver and academic note-taker. I would be driving to campus from Ellsworth, about seventy miles one way. I would spend one evening per week attending classes, totaling about four to five hours each time; turn around and drive back home; and then spend the rest of the week on independent study.

I can do this, I thought. After just one visit, I made it official. I enrolled at Maranatha for the fall of 2004. Although this would be very different from my first college experience, things seemed to be falling into place. For one thing, I resurrected a long-lost childhood friendship. Gretchen Stanford had temporarily moved to Hudson, Wisconsin, while her husband was deployed overseas for six months. He would be gone during my entire first quarter at Maranatha. Gretchen agreed to become my caregiver and note-taker for the start of my new program.

Despite the big changes from a traditional bachelor's degree, I loved my classes, and I did not have a problem keeping up. Since the coursework was so focused, in this case on theology, the workload seemed much more manageable. It did not hurt that this was a dream major for me, and I was incredibly motivated to succeed.

Early in November of my first year at Maranatha, I experienced what I thought would be a minor accident at home. I was done with my shower and preparing to be transferred into bed. As I slid out of the shower chair onto the sliding board with my caregivers on each side of me, skin underneath my right leg got pinched. I never felt it, of course. But one caregiver spotted it as soon as the transfer was complete. The spot on my leg looked like something Barb and Neil had warned me to avoid.

I had been lucky up to this point. At Winona, I had some minor blisters on my heels, but nothing that would threaten my overall health. This would be different.

I could not ignore what had happened, so I called the next day for a Mayo appointment. When my doctor saw the pinched spot on the underside of my leg, he showed less concern than I expected. "It's only a pinch—not an open wound. You can continue to be in your chair. Just have caregivers keep an eye on it for change. The mark will fade, but it'll take some time."

Relieved by his assessment, I left the doctor's office, headed home, and kept going about my everyday living.

Each day after my Mayo visit, my sore changed—for the worse. I made another trip to Rochester.

"Really, Tasha, I think you're doing fine. I agree, it looks darker. Appears to be worse. Keep the watchful eyes on it. But for now, I don't think you need to be out of your chair."

It was the week of Thanksgiving. I had come so far since that Thanksgiving Day when I awoke from my coma to give hope to my family. I returned to Rochester this time to hear that the sore had progressed to a large, deep, open wound.

"You'll need to be on bed rest until it's gone, Tasha."

This time, my doctor's orders set off my tears. Hadn't I been trying to avoid this? I cried, not only because I couldn't imagine my life back in bed, but because I believed I had done everything to avoid this as soon as the pinch had occurred.

How could I just lie in bed all day knowing I had so many things to do? For instance, I had a required interim class scheduled at Maranatha for the weekend, one of two required weekend seminars. I hated missing this and setting my academic schedule back.

When I arrived home, I followed doctor's orders and was transferred into bed immediately. For the first time since my accident year, I required round-the-clock care. I would need to be in bed indefinitely, until the sore closed up.

December 1, 2004: after a week in bed with no improvement, my doctor made an appointment with a wound doctor. The wound-care specialist declared that I "would have to be in the hospital for one month and probably be in bed for another three months."

Delivered the worst news possible, I felt powerless and defeated. I could only cry. I thought I had been doing everything right according to doctor's orders. Why was I hearing only bad news?

With a sore now the size of a softball and several layers deep, I didn't waste time informing every church that knew me, "Please start praying for me." I wiped my tears and truly felt the power of a miracle coming. This wound would heal a lot more quickly than the doctors had predicted.

I picked a date for my discharge: "There's no way I am going to spend Christmas in the hospital."

As soon as I could after being admitted, I phoned one of my professors at Maranatha. "I won't be able to make the weekend course—can I fulfill this requirement in another way?"

He told me not to worry, that I could make it up by attending a different weekend seminar. This made me feel a whole lot better. The stress was beginning to lift. I could focus all my energy on praying for my skin to heal quickly.

The next few weeks brought multiple surgeries in which the sore was essentially stitched together. I turned twenty-four in the hospital—not exactly my favorite way to spend a birthday, but I had done it before. As long as my goal to be home by Christmas was not completely out of the question, I could be grateful for my progress so far.

"You're healing faster than we ever expected, Tasha." My doctor delivered the good news one morning on rounds. "I think you're going to get your wish."

I was miraculously discharged on December 23. I had to be driven home in an ambulance since I couldn't sit up in my wheelchair long enough to drive anywhere. Out of the twenty-three days I spent in the hospital, I sat up in my chair only once, for fifteen minutes … the day before my release. Once home, I could be up four times per day, fifteen minutes at a time. I would spend those fifteen-minute increments eating and checking my e-mail. I had a lot of company during my time in bed, but I also spent a great deal of time praying, meditating, thinking, and focusing on my skin healing. Eventually, the intervals increased to thirty minutes, and then later, forty-five minutes, and so on.

By necessity, I would miss two weeks of the start of my new semester. I asked Maranatha if I could have someone sit in for me. Gretchen had moved back to Connecticut, where her husband was re-stationed with the navy. So my sister Angie agreed to attend classes and take notes for me. Angie was a perfect study partner since she was an excellent student herself—and we just had fun together, spending time as sisters again.

Once I was given the okay to return to school, we invented a few other tricks to keep the pressure off the troubled spot. For instance, I reclined my chair as far back as it allowed to simulate my position in bed. To avoid sitting on my sore during the commute, my sister would drive me to and from college so I could be reclined all the way there and back. An odd way to ride in the back of a van, but the reclining position took almost all of the pressure off of the spot where my sore had been and put it indirectly on my tailbone instead. I continued strict bed rest six days a week, adding increments of time at a very slow pace. My schedule at Maranatha granted me only one day per week to be up for an extended period.

By April, my life was back to normal—*my* normal, that is. No bed rest, no reclining tricks; I could drive without restrictions, and my Maranatha schedule seemed surprisingly manageable through it all.

While flat on my back all those months, I had time to think about life after college. I wanted to start a job, at least part-time. Within a week, my pastor at Abundant Life announced they were opening up three staff positions at the church. When I inquired about this, my pastor explained that these positions were for executive leaders—about twenty hours a week.

"There are a few other positions as well ... accounting, service coordinator ..." Accounting—yikes! Mom and Angie would be great at this, but bookkeeping was not my strength.

"Tell me about the service-coordinator job ..."

This employee would guarantee that Sunday morning services were done with excellence, working on publications, updating the church website—essentially using communication skills to coordinate Sunday events. This was it! This job was the right fit for me. I hoped that I wasn't biting off too much. I believed this was my chance to use the skills of my communications major, plus my theology knowledge gained at Maranatha, to support our church and its members.

I interviewed, and within about a week, my pastor invited me back to talk with him. "The job is yours." I was so excited! I wondered why he hadn't just told me this on the phone.

"But I have to tell you," he went on, "we unfortunately do not have the resources to offer this as a paid position."

Funny, this did not feel like a letdown to me. I was honored and humbled at the same time. At twenty-five years old, I would be a part of the Abundant Life leadership team and could now help make the top decisions for our Sunday services, as well as the entire church. In one moment, I felt inadequate and nervous because of my age and the fact that I was relatively new as a committed Christian. I wasn't exactly qualified to have a key role in the church's decision-making—I would be gaining those qualifications on the job. Yet after a month or so, I got over any feelings of inadequacy because I truly loved my role and the duties I had to perform.

Around the same time, Angie interviewed with our pastor at Abundant Life, and she accepted the accounting job. This meant we were now on the same team, working together with the pastor to help with any church responsibilities. My sister was extremely qualified for her new job. With a new leadership team now in place, I grew in confidence, developed deep friendships with the other staff members, and thanked God for this wonderful unpaid job.

In April of 2005, Angie announced her pregnancy with my youngest niece, Ella. I would be taking a course in Greek that upcoming fall, and as I suspected, Angie declined to be my note-taker and care provider on those evening trips to Maranatha.

My pastor's wife, Susan Humphrey, was looking for work at the time and gladly accepted my job offer. She was a tremendous help as I worked through Greek as well as my other classes.

I feared the Greek language class the most, but ironically my classmates soon wanted to know my secret. I had a photographic memory. I could study a page, close my eyes, and rattle off everything I had just viewed. Even though I had this edge, the language class was definitely the most challenging to me. I finally understood the cliché, "It's all Greek to me."

My time at Maranatha and Living Word were ending soon. I would be graduating and walking for a diploma for the third time ... but not walking.

Should I be disappointed that the miracle I prayed for did not occur? Should I be mad at God for making me roll across another stage to receive my document of success from a sitting position?

I spent those final weeks before graduation considering all of this. I admitted to myself that Maranatha became my college choice because of its stand on miracles, because of its policy of prayer and the power to heal. I wanted to literally *walk*, and I thought my faithful time and study at Maranatha would bring this.

Then I saw them—all the miracles. God's grace had come to me time after time in my short run at Maranatha. I just needed to pay attention. I needed to quit being fixated on my personal desire to walk so I could notice what really mattered in my life. I had just racked up a pile of miracles strong enough to rattle an atheist.

Gretchen suddenly appearing after all those years, with time and skills to get me started … Angie, my guardian angel, who covered class notes like my clone while I was flat on my back for weeks … friends, family, even strangers who prayed diligently while Mayo, absolutely stumped, discharged me before Christmas … my ability to focus on my studies when I could have wasted away in bed, feeling sorry for myself … and, of course, my pastor's wife coming to my rescue after Angie had done so much for me already. The miracle of this graduation, this second bachelor's degree, in theology, completed on time, in the name of faith, love, and patience, could not be denied.

I continue to read accounts of healing in the Bible. They inspire me and remind me that a miracle still could happen. But every year I grow stronger in my belief that my life is better not in spite of, but because I live it without the use of my limbs.

Chapter 21

There's No Place Like Home

SO OFTEN I'VE been reminded of Dorothy's poignant line in *The Wizard of Oz* ... when getting hooked up to my first traction bed, while coming out of the coma, at the Ronald McDonald House crowded with sadness, when I felt close to overstaying my welcome at the Carrs', when Mom announced we were selling my childhood home, during the hospital stay that interrupted my college studies ... I envisioned Dorothy holding Toto, stating earnestly, "There's no place like home."

With Maranatha coming to an end, Mom and I would be spending more time together—at home. We would be like college roommates sharing the same space. Yet we soon found that having two sets of friends and two different lifestyles meant we weren't the most compatible roomies. We both began to feel a very large house closing in on us. The thick walls became thin when Mom was trying to sleep and I had friends up late, laughing, ordering pizza, or watching a movie with the TV volume up high. I didn't want my friends to have chores after I entertained, but why should Mom wake up to a dirty kitchen the next morning?

"Leave it, Mom. I'll have one of my caregivers clean when she comes in later today."

But this would not fly with my mom. She was meticulous and driven. If she saw a mess, she got rid of it. "It's no big deal—I can have this done before anyone comes." But it *was* a big deal. I sensed her frustration, yet I couldn't jump up and clean for myself. I was reminded of my limitations again. This was not good for either of us.

I tried to contain my living space to just my bedroom, but I had acquired enough stuff to furnish my own apartment. Paperwork, collectibles, more paintings than wall space, my computer and accessories, two dressers, a bed—my clutter was out of control, and my clothes were inconveniently strewn throughout three different closets.

Meanwhile, my speaking career was launched! Sue, the wonderfully supportive pastor's wife who had helped me in my last stretch at Maranatha, drove with me one day while I began to think out loud.

"So, I want to speak—that's all I want to do for a career. This is definitely my purpose. But how? I'm an inspirational speaker! I'm ready for the job! But how do I get the word out to listeners?"

Sue's business sense kicked in. Without hesitation, she suggested, "Well, you could start by putting together some flyers." She showed me how to find the church addresses within a hundred-mile radius of Ellsworth. In no time, I'd mailed brochures to 250 churches and 250 schools. (Prisons—providing my favorite audiences, because I'm welcomed like a rock star—came later.) Then I waited ... but not for long.

I started getting phone calls, and the phone has never stopped ringing. Once again, I asked, and God opened doors. After those initial 500 flyers, my career evolved entirely out of word of mouth. I've never done any cold calls to solicit more events or venues. I have not hired an expensive marketing agent. Frankly, these ideas were a part of the original plan, but I've never had time to pursue them. I'm too busy!

After my initial two or three months in business, I no longer heard, "Say, I got your flyer, and ..." Instead, callers said, "I heard you speak! You have to come to my church, school, event ..." In recent years, I've also heard, "I saw your website—you have to come to my business."

People will ask, "What do you do to rejuvenate after the draining task of public speaking? It must be exhausting." Actually, speaking rejuvenates me. Because it is my passion and my purpose, a gig in front of many listeners can jolt me out of a bad day faster than any recreational therapy. In truth, the prep work is the work. I probably over-prepare, but I work best when I can research my topic, tweak my delivery to the given audience, add technology when possible and relevant, and then practice my delivery and timing. I don't just tell my story—I want the audience and event to drive the topic. Consequently, I have a long list of presentations I'm able to customize to each scheduled booking.

- *My Faith Story*: discovering my Powerful Partner in life
- *Media's Influence*: identifying modern media's misrepresentations of disabled people and dispelling the myths
- *The Power of a Positive Attitude*: the theme of perseverance at every roadblock
- *Motivation and Inspiration*: to those who feel all alone in their struggle
- *Inspiration and Hope*: understanding that you can make a difference
- *Bullying and Harassment Must Stop*: a new topic for schools in a society where cyber-bullying makes cruelty to peers far too easy

My favorite? When I'm given a topic and trusted to create a speech.

My entire business was launched from a computer in my mom's home. I had no office, no staff. This challenged Mom and me even more as roommates, since my work was not the typical eight-to-four-p.m. job.

Soon Mom felt grounded in her own home. Feeling obligated to go to her bedroom or leave the house at times to accommodate my business or social schedule, Mom tried so hard to give me privacy when I had guests.

I attempted to schedule visitors only when she had something else to do. But that felt a little businesslike for her as well. I wanted spontaneity—I wanted flexibility for friends or potential clients to stop in on the spur of the moment. I had just celebrated my twenty-sixth birthday, yet I felt I was regressing in my independence.

I called my sister with my frustrations at an all-time high.

"Sorry, Angie, I just need to vent. I love Mom. But this is so hard. I hate to complain—how can I, when I think of all she's done for me? But this is not working."

Angie surprised me with the most unexpected reply. She didn't say,

"You don't have a choice—deal with it." She didn't take Mom's side, "I couldn't live with you either." She simply stated, "Build a house. Get your own place. Why do you need to live with Mom? Why do you need to live with anyone?"

My first reaction was, "What? That's a ridiculous idea." Why would I build a house? I'll just wait until Mr. Right comes along. Building a home is not something you do alone.

"I'll do what you did," I told Angie. "I'll wait until I'm married to build my own home."

But the idea would not leave me. I obsessed over Angie's suggestion. And Dad liked the idea too. "Why not? Tasha, you can do anything you put your mind to. You've proven it over and over again. If you want to build a house, I believe you can do it."

Surprisingly, I couldn't find any reason to completely rule it out. The list of advantages of living alone got longer and longer. The only disadvantage: I was extremely nervous about planning the whole thing.

I spent spring break in Arizona that year, where I would soak up some sun and think more about the building idea. I gained such clarity on the whole topic. My anxiety lifted, so I knew it was time to tell Mom.

When I got back from Arizona, Mom reacted as I thought she would. She first offered to house-hunt herself. *She* would leave, and I could have our custom-built home to myself. But there were too many features built for a quad patient, and not for an active business woman who just happened to employ a team of caregivers. Even an extensive remodel would not make sense. Mom could not support my decision. I set out to change her point of view.

"I know this house was designed with me in mind. If we could remodel ... so we each had our own place ... but we both know that can't happen. We cannot convert this beautiful home into a duplex. And even if you moved, I'd spend a lot of money on changes that wouldn't result in the best outcome, anyway."

I tried another angle.

"I have no idea if and when I'll get married. I can't count on that. But I can count on myself, and the people I hire as caregivers."

Okay, that point always made Mom sad and more worried. Better try a different approach.

"We need our own space. We both deserve it. Yes, you too … to have your own house the way you want it. You have waited your whole life to be independent. You have always taken care of others. This is your house, and you should live in it the way you want."

Enough said. Now I had another thing to pray for … Mom's understanding and acceptance.

At first, my vision of my own home was small, similar to that of a townhome. But my hopes to entertain, not only with friends but with Angie, Ryan, and their families, made me rethink this. By now, Ryan and Nikki's two boys, Cameron and Connor, were almost big enough to spend time with Auntie Tasha too, like Isabel and Anna were already doing. Ella, Angie's youngest, wasn't far behind. I needed a builder who could tackle the accessibility needs as well as make room for my extended family. In addition, my career was branching out, which placed me more and more on the computer, working from home. A large office was a must.

Al Hines, the builder who designed my parents' home after my accident, gave me the name of a draftsman who could likely bring all my ideas together. The draftsman came over, and we made some progress, but we struggled with the design. I wanted two bedrooms, two-and-a-half bathrooms, an office, a living room, an open kitchen, and a laundry room. The draftsman did not intend to give up, but he clearly needed some insight to squeeze all of this living space into one floor. Suddenly, I thought of someone who could help.

My friend Chad had endured almost the same level of injury as me in a car crash one year after my accident. He worked as an engineer and had visited my mom's house a few years back with hopes of building his own home.

"Come and see my house, Tasha." I was so glad I did. Chad had a perfect layout that I loved instantly.

"Can I steal part of the floor plan—just the middle section—for my house?" Chad consented. I came home, shared ideas with my draftsman, and within days he had my house officially underway.

Mom was upset with much of my plan. She worried so. Even as

I finalized a good floor plan and secured Al Hines as my builder, she questioned how I would manage everything that comes with being a homeowner. She argued some valid points. For instance, living with Mom meant my meals and laundry were covered. She feared that I would need even more caregivers—that I was not prepared for the financial strain.

I, on the other hand, worried very little. I had so much peace about the transition. I truly believed I could deal with these issues as they came along.

I found a beautiful one-acre piece of land in the country—a hillside lot in a new development about a mile out of Ellsworth. We broke ground on June 6, 2007. That's when Mom's concerns became my reality. I was suddenly overwhelmed by all the decisions that came with the building process.

My second mom, Jan O'Meara, who provided design direction for our Piety Street home and visited me multiple times while I lived in Rochester, came to my rescue in more ways than one. My lot fell under some strict development rules. The siding, the shingles, the trim—everything outside had color specifications to ensure an aesthetically pleasing neighborhood where homes blended into the landscape beautifully. Once Jan helped me pick out the exterior colors, I eagerly held on to her for the interior designs too. Everything from appliances to doorknobs to dramatic lighting and warm colorful walls came through Jan's creative mind's eye. I don't know if I will ever be able to thank Jan O'Meara enough for her creativity, her patient support, and her enduring friendship.

Outside of work and home, my social life seemed to center around an endless list of weddings that year. I intended to look my best for these special events, so I set a goal to lose some weight. I was excited for the change—a smaller dress size, self-control with my appetite … until I experienced some adverse side effects. In particular, I was blacking out after every shower. Plus, I developed an annoying cough that really bothered me in the mornings and at night. My caregivers encouraged me to go to the doctor, but I refused. Weight loss was not on my current health chart.

Weeks into the annoying cough, I decided to see a local Ellsworth Clinic doctor before Angie would have to revert back to her Heimlich maneuver days of coughing me. Mom and Anna accompanied me to the appointment in plenty of time to still have lunch at the Pierce County Fair. The doctor ordered blood work to see if an infection might explain the mysterious cough and fainting spells. The lab tech drew blood from my feet—the usual source, since the veins in my arms were virtually invisible from previous pokes. I waited in an examination room for the results.

My doctor returned from the blood lab looking especially pale himself. He stated that the nurse needed to draw blood from my hand also because something registered wrong. Somehow they managed to take blood from my hand, and I waited again for results.

This time when the doctor returned, his first question was, "What hospital would you like to go to? I have to recommend that they admit you immediately."

Hospital? I was in shock. What was he talking about?

"Both tests show that your hemoglobin level is 5.3. Normal levels are between 11 and 15. This is the hemoglobin of a very sick person," I was told.

Mom called Angie. "Come and pick up Anna. Tasha's going to the Red Wing Hospital."

All right, I thought. *I'll be given blood transfusions as an outpatient, sitting in my wheelchair. That can't take more than a couple of hours. I'll get back to the fairgrounds for supper. I can handle this.*

But when I arrived at the hospital, I learned that I was being admitted for the weekend. I was so upset. I can usually cover, but this time everyone knew—I thought this was outrageous.

"I'm not sick. A little run down, maybe. It must be the dieting. I don't need to spend the entire weekend here and miss the fair."

I was so worked up that I was missing the fair! I cried to the point of sobbing aloud. Looking back, I now understand the alarming nature of this low hemoglobin. But at the time, I couldn't fathom how dangerous this was, and that I could have died if the source wasn't found.

Once I settled down, I received four bags of blood. A doctor explained that I clearly was bleeding internally. "We have to get to the bottom of this so we can stop the bleeding. Transfusions are Band-Aids that won't make the real problem go away. We're going to have to run some tests."

My skin was gray—the entire staff commented on it. "Did this come on quickly today, this poor coloring?" Mom and I both felt it must have been gradual—so gradual that the caregivers didn't notice either. With transfusions now going, my complexion changed on the spot, as if I were getting an instant spray-on tan.

Monday morning, we decided to make our way to Mayo for more tests. By Monday afternoon, those tests came back. One doctor explained, "We've narrowed things down to a couple of diseases."

I don't believe this, I kept telling myself. *They are way off this time. I don't have enough symptoms to be as sick as they think I am.*

While we waited for even more conclusive proof, one doctor casually asked, "Do you take ibuprofen at all?"

Curious, I answered, "Yes, I do."

With an unspoken reaction from him that I'll never forget, I knew that my reply was the missing piece to the puzzle. "How much?" he asked. "How often?"

I explained that I had been taking ibuprofen every other night for about six months. "It helps me sleep."

"Right before bed? On an empty stomach?"

"Yes. Every other night, after I shower." Apparently, when I would lie down, the medication was settling into one spot and literally eating ulcers into my colon.

I agreed to stop taking ibuprofen altogether. I haven't had any problems with my hemoglobin level since. I learned so much from that experience—mostly that I needed to be an open book about whatever I ingested. I would not take a chance to self-prescribe even a casual, seemingly safe medication ever again.

With summer nearing its end, I would take frequent drives to view the progress on my house. I got more and more excited for moving day, scheduled for September 27, 2007. When this date finally came, Stevie drove to Piety Street with his enclosed trailer to haul most of my belongings. Mom, Dad, and fifteen close friends and family members volunteered to load and unload my stuff. As things poured into my new house, I struggled with the job of directing everyone. Finding a place for every item overwhelmed me. I was thankful there was no trapdoor to maneuver around.

At the end of the day, I sat in utter awe. Feelings of pride and fear collided with nervousness and amazement. I was about to spend the first night in my own home.

It took some time to adjust to the quiet noise of country living on top of a very windy, open hill. But once I got used to it, I slept well in my big house. The pride and amazement quickly smothered any fears.

Mom's concerns that I would require more support from caregivers proved inaccurate. The caregivers I had employed up to that point stuck with me; they made a few adjustments but required no extra hours to complete the tasks they were hired to do. I've had a great team, which changes from time to time, who have accepted my desire for more methods of independence. My most recent skill has been my ability to do my midday cath cares unassisted, entirely without a caregiver in the house. I still find the need for help each day, about four to five hours—fewer than during college life or even when I roomed with Mom. By doing suppers on my own, and multitasking two caregivers to maximize efficiency, I've added considerably to my hours of independent living.

Certain high-tech upgrades on the house help maintain my independence. For instance, I had an automatic door system installed. This allows me to get in and out of my home by pressing a button that swings my entry door open to my garage. The remote control for this feature attaches to my wheelchair armrest via Velcro so it is always within my rather limited reach. Consequently, I don't need anyone to turn doorknobs for me, and I never have to worry about placing keys in precise keyholes. This provides excellent security for me while still giving me freedom to come and go as I please, since I can enter my van and use my garage door opener all without assistance. I may need my initial morning caregivers to get me ready for the day. But once those tasks are behind me, the caregivers can leave and I am prepared to come and go as needed. For example, I can go get an oil change on my own, go to a speaking engagement by myself, attend church by myself, or go to a doctor's appointment alone.

With my newfound freedom, I felt bold enough to take my first recreational drive into the Cities on my own. This was a big learning curve—I wasn't always brave enough to venture out alone in this way. Although I had been to both Minneapolis and St. Paul many times before, it was always with a companion. I feared city driving by myself. I didn't want to get lost, but it was time to get more daring.

I called Darcy Pohland to update her on my new home and to see if she could find time to hang out with me for a night. I suppose you could say I wanted to show off—prove to her that I was inspired by her daring spirit. I needed to go out and about with someone who would truly know what a leap of independence this was for me.

Darcy's life was extremely busy with her job at WCCO, but I called anyway. Like always, Darcy heard my message and returned my call as soon as she could.

"So good to hear from you, Tasha! How are things?"

I caught her up on my recent changes. She told me that she hated days off. "I love a busy work schedule. But if you can join me, I'll take some time off. Let's do something fun."

Darcy loved theater and sports. She often covered the Vikings, Gophers, Twins, and Timberwolves games. But this time she thought we should try the theater.

"Let's see what's playing at the Guthrie." The Guthrie Theater in Minneapolis is arguably one of the most impressive theaters in the Midwest—perhaps in the entire country. I was so excited to see anything there, but Darcy knew the musical *1776* was playing. She continued to plan: "I'll get two tickets and meet you there—let's say, early enough so we can have dinner before the performance."

"Two tickets—plus yours, you mean."

"No, Tasha, I mean two tickets total. Come on! You can do this without a caregiver. Have faith. I will meet you near the parking ramp. You'll see—that extra person you usually bring along is not a necessity."

There was no turning back now. I had to follow through with this self-inflicted challenge. I would map out the directions, memorize my route, and meet Darcy without a glitch—or so I prayed.

Street by street, I memorized the directions. Of course, when I left home it was still daylight. I was already worrying about my ride home after dark. But as soon as I arrived at the Guthrie and saw Darcy waiting patiently in her wheelchair outside on the sidewalk, my worries of driving home completely faded. I parked in a nearby lot, and as I made my way toward Darcy, I soon felt underdressed and plain-Jane in her presence. She wore a stunning green dress, and her glamorous look made me wish I had asked her on the phone what the evening dress code was.

"Darcy, you look beautiful! Here I am in my jeans. Will they even let me in tonight?"

"Tasha, you look gorgeous, as always. Come on—this show is supposed to be fabulous."

I will never forget this beautiful, sunny day when we found outside seating at a trendy cafe called Spoon River. Once in the theater, Darcy and I wheeled into our spots and sat back to take in this talent-filled production of spectacle and history. Only a few years later, I would sit in that very spot for one of the saddest events of my life. But Darcy would not be in her chair next to me.

At the end of the night, Darcy agreed that our next meeting would take place just outside of Ellsworth—a visit to my new home once I was settled in. My final request of the night: "Darcy, can you verify my directions to get back to I-94? I just want to drive out of the Cities without any problems."

She told me the turns to take to get onto my exit, but within a block or two, I second-guessed myself and was completely lost. My eyes welled up with tears. I tried calling Darcy, but she didn't answer. Thankfully, I had OnStar in my van. My initial installation gave me one free service call for directions. But in order to hit the button for the OnStar service, I had to pull off the road into a gas station parking lot. Unlike most drivers, I can't take my hand off the steering wheel to press a button. Suddenly I wished I had a second set of hands.

Just my luck, the parking lot of this particular gas station was teeming with fifteen to twenty men, all covered with tattoos, looking ready to add a little drama to my night. I wasn't about to ask any one of them for directions. I just hoped and prayed they didn't interrupt my need to talk to an OnStar rep. I hit the button and veered back into traffic. I wasn't compelled to find out if my wheelchair would trigger the best or the worst in these characters.

Like an actress in a cheesy commercial, I sounded so happy to hear that OnStar rep's voice! "Oh, thank you for being there! I'm lost. I need to get back onto east I-94. Can you help me?" After the guy calmed me down, I found out that I was literally a block away from I-94.

"Oh, thank you, thank you, thank you! I don't have to die tonight."

"No, Miss Schuh. Drive safely. Happy to help." The rep asked me if there was anything else I needed. I blessed him three more times, and then finally let him disconnect.

As soon as I got back home, I called Darcy.

"I almost died on the streets of Minneapolis tonight! You could have reported my story as breaking news on Channel 4 tomorrow morning!"

She laughed and told me how proud she was of me. "I've lived in the Twin Cities most of my life. I've asked many tattooed guys for directions. I think you would have been fine. You're learning, girl! See—you can do these things! If OnStar makes you feel more secure, what the heck. Just don't be afraid to do what you want, to do what every other person has a right to do, with or without a wheelchair."

I heeded Darcy's advice, and didn't waste any time purchasing my next electronic gadget—a GPS for my van.

When she came to visit a month or two later, we talked on my new deck, ordered takeout food, and solved problems ranging from men to cats. Darcy and I coincidentally owned two cats each. A few months back, I added Jewel and Lily to my household. As soon as Darcy answered questions regarding my feline friends, the conversation suddenly switched to another of my constant concerns. I was considering an attempt at the whole dating scene again. I had so many great friends in wheelchairs who were men. But Darcy was my only girlfriend in a chair who could share my curiosity about dating.

This would be the last time I would meet with Darcy. Had I known, would I have done anything differently? Said anything profound and memorable? Maybe, maybe not. I'm just grateful that, as she left, I thanked her for her friendship and shared with her how much the evening meant to me.

Darcy Pohland tragically lost her life in the spring of 2010 because of a bleeding ulcer. The very thing that baffled the doctors when my low hemoglobin numbers were discovered took Darcy from us far too early. Darcy had become one of my favorite people—a mentor and dear friend. She inspired so many by choosing to be a field reporter rather than an anchor, pursuing stories that ranged from grueling NFL Vikings tryout camps to the tragic losses of Interstate 35's bridge collapse. Darcy feared no one and traveled everywhere. Dragging a camera crew with her, she visited me four times to report on my accident as well as my progress. As a young college student, wheeling off to a strange campus, I felt Darcy's expectations going with me to Winona State University. As we kept in close contact over the years, she inspired achievement within me—a gift of confidence that cannot be measured. My family knows how devastated I felt when Darcy passed away at the age of forty-eight. During her funeral, I sat in the Guthrie Theatre alone, in the very spot I wheeled to on the night of *1776*. I just hope she knows how much I treasured her friendship and how her gift of time and attention changed me forever. Darcy Pohland was my hero, and I miss her more than words can express.

Chapter 22

The Trapdoor of Opportunity

I AM WRITING this final chapter from my hospital room on the seventh floor of Gillette's adult unit, Regions Hospital, St. Paul, Minnesota. While finishing this memoir over the past year, I have been nursing a skin wound that finally required surgery and complete medical supervision. My prognosis is good, but I am only halfway through my bed rest. Thankfully, this is a rare interruption to my otherwise healthy, full life. I've gone years with nothing but routine physicals. My doctors glow with pride as they give me a perfect report at my annual checkup. Yet these occasional setbacks come with the territory of spinal-cord injury. This time, I continue to pray for a full recovery—and for patience to lie here with a grateful heart since, once again, I am blessed with support that astounds me.

Healing starts with my family. If love alone could heal a wound, I wouldn't have to come to the hospital. Mom, Dad, Ryan, Angie, their families, aunts, uncles, cousins, and friends can be counted on for love, attention, and prayer support. I am blessed with calls, visits, e-mails, and texts. My iPhone and iPad are close to my face, since they are duct-taped to my hospital rolling table. As I lie flat in an automated sand bed designed to keep all pressure off the surgical spot, my right arm is strong enough to get one knuckle within reach of either screen. I can reply with a quick "thank you" to those who send messages of encouragement.

This time, my stay began right around Easter. While I dreaded spending this holiday in the hospital, Mom made sure I had plenty of company—and food—to know that it was indeed a special day. Angie's French-silk pie complemented all the high-protein nutrition that is prescribed for quick healing. Of course, one of the best changes with time is that my family is my *family*—not one of them works as a caregiver any longer. They help me heal in a different way. Spending quality time together as independent adults is what family should do at this point in life. Sure, any one of them would help me out in an emergency, I know that. And they certainly shared added support during my hospital stay. But keeping family off the regular caregiver personnel list is so important to me. There is a different dynamic that develops when one is too dependent upon a family member, so I am grateful that I have worked away from that level of need.

Speaking of caregivers, my healing continues thanks to my excellent care. Anyone with health issues will tell you that you cannot put a price on smart and perceptive medical attention. My hospital care has been both those things and then some. In addition, my personal caregivers drive almost an hour to St. Paul to help me on days with special requests. I know I could have the hospital staff do all of my cares if needed. But I am aware of the financial setback my absence from home creates for caregivers who rely on me for steady employment. I do not want to lose an excellent employee because of a hospital stay. And of course, there is the comfort that accompanies an experienced caregiver who can perform every duty without direction. She might ask for advice out of kindness, but she knows exactly what she's doing. Why train a nurse only to find that she won't have another shift for three more days ... or discover that she applied my makeup like the 1980s cosmetic expert I met right after my accident? Communication is simplified and stress is minimized when a hospital allows your personal caregivers to add to their facility's quality treatment.

There is one change that I adapted to throughout the past year of trying to heal and trying to avoid this very hospital stay: I now use a Hoyer lift for bed and chair transfers. I hope to eventually go back to the simplicity of a sliding board, but after two serious wounds because of transfer impact on my skin, I am resigned to the Hoyer for safety reasons. Of course, my shower chair is the biggest culprit, since I am much more vulnerable when transfers involve unclothed skin. As far as I'm concerned, the Hoyer lift has a melodramatic factor I'd rather do without.

Imagine all six-foot-two of me dangling from a giant hammock, as a caregiver gently hoists me over the bed and then sets me down in my wheelchair, only to have the entire hammock tugged and pulled from underneath me. It's safe, and it works. However, during this recent recovery from surgery when I am only permitted to be in my chair four times a day, twenty minutes at a time, the multiple transfers exhaust me because I've been completely flat on my back the past three weeks. Some patients might say, "It's pointless. I'll just stay in my bed until I get full clearance to be in my chair twelve-plus hours per day." But that's not me. If I'm allowed twenty minutes, I'm going to take twenty minutes. Of course, twelve hours per day in my chair is not me either. I prefer the clearance of unlimited hours since some of my busiest days are more like eighteen hours out of bed. In my chair, I feel the closest to upright that I can be. I'm not passing that up.

I wish I could say this will be my last medical incident—that I will prevent this type of event from happening again. But I can't. As hard as we try to avoid such wounds, the potential for pressure sores exists. I could let this depress me. I could say "Woe is me ... no one knows what it's like to live with the fear of recurrence." Or I could face the treatment with a positive attitude, find goodness in the people who care for me, and try my best to get out of here ahead of schedule.

Every hospital stay reminds me that my condition brings out the best in others. Part of my purpose in life is to give, but the other part is to receive. My needs as a quadriplegic prove that when we are vulnerable, when we truly depend on others—and we all will—most people rise to the occasion and find a deep, compassionate capacity to help. This may not be realized if human suffering is not placed directly in one's path. Sure, I do everything to avoid setbacks. I don't relish being taken care of. But I recognize God's grace in action when I bring the best out of people who have time and talents to support me.

Maybe because of this occasional setback, I cherish the times in my life when I *give* to others. Like the times I speak to groups of students who wonder how I accomplish so much in a given day. Or the time I counseled a college student who had recently lost his father. He heard my speech and believed if I could overcome so much, he could also defeat the grief that paralyzed him from moving forward. Or when I visit the juvenile detention center where I meet young men who ask sensitive questions. They often say their lives could be different if they could find just one ounce of the tenacity it takes for me to go about my daily living.

Sure, I cried—for about six hours—on the day my Gillette doctor informed me, "Go home, get your things in order. I need you to be admitted on Wednesday. Plan to stay for a minimum of six weeks." What? I'd been praying for all these speaking engagements, and now that I was booked, I couldn't do them? I had to cancel all fifteen engagements?

I was temporarily devastated. But after that good cry, I dried my tears and thought about how I had spent my last week. I received my bad news just after speaking at a Minnesota college where I discussed the need to choose a positive attitude regardless of our circumstances. *Come on, girl! Practice what you preach—live what you tell people.* I dried my eyes and packed my bags for a six-week challenge that I hoped would end in my favor.

After living nearly half my life as a quadriplegic, I can tell you this— there's always hope. In fact, Sarina and I talked about this on the phone today. She called, concerned after hearing the news that I was admitted for surgery. I was happy to hear things continue to go well for her as she works at a supervised facility and still lives in a group home, independent from her family. I was touched by her concern for me and reminded that both Sarina and I are living proof that hope is worth holding onto—better times are always ahead.

If you are depressed, someone is out there who needs you. Listen, counsel, and you will find relief for your own sadness. If you are broke, feeling financial stress, volunteer to help the poor. You will find a new perspective by serving those who truly do not know where their next meal may come from. If you are in chronic pain, visit a children's oncology ward. I believe you will leave with your mind full of concern for the children who take uncertainty in stride. Your pain will seem absent, at least for a while.

I have to admit, much of my devastation in getting this six-week medical sentence was because I have met someone special. Yes, I have met someone wonderful—someone I want to spend all of my time with. And just when this relationship seems to be taking off, I have to leave for a St. Paul hospital room. We already struggle with distance, living in two different towns about an hour apart. However, I have faced my fear of relationships, taken a chance with someone new, and now must test things by revealing just how difficult my life sometimes gets. No secrets, I guess. This man will learn about my cares, about my surgery and recovery, and he will have to find the extra time in his busy schedule to drive to St. Paul to visit me.

I almost missed the chance to meet someone so amazing. I spent most of the previous year recovering from a painful relationship where someone had stripped me of all my confidence—had nearly convinced me that I was a burden and should be utterly grateful that he stuck with me. I sank so low. After our break-up, I believed I was done with relationships, probably forever.

As awful as it was, I will give him one thing—he taught me that I *do* want to get married one day. Like so many relationships, it was good in the beginning. I loved having someone to count on, someone to share time with on a personal level. And then things got bad. In his life, he had been dealt an unfortunate set of circumstances. I thought I would bring him up to my positive way of seeing things, but instead he sucked me down to his. It was so painful. I quit asking for anything from him, for fear he would yell or act like he was giving me the world. I began to wonder, what if his hurtful words are true? When he tells me I'm demanding, that I expect too much, that I'm self-centered, should I believe him?

After all the years of being the Gingerbread Man, I took a chance on someone, and when it ended, I feared that I would spend my life alone after all. I thought, *God brought me here, to the point where I want to get married … but no one's left*. Little did I know that this failed relationship was preparing me to be with just the right one.

It took lots of time, but I built myself back up again. I replayed the times this man told me I expected too much and that everything was my fault. It took the better part of a year, but I eventually saw, again, that I was worthy—worthy of being loved, worthy of someone who loved me unconditionally for who I was. That person has to be out there somewhere.

Just when I thought rejection would kill me, I began to see that this failed relationship actually made me stronger. I was all the more prepared to be with the right one—all the more prepared to know him when I met him.

Here's a stereotype I'd like to dispel: "Gee, Tasha, it'll take a special person to commit to you … I don't know if just anyone can do that." Well, I don't want just anyone. I want someone special enough to see that I have a lot to bring to a relationship. I want a man who sees just how much I have to offer. If you think you're the only one bringing something to the table, don't apply. It won't work for the guy who overlooks just how lucky he is to be with someone like me. Is this arrogance or wisdom? Maybe a healthy dose of both. I wish all women could have the same view of themselves. With this attitude, relationships may take longer to establish, but I predict they will last.

I came across an online quote that became my temporary mantra: "Being single is not weak—it's being strong enough to wait for the right one." Ironically, the day I let go of the pain of being single, Doug Drogorub introduced himself to me.

We all avoid so many things because of our fear of failure. I knew very quickly that resisting Doug would be a product of fear. We had so much in common; there wasn't one red flag warning me to stay clear. If I ran away from this opportunity—if I pulled a Gingerbread Man—the fear of repeated hurt from a failed relationship would win.

Is this relationship "the one"? Is this destined to last forever? I hope so! But I remember clearly the days when I didn't want to get married—had no desire to have kids. To be honest, marriage and children are probably the most popular questions at my speaking engagements. Depending on the time in my life, I have given varied answers to these personal topics. But now, all that has changed. Sitting in my audience today, you will likely hear, "Yes, I can have kids, and I'm seriously thinking about it." Parenting is a huge responsibility. Yet I'm not so afraid of the physical part—carrying a child in this paralyzed torso. I am more intimidated by the sheer impact a child would bring to my independent life. Like every parent should, I fear the balancing act, balancing family with job and other personal hopes and aspirations. Parents—the really good ones, like I see in my own family— undergo self-sacrificing experiences I can only imagine at this point.

With all the change I have endured from past relationships, I am now convinced I deserve somebody to love—I deserve to be with someone to whom I am attracted and who finds me attractive as well. All of us deserve to be with someone who not only has the same values and shares similar interests, but is desirable. As I rest in my hospital bed, knowing Doug will call at any moment, I believe I have been strong and wise in waiting for the right one.

My life is not perfect. But God has a good plan for me. His promise is that no matter what happens, I am not alone—He is by my side. Do I have hard days? Have I felt the disappointment that comes with the loss caused by my accident? Absolutely yes. But if I trust in Him, no matter how dark things get, no matter how difficult, He will turn it into good (Romans 8:28). There will be triumph in tragedy, goodness from grief.

Epilogue

WHAT IS YOUR trapdoor? We all have one. It's a part of your story. Maybe it's a health problem. Maybe a learning disability. Indeed, some lives seemed ruined by external obstacles. After many of my speaking engagements, people share with me their sad times.

"My family's messed up ..."

"I'm broke—can't seem to change things ..."

"I've been doing drugs since I was a kid ..."

"I come from a family of alcoholics ..."

"I have no talents. How can I achieve like you when I have nothing to offer ..."

"I'm depressed all the time ..."

"I just got out of prison. No one will give me a job ..."

I've heard all the excuses. But excuses are nothing compared to the power you possess to turn things around.

I am saddened by the stories of so many who suffer in our world. I feel blessed when I hear others' excuses, because clearly my greatest strength is my attitude. Attitude is a choice I make every day. I wake up and decide: *I can whine and complain about my circumstances, or I can confront each day for what it truly is—a gift from God.* You also have this choice. You may not be able to control many things in your life, but your attitude is one of them. Take charge because you can.

I am living proof of the difference that attitude makes. Instead of taking six weeks or more at Gillette to recover from my surgery, I was discharged after only four weeks. My skin healed without a glitch, even though complications are common with this procedure. By choosing to be positive, I made the days fly by and found that I gained, rather than lost, once again. I gained perspective, new friends from the staff, and quality time with so many visitors. I am convinced that I healed quicker than expected because of my positive outlook.

In the little bit of time I spent alone, I reflected on my Miracle Journal, a document that I started during my struggle with scoliosis. I began to list all the good that was happening while I adjusted to life as the new Tasha Schuh so I wouldn't be consumed by the setbacks and changes. My Miracle Journal is full of what some might see as big miracles—"the scoliosis surgery is unnecessary" ... as well as small miracles—"I can taste this sherbet again!" My stay at Gillette proved that if I took inventory of all the positive elements of each day, I would see a miracle unfold again.

Even before I knew how to ask God for guidance, I can trace back to times when He was surely there for me. This book recounts them. Before I knew how to pray for patience, acceptance, and perseverance, God pumped me full of resilience so I could move on after letdowns, advance after despair. Look for strength—it will be there. Take inventory each day. You too can experience miracles.

I am only in the middle of my movie. I know there are great things yet to come. Besides having this wonderful man in my life, in September of last year I was selected as an ambassador to my home state. I became a spokesperson for those who rise above their disabilities by being named Ms. Wheelchair Wisconsin. I recently traveled to Ohio for Ms. Wheelchair USA, where I competed with the top finalists from various states. Each contestant embodied the level of self-worth, empowerment, and achievement that the Dane Foundation, our pageant sponsor, strives to inspire in all who face adversity in their lives.

Mom, Doug, Angie and her family, plus some of my closest lifelong friends all contributed to the biggest entourage there. They supported me through a challenging week of interviews, community events, and rehearsals for a televised and webcast show. The pageant itself consisted of three wardrobe changes—a hippie outfit, fitting the "Peace, Love, and Understanding" theme of the pageant; a professional outfit; and an evening gown. Imagine women in wheelchairs making a quick change while the program took a short commercial break. Our speaking demands included a friendly introduction to the audience, a platform speech on individual chosen topics—in my case, the power of a positive attitude—and two impromptu answers to questions posed by the judges.

As the pageant closed, it was clear that the crown could have gone to any one of these worthy participants. As we gathered onstage, some contestants were honored with unique awards like Miss Congeniality, the Photogenic Award, and the Mayor's Award, presented by the current mayor of Stow, our host city. My family told me later that they feared I would be overlooked, since each of these special awards went to the other contestants. With the final prize of the evening still to come, I felt the anxiety that comes with a suspenseful buildup, but I also felt peace in knowing that, whatever happened, I had already gained so much from the experience.

The official envelope was delivered to the pageant emcee, Christi Nichols, the local WONE radio news-show host. "Our fourth runner-up is ... third runner-up is ... second runner-up is ..." Ms. Nichols took a moment to explain that if Ms. Wheelchair USA could not fulfill her duties for the year, the first runner-up would take her place. "First runner-up is Ms. Wheelchair Florida, Ashley Cooper Heath!" I was thrilled for Ashley, my newfound friend, but anxious for the final announcement.

"And the winner of the 2012 Ms. Wheelchair USA is ... Tasha Schuh!"

I remember closing my eyes in disbelief. I wanted a playback to confirm what I just heard. I opened my eyes to my family's loud cheers in the audience, and I knew it was true. I felt the crown placed on my head within seconds of the announcement. Someone put flowers in my lap and placed a tall trophy on the floor next to my chair. Cameras flashed all across the audience, and the roar from my entourage verified that I did not need to pinch myself. This was really happening.

I am crowned Ms. Wheelchair USA on July 21, 2012.

Ms. Wheelchair USA pageant, Cuyahoga Falls, Ohio, July 2012

After I attended the post-pageant gala, I had time to think about how much I had gained from this week. I came away with much more than a crown after the announcement of this title, Ms. Wheelchair USA, 2012. The true highlight of the experience was meeting other talented and accomplished women who did not back down in spite of their obstacles. Their feats ranged from training for the Paralympics to graduating with a doctorate in psychiatry and practicing in New York City. It's hard to measure the positive impact of people so driven to achieve personal fulfillment, with or without limits on their physical movement. My advice to you: surround yourself with people like this. Pursue friendships, jobs, and volunteer experiences that allow you to meet people who no longer see obstacles as anything more than speed bumps in the path of bringing good to the world.

This pageant experience reminds me how much I have changed. Before my accident, I was a self-conscious teenager with low self-esteem. Now I believe in myself, knowing that, with God's help, I can accomplish anything I put my mind to. I use to feel pity when I saw someone in a wheelchair. Now, when I am the reason for that same look, I wish I had time to stop and tell each person how happy my life is, how thankful I am that my accident occurred. This accident—this life-changing event in a theater so many years ago—has been the best thing that could have happened to me.

I had mediocre goals before my accident. My dreams now are so much bigger. As a selfish sixteen-year-old, I never imagined that my recovery would inspire others to the point that the Mayo Clinic nominated me for a national rehabilitation award. I found out recently that I have been chosen to receive the 2012 American Rehabilitation Champion Award. The Foundation for Physical Medicine and Rehabilitation will fly me to Atlanta, Georgia, this fall to receive this honor at a national convention for the inspiring people who work in this demanding health-care field. With accolades come opportunities. I look forward to the doors that will open as I attend a full calendar of events this year.

I will never step backward again—literally or figuratively. It doesn't mean that I won't make mistakes or have regrets. But I will choose to learn from my mistakes and move forward. I acknowledge bad days. I am not immune to sadness. I will feel loss in my life, as I have in becoming the new Tasha Schuh. But let me leave you with this: we all must press on after discovering our trapdoors. God's love and support will be found on the other side. Trust in His plan, ask for answers to your questions, and you will find peace knowing that you can travel beyond the trapdoor with a powerful partner. With God's support, I know I will have both joy and disappointment as my movie plays on. But I will not let what I *cannot* do interfere with what I *can* do, ever again.

I took my last step backward. I really thought that my life was over, that I had to walk again to be happy. I have found that I am happy right here—right where I am—right now. Every day is a gift, and I refuse to waste one.

This is my life. Tasha Schuh's life. I wouldn't trade it with anybody. I'll move forward in peace and happiness no matter what comes.

Okay—it helps that I have a sweet boyfriend …

I am only one, but I am one. I cannot do everything, but I can do something.
And I will not let what I cannot do interfere with what I can do.
—Edward Everett Hale

Doug and I celebrate six months together on a boat ride down the Mississippi River.

Bibliography

Ballard, Glen and Alanis Morissette. "Ironic," *Jagged Little Pill*. <u>Warner Bros. Records</u>. 1995.

"IDEA, ADA, IEP's, and Section 504 Plans: What Happens in College?" *Office of Disability Services for Students*. Rutgers University, 14 May 2010. Web. 20 Oct. 2012.

Quotations. *Edward Everett Hale Quotes*. Think.Exist.com, 1999-2012. Web. 23 Oct. 2012.

Spinal Cord Injury Rehabilitation. *Diseases and Treatments*. Mayo Clinic, Rochester, Minnesota, 2001-2012. Web. 10 Oct., 2012.

"Tasha Talks," *News and Info*. Ms. Wheelchair USA.org, 2012. Web. 23 Oct., 2012.

Whitman, Walt. *Leaves of Grass*. New York: New York University Press, 1980. Print.

54560634R00162

Made in the USA
Lexington, KY
20 August 2016